Thomas Holley Chivers

CHARLES HENRY WATTS, II

Thomas Holley Chivers

His Literary Career and His Poetry

UNIVERSITY OF GEORGIA PRESS

ATHENS

TO MY
MOTHER AND FATHER

V

Contents

✐ Preface

THIS study of the literary career and poetry of Thomas Holley Chivers, a poet neglected by his contemporaries and scarcely known today, is an attempt to understand Chivers within the literary world for which he wrote, and an effort to analyze his poetry in terms of his own literary theory as well as in the light of objective critical standards. It is based upon a belief that Chivers, as both man and poet, deserves considerably more recognition than critical opinion has as yet provided, and that, furthermore, a study of his literary career may illustrate some of the aesthetic problems which faced the American artist in the first half of the nineteenth century.

Born in Washington, Georgia, in 1809,[1] Chivers moved through the literary world of pre-Civil War America with an outward confidence startling in the light of the virtually complete critical silence which met his literary efforts throughout his lifetime. Educated as a physician, he had determined to write poetry before he was out of medical school, and the history of his efforts, prolific as they are, is one of continual determination to establish for himself a place among America's men of letters.

The materials for a study of Chivers, beyond his published volumes, consist of a variety of manuscript poems as well as essays and poems published during his lifetime in a wide assortment of periodicals. The volumes of poetry themselves are now exceedingly rare. The most nearly complete collection of Chivers' books is in the Harris Collection at Brown University, where there are copies of all his volumes except *The Path of Sorrow*, only one copy of which is now known to exist, and *Atlanta*, both represented in the Harris Collection by photostat copies, and *The Constitution of Man*, of which no copy has ever been found.

While the Harris Collection contains all of Chivers' collected work now extant, manuscripts of poems and prose articles are located in the Henry E. Huntington Library and the Duke University Library. These manuscripts include a variety of texts of Chivers' published (and a number of unpublished) poems, as well as the text of Chivers' recently published biography of Edgar Allan Poe. A further collection of great importance is in the Washington Memorial Library, of Macon, Georgia, where the only known files of the *Georgia Citizen,* a paper which published more of Chivers' work than any other journal, are located.

The Chivers manuscripts now at the Duke and Huntington libraries are but a part of those left by the poet at his death. Chivers appointed a close friend, John Gierlow, as his literary executor. Perhaps the storm of the approaching Civil War kept Gierlow from editing Chivers' work for final publication, as the poet had requested; in any case, the war came and Chivers' home in Decatur was in its path. Mrs. Chivers, a Northern woman, almost surely was instrumental in preventing complete ruin of her home. But, perhaps in preparation against Sherman's troops, or simply to preserve the poet's masses of manuscript, an attempt was made to file them; only one box of what was reputed to have been a larger manuscript collection survived. Its whereabouts directly after the war are not known, but finally it came into the hands of Chivers' son, Thomas Holley, Jr. From him it went to one of Chivers' nephews, John Q. Adams, son of the poet's sister Ann. It remained in the Adams family until 1924, when the Huntington Library purchased a selection of the manuscripts dealing with Poe. In 1929, largely through the efforts of the late Dr. Lewis Chase, the remainder of the manuscripts were bought by Duke University.[2]

That such a large body of manuscript material, promising to aid so much in a clearer understanding of the literary world of the 1840's and 1850's, escaped the hands of scholars for so long is indeed ironic. Had Professor Gierlow ever executed the request in the poet's will and edited the manuscripts, or had the collection been sold and edited during the lifetime of Mrs. Chivers, who died in 1888, we might today know the answers to the great number of perplexing questions which surround the poet's life. Certain it is that many of his works were irretrievably lost during the rough passage which the iron box containing the manuscripts underwent. It is a sign of the fragmentary nature of the information which had been available to those concerned with the manuscripts that in 1897 John Q. Adams, the man into whose hands Chivers' son had put his father's manuscripts to insure their being given some sort of lasting form, had never seen a copy of *Eonchs of Ruby, Memoralia,* or *Virginalia,* the volumes which contain the best of Chivers' work.

Indeed, aside from several interesting but fragmentary comments on Chivers at the turn of the twentieth century,[3] until S. Foster Damon's *Thomas Holley Chivers,* published in 1930, no attempt had been made to establish Chivers' position in or value to American literature; furthermore no correct bibliography of Chivers' published volumes was in print, nor was the world of scholarship generally aware that a large body of manuscript poems was still extant.

However, when in 1930 Dr. Chase came to Brown University to work with Professor Damon on an edition of the Complete Works of Thomas Holley Chivers, photostat and typed copies of all the manuscripts of poems and prose articles in the Duke University Library, as well as those in the Huntington Library, were collected at Brown for the project. Professor Damon had already begun his work in compiling a bibliography of the magazine publication of Chivers' work, and that effort is now approaching completion. It is hoped that the long projected edition of Chivers' Complete Works may soon take final form. Professor Damon has been extremely generous in allowing me access to this bibliography, as well as to the critical notes which he has drawn up during his work on Chivers. Mrs. Lewis Chase has allowed me to check my findings with her valuable files of Chivers' correspondence, and has provided biographical detail otherwise unavailable. My wife's confidence and patience have always eased the difficulties inherent in my task. Without the assistance herein noted, this study could never have achieved whatever definitive elements it may now contain.

Chapter One

⟋⟍ Literary Career

INTRODUCTION

THE fascination which Chivers holds for today's reader stems as much from the portrait he presents against the background of nineteenth century American letters as it does from the variety of his poetic experiment and accomplishment. That the literary world he moved in almost never spoke of him, despite the startling figure his Southern transcendentalism and adamant confidence must have created, only adds to the uniqueness of his position. Independently wealthy, Chivers made his way from Georgia to the literary centers of the Northeast—Philadelphia, New York, and Boston—recording what he saw and heard in a long series of published letters, and regularly submitting his poetry to any and to all periodicals. He published, over a period of twenty-six years, nine volumes of poetry, two verse plays, and two prose pamphlets. Yet despite the number and variety of his efforts, only three of his volumes ever received contemporary notice of any import. His name is not to be found in any nineteenth century collection of American poetry,[4] though his work was known to E. C. Stedman and to R. W. Griswold; and virtually no critical comment on his work, beyond incidental magazine squibs accepting or rejecting submitted poems, was ever made by any commentator who knew him personally.

Against such silence Chivers wrote poetry of greater force and subtlety than his contemporaries suspected. His failure to achieve public recognition had its effect upon him of course, generally increasing his innate tendency toward extremes of emotional reaction and deepening his dependence upon the inward, almost mystical world his poetry evoked with increasing frequency. When Nathaniel Hawthorne, in 1844, considered the problem of the artist's need for inward strength and determination in the face of

1

public neglect or misunderstanding, he might almost have been speaking of his Georgia compatriot, a man whom he never knew but who suffered from the same failure to find an audience. Hawthorne dramatized such a situation in "The Artist of the Beautiful":

It is requisite for the ideal artist to possess a force of character that seems hardly compatible with its delicacy; he must keep his faith in himself while the incredulous world assails him with its utter disbelief; he must stand up against mankind and be his own sole disciple, both as respects his genius and the objects to which it is directed.

Hawthorne's artist, Owen Warland, achieved a calm, inward assurance which Chivers' enthusiasm kept from him. Yet while inward peace and satisfaction were never to come to Chivers, in a sense their absence drove him to the further experiment and trial which produced some of his most effective poetry.

Despite contemporary America's refusal to accept Chivers as a poet worthy of study, somehow his poetry reached England not long after his death. Clarence Stedman, literary editor and critic, paused in the midst of a comment on Poe to say that he had often heard Swinburne "rehearse [Chivers' poetry] with shouts of delight,"[5] and, indeed, the first stanza of Swinburne's "Dolores" has a very close resemblance to a descriptive passage in Chivers' "Lily Adair."[6] Furthermore, Dante Gabriel Rossetti, as early as 1866[7] was inquiring about Chivers, hopeful that Horace E. Scudder, later editor of the *Atlantic Monthly*, might provide information. Scudder replied in a letter to W. M. Rossetti which, as much as any other testimony, indicates how little America had been concerned to investigate Chivers:

My dear Sir,—Since my return to America on November last I have kept in mind a request of your Brother's that I should find out something about the astonishing Chivers—a poet in spite of his name; but, though I have asked Professor Lowell and Mr. Fields, both of whom had correspondence with him, they could tell me nothing beyond the fact that he was a Georgian by birth (American, not Asian Georgia), but recently was living in Washington. Further productions may no doubt be expected, for Fields declared that one of his letters mentions a poem on which he was engaged "of the size of Paradise Lost." So you see what is before you. Fields irreverently described him moreover as a bore whose foolscap-letters—the poet always using that style of paper—he had unfortunately destroyed; for he began to think that they possessed a value aside from that intended by the author. Mr. Lowell told me that Chivers had sent him his poetry, and he had presented half of the volumes to the Harvard Library. He thought him a rather droll illustration of the shell of Shelley. I have tried in vain to get hold of his books. Somebody else must be on his trail—if it is not the doctor himself—for one of our most knowing second-hand booksellers told me that he had been enquired about at his store . . .[8]

That Chivers could have dropped so far from sight but eight years after his death, and that literary gossip could not inform Scudder better than his errors suggest it had, show how completely Chivers had failed to achieve his goal of man of letters. If Rossetti had been serious in his request, Scudder's tone must have shocked and disconcerted him.

Yet Chivers was known by a select few. Stedman wrote to J. Q. Adams that "Chivers was a crazy poet, but had an ear for melody. I have long been on the hunt for the rare vol. of his poems [EofR] . . . ." And again: "I have a copy of 'Lily Adair,' which shows that the Dr. was a blind devotee of Poe, &—a sort of Poe-run-mad!"[9] Apparently one of Bayard Taylor's favorite entertainments for his friends was a recitation of Chivers' verses; it is recorded that he "brought down the house" with a poem from *Eonchs of Ruby* while he was at Cornell on a lecture tour.[10] Charles A. Dana, of Brook Farm and Greeley's *Tribune,* said he "knew" Chivers and thought him a "literary freak."[11] No one, it seems, took Chivers seriously, and few had read his poetry. Chivers, the poet, stood forgotten behind parodied stanzas, a literary footnote.

The critical audience Chivers hoped for among his contemporaries never really materialized. How that failure to achieve contemporary fame grew out of Chivers' own personality as much as from the circumstances of literary America before the Civil War, as well as the nature and development of Chivers' poetry itself, will, I hope, be made clear in the following chapters.

1832-1837

Sometime soon after November 15, 1832, Chivers published *The Path of Sorrow, or, The Lament of Youth: A Poem.* Printed at his own expense at the office of the *Western Weekly Review* of Franklin, Tennessee, the volume is his earliest known collection of poems, most of them devoted to a defense of his own actions amid the distressful circumstances of his first marriage, the details of which are still shrouded in local gossip and conflicting testimony.[12] There is only one known copy of the book, and it is the property of Mr. Robert Housum, of Cleveland, Ohio.[13]

The poems contained in this first volume are without date or place lines, but ten of the eighteen poems concern themselves with the essentially autobiographical material of his first and unsuccessful marriage, and were obviously written some time after this event (1828) and November 15, 1832, the date line of the dedication. It may well be that the majority of these autobiographical poems were written after he arrived at the medical school of Transylvania University, Lexington, Kentucky, in 1828, because it seems certain that Chivers would not delay in Washington, Georgia, long after the disruption of his marriage. In his dedication to John Rhay, Esquire, of Newnan, Georgia, he says, "John, these Poems were written during my leisure hours, when a student of Medicine in Lexington, in 1828-9." He was probably led to Transylvania by Leonidas B. Mercer, himself a physician, who had been Chivers' preceptor. He registered for one course in 1828, and for two in 1829.[14] Graduating in a class of seventy students, Chivers obtained his medical degree in March of 1830, having prepared a thesis of thirty-four closely written pages on *Intermittent and Remittent Fevers.*

Chivers had been preparing for publication as early as June 14, 1832, for there exists a cancelled dedication page so dated, containing eulogistic praise of John Rhay; the title reads *The Path of Sorrow; or The Flower of Youth Lies Bleeding.* Also in the Adams Collection are a number of manuscript poems, published in *The Path of Sorrow,* which bear dates, in Chivers' hand, from the later 1820's. The earliest, published as "An Elegy," bears the date of April 1, 1829; there are two others dated from that year, and two from 1830.[15] Thus Chivers began his versifying early, certainly before he was twenty, and was prepared to issue a small, personal volume by the time he was twenty-three.

The poems of *The Path of Sorrow* vary from the thirty-two lines of "To a Friend" to one of 945 lines, and the average poem length is 225 lines. Chivers was primarily interested in stating his opinions about his marriage, and utilized whatever form seemed to suit the intensity and duration of his emotion. At the same time it seemed natural to him to express himself in poetry, and the variety of the techniques employed makes his interest in the art of poetry clear. The youthful experimenter attempted several different meters, including blank verse, double quatrains, Spenserian stanzas, and rhyming five- and six-line forms, most of them in iambics with an occasional anapestic line. He was not deviating violently from the norm, but who would expect extreme experiment in poetry from an inexperienced, lonely young student of medicine? Yet the variety of form prefigures his later experimenting. He did attempt a new stanza form, *ababcdcdd*,[16] in "The Minstrel's Valedictory," which he found useful later.

The probable circumstances of composition may be easily surmised. Chivers' home had a decent library, and certain of his autobiographical poems indicate that he was a quiet youth given to reading in the English poets; Byron he discovered in time to draw the parallel between that poet's personal tragedies and his own, and we may assume that he had the usual acquaintance with the English classics.[17] It is my belief that certain very early efforts appear in *The Path of Sorrow*. "Kosciusko's Resignation." (pp. 124-126) seems an exercise after Campbell's lines on the Polish hero Sobieski's relief of besieged Vienna in 1683; likewise, the two other heroic adventures, "The Siege of Vienna" (pp. 72-83) and "Anastasius" (pp. 114-118), appear to be youthful exercises. Their appearance in a volume so exclusively dedicated to an apologia for his own actions indicates that he may have taken the manuscripts out of whatever collection he had from his adolescent days. They are of a completely different (a wholly literary) nature, having no personal connotation whatsoever.

It is doubtful that Chivers had published any poetry before the appearance of *The Path of Sorrow;* he was busy enough with medical school, and the poems which the volume contains (except those just noted above) were the product of reflection upon his late marital difficulties. In no sense were they prepared for public, magazine publication. His November 15, 1832, dedication says, in part, "I have only had a few copies printed for the perusal of my friends; and I hope you will not uproot the scion, because it is not, intuitively, a lordly oak." This was his first trial, we may presume, and that he had published in magazines before is possible, but not overly probable.

On November 18, 1837, a year which saw Chivers traveling over the middle and northern seaboard states, he had returned to Oak

Grove (one of the names he gave his estate in Washington, Georgia) for a visit. While at his brother's home, he apparently came upon the manuscript of several of the poems which had been published in *The Path of Sorrow*. He says,

They were printed for private circulation in 1832. . . . While I was at my brother's, not long ago, I found them in an old Library, where they had been carefully stored away during my long pilgrimage from home. The sight of them was like a vision of my lost children in Heaven. Being the first birth of my Minerva, I cannot but treasure them highly . . . .[18]

This statement is interesting in the light of one of Chivers' most characteristic habits, that of carefully preserving the manuscripts of his poems, utilizing images, lines, conceits, or stanzas from one poem in a second. His file of literary magazines and journals further suggests a habit of more or less scholarly investigation and comparison.[19] Yet he says that he came upon these *Path of Sorrow* poems by chance. This discrepancy may cause us to wonder whether Chivers did not destroy whatever copies of *The Path of Sorrow* may have remained after the "private circulation" he speaks of. The reasons for such an action are obvious. They were intensely personal poems, restricted in their application to events recently past, if not forgotten. The poems may well have brought an unfavorable reaction from the friends among whom they were circulated; certainly the scarcity of the volume testifies that few of them preserved their copies. Chivers said that the sight of the manuscripts struck him forcibly, and their presence seems to have stirred up in him the old hatred and disgust that are so obvious in *The Path of Sorrow*: "my whole soul has been on fire ever since the day that I heard my precious name slandered by the polluted lips . . ."[20]

Once he had gotten over the shock of the memories aroused by the poems, Chivers began to construct a new volume, to be entitled *Songs of Sorrow,* a collection never published as a whole. The manuscript title page reads, *Songs of Sorrow; or, Cantilodes of Rosemary Gathered From the Grave of Joy.*[21] There are seventeen sheets of manuscript, in his hand, containing ten poems, of which seven are poems from *The Path of Sorrow*.[22] Chivers revised almost all of the autobiographical poems, and generally the revision tends to sharpen his statements where previously the desired emphasis had been achieved through repetition. However, he had been away from the poems too long or did not review them carefully enough to produce obviously improved poetry.

The four "new" poems in the *Songs of Sorrow* manuscript are variously concerned with autobiography and philosophy. "The Separation" and "The Farewell" add several details to our knowledge of Chivers' disastrous first marriage, particularly with regard to his first wife's actions after having left him:

> She left his home, but never more returned,
> Although he importuned her oft to come.
> In garb of widowhood she sate alone,
> Gazing like one forlorn in wretchedness,
> With none to comfort her, or help her weep,
> But one lone babe, the orphan of his love,
>
> . . . .
>
> She did not yet return — nor ever did —
> But lived in voluntary exile, far
> Away from him — forlorn in weeds of wo!
> And would not let him see his only child,
> Then born unto his name — nor ever did![23]

The accuracy of this description may be questioned in part, but such is his memory as he looks back some ten years. The passage of time had performed a humanitarian service, it would seem, for throughout his revision he has toned down his attacks on his wife, which in several of the published poems were extreme,[24] and concentrated his fire on the causes of their separation.

The other two poems in *Songs of Sorrow* are "To My Little Book" and "Death," the latter dated March 8, 1829, at Transylvania University. It was never published, here or elsewhere, and its presence would increase proof that Chivers was revising from his older manuscripts and not working from a copy of *The Path of Sorrow*. "To My Little Book," evidently intended as a sort of introduction to *Songs of Sorrow*, indicates Chivers' occupation at the time he was compiling the manuscript, for it appeared as "To Idealon" in the volume Chivers published in 1837, *Nacoochee*.[25] The manuscript is dated first 1836, which is the probable date of composition, and 1830 is written in over it; Chivers intended to back-date it so that it would appear, as his Preface says, that all the poems were products of his college days. *Nacoochee* is also represented in the manuscript by a table of contents. *Nacoochee* appeared in late 1837; the Preface is dated September 10, 1837. The coincidence of the presence of *Nacoochee's* table of contents in this manuscript collection indicates pretty fully that the date (November 18, 1837) which Chivers gave to the Preface of *Songs of Sorrow* accurately fixes the time of revision.

Other than the reappearance of *The Path of Sorrow* poems in this manuscript Chivers found only three further occasions for reference to them. "Though the Rose of My Eden is Blasted" (pp. 122-123) appeared as "Song" in *Nacoochee* in a much shortened (and improved) version.[26] "The Prophet's Dream" (pp. 44-72) was never republished, but one revision appears to have been written in the 1850's, apparently with the intention of republication.[27] "The Lament of Youth" (pp. 84-109) exists in two manuscripts; the first bears the date "Transylvania University, Lexington, Ky., April 10, 1829," and the second is first dated "Boston, Aug. 18, [185?]" and then "Oak Grove, Ga. March 8*th* 1829" is written over it. The first date probably represents the date of attempted revision, the second the date of composition. The revision indicates that Chivers was attempting to recast the entire poem without discarding more than a few lines. The 1850's found Chivers republishing a number of his early poems in the *Georgia Citizen,* a weekly journal published in Macon, Georgia, which kept its pages open to him when other magazines had ceased accepting his work; it seems probable that the revised "The Lament of Youth" was intended for this paper.

Phrases, lines, and stanzas from these early poems do not appear in his later work as often as elements of some of the poems published in the mid-thirties. Personal in the extreme, they were so much a part of the catastrophe they describe that even when he attempted to revise one of them twenty years later he found himself unable to complete the job.

Testimony of his continuing literary activity after the publication of *The Path of Sorrow* is found in five pages of the *Western Monthly Magazine,* published in Cincinnati, for the month of July, 1833.[28] There, a review entitled "Chivers on the Constitution of Man" offers the only known reference to the second of Chivers' published works. There is no manuscript among the many found in Georgia, and no other magazine of the period believed Chivers' work worthy of review.

The Constitution of Man was apparently printed in pamphlet

form in Memphis, in 1833, for the review takes quotations from
pages numbered up to seventeen, and notes the place and date of
publication. The reviewer, Dr. Charles Caldwell of the University of Louisville, introduces Chivers as follows:

When a friend handed [the pamphlet] to me and I read the first sen-
tence, I promised myself much pleasure in the dissection of it; but when
I ventured a little deeper into the essay, I found absurdities as thick as
pigeons, and all hope of sport was gone.[29]

Such a beginning hardly promises well for Chivers, and the excerpts offered at least in part justify Caldwell's objections. He
satirically elevates Chivers when he adds, "Have at you, England
and Germany; Kant and Coleridge; mystifiers and double-mysti-
fiers. . . . Show me in all your boasted fog-volumes . . . a passage
equal to that. . . ."[30] It is interesting that the first published notice
of Chivers' work, which this is, should link him with Coleridge,
for certain of Chivers' later poems are very much in the style of
"Kubla Khan" and "Christabel." Yet surely this was no ordinary
scribbler of the Georgia pine barrens! Obscure he might be, but
never dull; Chivers was to continue to avoid mediocrity, no matter
how often his efforts ended in failure.

One who signs himself only "N. S.," presumably an assistant editor of the magazine, continued the comment on Chivers for three
pages after Dr. Caldwell had specified his objections. The laughter
evident in Caldwell's review grows in volume in this extension
of it. Suggesting that a phrenologist might find an examination
of Chivers interesting, "N. S." quotes a passage in which Chivers
appraises his subject, a passage which he believed might have been
inspired by an intermittent reading of Webster's dictionary:

The beauty and excellence of its intentions and inculcations, the
glory evinced in its contemplations, the benefit derived from its inculcations, and the sublunary felicity contained in its making, constituting
an insight to that superior bliss which shone upon the sons of Jacob,
when the land of Nile was dark; and that bright, shining lamp which
irradiated the horizon at creation's dawn, when all the sons of God
shouted for joy; and the stars of creation, sentients of God, illuminated
the pavement of the sky, and gave gracious audience to the eternal serenade: while all created things responded to the manumission of the
Lord, that every thing was very good.   —p. 1.

"N. S." adds that Chivers should have provided a glossary and
marginal notes; already Chivers is trying his powers at language,

and despite his evident failure the attempt is well motivated. He needed such practice when he came to break away from established standards later in his life.

From the parody of the essay's contents which Caldwell and "N. S." wrote, it becomes clear that Chivers' *Constitution of Man* was a theophysical explanation of man, his nature, his motivations, and his physical body, all seen from the perspective of a belief that regards man as essentially divine, and inspired by divinity. It may be assumed also that in some manner Chivers managed to connect man and his divine nature with America and her divine, foretold duty as prophesier of the New Jerusalem of liberty. Passages quoted in the *Western Monthly* show that Chivers' love for extreme metaphor was born early; speaking of the long years of the American Revolution, Chivers describes Washington as " 'the farmer of Mount Vernon, [who] led the van, thanks be to God, on the fatal night of impending peril, wading [sic] hand in hand for seven years with the python of British domination.' "[31] Exaggerated images of this sort appear first in his prose. It seems possible that the transference (and refinement) of imagery from his prose to his poetry was one of the developments of his growing poetic power, for the poems of these early years are not as striking in imagery as later work, while Chivers' prose never lost the metaphysical quality of yoking extremes by violent metaphor.

While Chivers' early prose, if *The Constitution of Man* is accepted as example, was extreme enough to call an editor's attention to his name, his early poetry, lacking much of this power, may have passed unnoticed, if ever it was submitted to a magazine. Yet there remains the possibility that a journal like the *Western Weekly Review,* of Franklin, Tennessee, which had printed his first collection of poetry (1832), accepted his incidental poems at about the same time. The original files of this magazine, except for the years 1832 to 1834, were destroyed by fire, and our knowledge of Chivers' later publication there comes from his own clippings of his poems from the magazine; so there is no positive proof. Old residents of Franklin remember Chivers vaguely, and associate him in their minds with the *Western Weekly Review.* Apparently during the early 1830's Chivers visited the town often enough to establish himself not only as a contributor to the magazine but also as one intimately connected with it.

The first piece of Chivers' work known to have received magazine publication did appear in the *Western Weekly Review*. "Lines Written on Receiving the *New Monthly Magazine*" was published on February 7, 1834; it is a satire on James Hall, the editor of the *Western Monthly Magazine*. This, of course, was the journal which had printed the damning review of his *The Constitution of Man* six months before.

Chivers frames his reply to what he mistakenly believed was Hall's personal attack upon his work, in the form of a tall tale. It contains the colloquial diction, homely metaphor, and grammatical errors common to the humorous pseudo-realistic tall tales. Hall is satirically characterized as one who can " 'wade the Ohio! walk the Mississippi, and tote a steamboat! and grip a bear too close to be comfortable! grin a raccoon to death in a minute! drink branch water! snigger any epidemic out of America—grin the cholera out of his own liver!' " He is, in short, " 'the real *Cerberus* of old grand daddy Jeffrey!' " [32] His criticism, Chivers says, is best likened to the blast of a hunter's smooth-bore loaded to the muzzle, never killing the game but severely injuring the hunter. This description comes close to that used in the tall tale, although the animus behind the humour is more obvious here,[33] and his oblique reference to *Blackwood's* gives the whole a decidedly literary cast. Chivers was seldom content with moderation, as the extremity of his reply testifies.

Such was Chivers' introduction to the none-too-polite world of magazine publication. Cross fires of this sort were in all probability fostered, up to a certain point, by the respective editors, for they boosted circulation. Perhaps it was partly with this in mind that the *Western Weekly* accepted four more of Chivers' pieces over the following eleven weeks, although none of these refers to Hall. One, "Squire Bunkley of Sandy Cross," is a prose lampoon of some local character, now unknown, another is a study of "western" versus "eastern" female beauty, and the two final pieces are poems, the first to be published in a magazine.[34]

The two poems indicate that Chivers began his public career in a most orthodox fashion; one, "Lines on Parting," derives its power from the fact that it is based on a popular song from Thomas Moore's *Irish Melodies*, "Come, Rest in This Bosom," while the second, "The Burial at Sea," is modeled on Charles Wolfe's "Burial of Sir John Moore."

· 11

This poetic derivation and the presence of the satiric prose articles within a very few months of his first public appearance show that Chivers was testing his abilities and desires; having commenced with prose work, he was as yet unsure of his poetic idiom, form, and style. *The Path of Sorrow* had been a most intimate sort of poetry, inspired by the most personal of emotional circumstances, and these pieces in the *Weekly Review* are quite orthodox as compared with it. It becomes obvious later that Chivers needed exactly such personal stimulation or motivation to achieve real success in his work. Not a glib versifier, though astoundingly prolific, it is as an occasional poet or as an incidental poet that Chivers most often fails. At this early point in his career his genius was probing several different mediums, and not succeeding entirely in any one of them: *The Path of Sorrow* is evidence today of his attempts to expand both poetic form and diction; *The Constitution of Man* seems an attempt to combine his training as a physician with his theological beliefs, all expressed through extreme metaphor, a device which he was to use more and more; and these magazine publications were the attempts of a still young man to get himself published, to establish, in his own mind as well as in the minds of his family and neighbors, the fact that he might be a "professional" poet, and as such respected.

Shortly after November 8, 1834,[35] Chivers published his first play, *Conrad and Eudora; or, the Death of Alonzo,* which was, as the title indicates, "Founded on the Murder of Sharpe, by Beauchamp, in Kentucky."[36] The circumstances of this killing, as melodramatic and bloody as any tabloid writer might desire, have inspired no fewer than four novels, four plays, one short story, and three ballads. It is doubtful that any other contemporary event so caught the public's eye as the colorful proceedings of the trial of Jereboam O. Beauchamp, who, spurred on by his wife of less than two years, the former Anne Cook, murdered Colonel Solomon P. Sharp, ex-Solicitor General of Kentucky and member of Congress, on the night of November 6, 1825, when Sharp came to the door of his house in answer to Beauchamp's knocking. Within a few days Beauchamp had been caught, and on May 19, 1826, was sentenced to die by hanging; between this date and his death on July 6, 1826, Anne smuggled a case-knife to her condemned husband, and in a double suicide pact, decided upon after an unsuccessful attempt to kill themselves by laudanum, they wounded themselves severely. Anne died before her husband, who recovered enough to be hanged.

Newspaper accounts turned the tragedy into a closet drama almost as soon as news of it was out. Anne became the wronged woman, and Beauchamp her heroic defender. The facts of the case, as seen through the haze of partisan interpretation of the time, seem to suggest that no one's hands were completely clean. Sharp had seduced Anne Cook, who had borne him a child, and who was apparently less virtuous than newspaper reports indicated. Beauchamp, who had married her not long after the birth of her child, seems to have been encouraged by his wife to revenge her sullied honor. Further motivation lay in the fact that the political groupings in Kentucky in 1826 found Sharp and Beauchamp, both involved in politics, on opposite sides of a popular issue. Such multiple motivations had been added to by Sharp's countercharge to his political enemies' accusations of his having seduced young Anne, for he stated that her still-born child had been a mulatto and provided a signed statement from a midwife as proof.

For all or several of these reasons Beauchamp, in part spurred on by his wife's wishes, killed his political opponent and his wife's seducer. The evidence presented at the trial was wholly circumstantial and in certain areas less than convincing, but the jury remained out only an hour to find him guilty.

Chivers not only followed his countrymen in scanning the newspaper accounts of the tragedy (he was sixteen at the time); he had as his personal friend and one-time tutor Thomas Lacey, who was, in all probability, the "Th. J. Lacey" who served with two others as Beauchamp's counsel during the trial.[37] In the Preface to *Leoni,* a later play which is a revision of *Conrad and Eudora,* Chivers specified further acquaintance with the tragedy:

When I was a student of Medicine in Transylvania University, some person gave me a pamphlet containing the confession of Beauchamp . . . I then made a sketch of the outlines of a Play which I intended to write upon that remarkable occurrence; but before I had finished it, some person took the pamphlet away from me, and I then wrote the following play.[38]

Although Chivers does not say so, the play he had written was originally published as *Conrad and Eudora.* The pamphlet which he had seen was probably that written by Jereboam Beauchamp himself just before his death. In a thoroughly heroic manner, Beauchamp had requested a stay of execution until he had written his "confession"; this appeared as *The Confession of Jereboam O. Beauchamp* soon after the execution.[39]

Chivers was not alone in his interest in the literary possibilities of the occurrence; before July of 1826 was over notice had appeared in the *New-York Mirror* of a "new tragedy" by a "native dramatist" based on the Sharp-Beauchamp murder,[40] but the play, if indeed it were written and produced, has never been found. The critic of the *New-York Mirror* continues his short notice to suggest that "Perhaps there never occurred in real life a combination of incidents so admirably calculated to produce stage effects," and Chivers shows by his use of the materials that he was well aware of this fact.

Conrad and Eudora, in blank verse, suffers indirectly from the fact that closet dramas were particularly popular in America and England at that time, and it suffers further from the youthful poet's attempts to create atmosphere through rhetoric, although some of it is effective enough:

> then scandal's fast asleep,
> And rumor, with her snaky tongue, has found
> Some confine in the earth, and buried envy!
> When a man sets fire the lips of hell, and makes
> Black passion stare young virtue in the face,—
> Then fix a pivot in thy heart for doubt to turn on![41]

Such figures of speech take us back to the seventeenth rather than the nineteenth century, and the Byronic echoes which sometimes occur in *Conrad and Eudora* are subdued by such imagery.

Among the four dramatists who utilized the material,[42] Chivers stays closest to the facts of the murder and seduction, and the first two acts of the drama move at a respectable pace. In these early scenes, which open dramatically as Chivers presents the facts of the seduction itself and lets the action carry quite naturally into the classical five-act division, there are few expository pauses in the development, and were the language controlled, the result might be effective theatre. The atmosphere of the play seems to approximate Lear's mad world, but Chivers failed to provide the irony and contrast which Shakespeare's "comic" fool affords. Toward the conclusion of the fifth act, the reader is strongly struck by the parallel afforded to *Romeo and Juliet* and the double tragedy their deaths provide; actually, the parallel existed in the facts as Chivers read them in Beauchamp's *Confession*.

One further point may be noted. Chivers' probable acquaintance with the Thomas Lacey who acted as one of Beauchamp's counsel may have led him to provide the reader with the occasional glimpses into Anne Cook's true character which we find in *Conrad and Eudora*. Young, sweet, and wronged throughout most of the play, she infrequently achieves something close to the strength of a Goneril or a Regan, and can swear to "live to see the mirror of his blood / Reflect the deep damnation of his deeds!"[43] These hints of a more complex character than mid-nineteenth century drama is likely to afford provide plot interest which would otherwise be lacking. Lacey may have suggested her underlying qualities of passion and sensuality to Chivers, or it may simply be that Lacey's presence at the trial stirred his young pupil's imagination.

The Beauchamp tragedy has offered native material throughout the history of American writing, the latest use occurring in Robert Penn Warren's *World Enough and Time* (1950). Before him, W. G. Simms had utilized the details in *Beauchampe* (1842), and in *Charlemont* (1856). Charles Fenno Hoffman's *Greyslaer* (1840) was the first novel built around it. By a happy combination of circumstances, Chivers (if we disregard the *New-York Mirror's* notice of a play to be written) seems to have been the first literary man outside the contemporary newspaper columns to realize the naturally dramatic qualities of Kentucky's most notorious of murders. This, too, as he notes, while Chivers was at college; the volatility and sensitivity of Chivers' imagination are evident early in his career, and his later development as an artist became a matter of direction and control.

When Chivers worked the play into publishing shape is unknown, but the year preceding its publication in 1834 was a busy one. Although he had not achieved a place in the magazines, he was writing lyric poetry which is very similar in nature to the typical column-end lyric or occasional poem found in those journals. The poems dated 1831 were generally written in what was then the West, Cincinnati, the Cherokee Nation, and St. Louis. Apparently the young doctor had decided to explore his own country before returning to Georgia from medical school, and

· 15

while there is little in the way of natural or geographic detail in his poetry to indicate that he absorbed and used much of what he saw, a trip of over a year, probably, swinging west through Cincinnati and St. Louis, in 1831 and 1832, shows a certain strength of spirit; civilization, except for certain surprisingly cultivated outposts like Cincinnati itself, was left behind. It is indicative of the kind of inspiration which Chivers was to depend upon later in his life that he did not utilize as the basis for poetry the fact of his presence in the but partially explored western land.[44] Several poems express homesickness, but only a few are devoted to describing the natural scene, which seldom served him as anything but a starting-point from where he could move on philosophically, theologically, or emotionally into another sphere.

What the young doctor did during his extended western tour is nowhere recorded; he probably traveled by horseback, and it seems particularly perplexing that he did not, at least in his later letters to the *Georgia Citizen,* in which he indulges often enough in reminiscence, mention the journey. The business of his father's plantation would not draw him to the West, and although he had just received his medical degree he probably was not practicing medicine, for the only reference to his ever having established a doctor's office places him in Sandy Cross, Georgia, in the summer of 1831. His nephew, J. Q. Adams, recalls that he practiced medicine "for a few years,"[45] but it seems improbable that he became an itinerant doctor while traveling in the West. Chivers utilized his knowledge of medicine to only the most speculative and philosophical ends. His stay in the West continued from 1831 until the summer of 1833, when he was somewhere in the Mississippi Valley, and those poems which show acquaintance with local detail and subject matter do so in a most commonplace manner, indicating that whatever he was doing it did not provide him with any particular stimulation towards poetic expression.

That the trip to the West was dictated at least partially by his desire to escape completely from the scandal of his first marriage, and possibly to avoid direct participation in his wife's suit for alimony, helps to explain something of his silence; a period of readjustment, perhaps relaxation, after the emotional rigors of unsuccessful marriage, and after the taxations of medical school, would be logical for a young man whose father was wealthy enough to provide the means. Whatever poetry he wrote during

16 ·

this leisure was published in the *Conrad and Eudora* volume, in a final section of short lyrics entitled "Songs of the Heart."

As has been suggested, lyrics like "Sonnet to my Mother" (p. 133) or "To a Lady" (p. 144) are orthodox in construction and sentiment; many of the lyrics collected here find their inspiration in songs and poems popular in Chivers' day,[46] and show a young poet still not sure of his own talents, trying to develop facility and ease through standard themes and forms. The years of composition represented by the lyrics of *Conrad and Eudora* were not particularly fruitful ones; in a sense, they are reactions against the personal tragedy of his marriage, for the majority of them concern themselves with themes of flirtation, romance, and love, in a literary and impersonal manner just the reverse of that found in *The Path of Sorrow*.

Chivers' movements through the 1830's can be charted but vaguely, for we are guided only by the places of composition of his poems, and the place and date of his second marriage, in 1837. *Conrad and Eudora* was published in Philadelphia in 1834, and until 1837, when his third volume of poetry, *Nacoochee*, was published, Chivers seems to have moved about the South and into the North quite as he wished. Four poems place him in Philadelphia in 1834, and since they were included in *Conrad and Eudora*, Chivers must have stayed in the city for some little time before the publication of his second volume.[47] In September of 1834 he traveled to Baltimore, and it was not until that year that Chivers dated any of his poems from Georgia.[48] If the testimony he offers in his indications of the place of composition is correct, he had not returned to his Georgia home since June of 1831. Kept away perhaps by the continuing scandal over his first marriage, Chivers had spent several years in the West, and a considerable period in or about Philadelphia before returning home. He must have come back a changed man from the youngster who had hurried off to medical school seven years earlier in the wake of a domestic uproar.

He returned in 1835 the author of two volumes of poetry (one of which included a verse tragedy), a pamphlet on the constitution of man, and five magazine pieces; no matter what the town might think of his marital habits, they knew he had obtained something beyond a medical education at Transylvania. Something of a curiosity, perhaps, when he returned, he soon furthered the impression of his position as a professional author by sub-mitting his poems to various local journals, and a goodly number were accepted. The *Christian Index,* of Washington, Georgia, accepted "The Jew's Lament" (October 13, 1835), the *Augusta Chronicle* included two moderately long poems in a single issue,[49] and there is reason to believe the *Atlanta Enterprise* took a poem during the next year.[50] So Chivers had begun his long task of proving his capabilities to his local audience. To have a resident poet must have pleased the town fathers, although it was not until 1856 that they called upon him for public utterance in behalf of the town.

Gradually Chivers' vehicles of publication increased in number until he could list the *Knickerbocker* and the *New Yorker* as among those magazines which had given him space.[51] He remained in Georgia during 1835 and 1836, publishing in the South and in certain Northern magazines, but the reception given his literary attempts was not always cordial. The *Southern Literary Messenger* was blunt enough:

There is a great deal of feeling in many of the communications sent to the publisher by T. H. C., M.D.; but to our poor taste, there is not much *poetry*. We question whether the Doctor will not find the lancet and pill box of more profit in that warm region to which he has emi-grated, than the offerings of his prolific muse. The poetical manufac-ture depends more upon the *quality* than the *quantity* of its fabrics, for success.[52]

There has been speculation that Poe wrote this squib, but the evidence is by no means conclusive.[53] The paragraph does indi-cate that Chivers had been actively soliciting the magazine in some considerable volume, and it also suggests that the *Southern Lit-erary Messenger* critic had seen *Conrad and Eudora;* the reference to the "warm region to which he has emigrated" postulates a more northerly acquaintance before this date (March, 1835), and the *only* publishing Chivers had done in the North to this time was the printing of *Conrad and Eudora* in Philadelphia. Con-ceivably Chivers might have sent a review copy to the *Messenger.* Despite Chivers' later fame, this magazine never changed its edi-torial mind, for only one of his poems appears in its pages. Within two months of the *Messenger's* notice, the *New York Mirror* commented, in rejection of Chivers' poetry, that his "Letters and verses are highly honourable to his own feeling, and to the gentleman alluded to; but the lines, though very pretty, require a more careful supervision than we have leisure to bestow upon them . . . ."[54] Within a month, not discouraged by such comment, Chivers had subscribed to the magazine, and the editor, apparently pleased by the subscription, noted that "The Dying Dove" was "very pretty."[55]

But the majority of Chivers' work during the years between 1834 and at the end of 1837 was devoted to writing poetry which did not receive publication until eight or more years later. Only one poem is dated 1834, and five are dated 1835, but in 1836, according to their date lines, Chivers wrote twenty-six poems. Of these efforts, seventeen appeared after 1850, while only four of them were published in his next volume, *Nacoochee* (1837). The number of poems which Chivers produced during this single year (in addition to the poems of *Nacoochee*, none of which are dated) indicates a sort of minor *annus mirabilis;* it suggests that he had finally begun to find himself in poetry, that his style was settling into the form he would later develop so effectively, and that his subject matter was being bent to fit his own desires and not those of contemporary magazine publishers or the public's tastes. None of his poems were published during this year of 1836, a fact which testifies further to the impression that Chivers had set himself the task of maturing his talents. He could not very well fail to respond to literary notices as critical as that in the *Southern Literary Messenger* rejecting his poetry, and even the *New York Mirror,* which had accepted his work, had warned him that his lines needed polishing.

During 1835 and 1836 Chivers wrote ten of the poems which were to be published in his most interesting volume, *Virginalia* (1853). These poems remained in manuscript during the intervening years, and surely must have been subject to considerable revision and alteration. Chivers was not the artist to discard an attempt once made, and in all probability comparative texts of poems written, say, in 1836 and published seventeen years later would show the process of his development. The primary image of "The Dying Beauty" (1837), effective even in its first context, was refined and sharpened for its republication in *Virginalia* (1853).[56] Much of the same sort of improvement has been effected in the change of "The Dying Poet" of *Nacoochee* (pp. 45-47) to that of *The Lost Pleiad* text of the same poem, published eight years later. The first text of the poem shows a very loose construction, and the two parts of the double quatrain hang together only haphazardly. When he came to use this poem later, Chivers cut it to a series of single quatrains, orienting each with the next so that the poem now presents a unified effect. The change Chivers made from the 1837 text to that of 1845 gives the final text of the poem whatever power it does have.

Chivers was learning the values of revision and careful composition. The number and variety of poems written during these years stand as proof that he was consciously testing his capabilities, going much further than the standard lyrics of *Conrad and Eudora,* which had been in themselves an extension from the topical poetry of *The Path of Sorrow,* toward poetry which, by 1853, he could revise to use in compiling his most striking collection. Although the middle thirties did not see the publication of this work, for he was not yet sure of himself, they did see the firing of his imaginative grasp and his first attempt to write in his later style. His trip to Philadelphia in 1834 may help to explain this surge of literary power, for it was during this trip, in all probability, that he first saw the collected works of Shelley, Keats, and Coleridge.[57] To the young Georgia poet, an amateur despite his two published volumes of poetry and his anxious desire to be considered a professional, the pages of their works must have been exalting; Keats and Homer conspired to produce one of the most provocative of metaphors, and Chivers surely gazed on Keats with the same delight. There were lessons to be learned from their poems, and the many manuscripts bearing 1836 dates are testimony to Chivers' application to the task before him.

During 1837 Chivers made another trip to the North, this time centering his activities about New York. Apparently he was in or near the city, except for various trips to the South, until 1842; it was the second long stay away from Georgia, and it was to mark the publication of a third volume of poetry, continuing magazine publication, and, finally, the beginning of his correspondence with Poe.

Nacoochee; or The Beautiful Star, with Other Poems was published by W. E. Dean, 2 Ann Street, New York, in 1837. The Preface to the volume is dated September 10, 1837, but, as Professor Damon has pointed out, one of the poems included in *Nacoochee,* when it was revised for inclusion in a later volume, bore the date of October, 1837;[58] so either Chivers had forgotten the date of publication of the volume by 1853, or the Preface was prepared well ahead of publication. This was his first volume to be published in New York, and, as always, he paid for the printing himself.

The book consists of fifty poems, varying from the thirty-two pages of the title poem, *"Nacoochee,"* to many short lyrics. There is clear evidence that he had been reading Keats and Shelley, and the overall atmosphere of the book is calmer, more controlled, and Chivers is less liable to slip off into extremes and excesses. He utilizes a variety of meters, from blank verse to Spenserians, but his use of them is characterized by the same increased certainty of touch that is present in the general tone and atmosphere of the book. The two years of comparative silence and intense poetic activity left evidence of improved technique; his themes seem closer to those which attracted him in his mature poetry; he shows a control over diction that indicates he has not given up his aim of expanding the available language but has realized the necessity of keeping his descriptive words and exotic names within certain bounds so that they may be effective within their context. The book is not a perfect specimen of his talents, but it is a distinct advance over the two earlier volumes.

The title poem of *Nacoochee* still holds interest for the critic of Chivers. Ostensibly a verse romance, it is actually one of the first evidences of Chivers' conscious use of symbolism; moreover, it is his first attempt to evoke the mystical world of the Terrestrial Eden, the paradise on earth, which held his attention and his imagination so forcibly in later years.[59] The poem concerns itself with an Indian youth's attempts to reach his loved one, who is hidden away from the world on an island of ideality and peace. As he finally approaches her retreat, she is carried away by the Angel of Death. The source of this romantic outline for the poem lies deep in Georgia folklore, involving a revision of a myth of a Cherokee maiden who, according to various versions of the tale, either dies in a fruitless attempt to save her lover, or dies with him rather than be captured by their enemies.[60]

There was a Cherokee village in the Valley of Nacoochee, in northeastern Georgia near the headwaters of the Chattahoochee, as early as historic times. The Spaniards of De Soto speak of reaching the village of Guaxule, in May of 1540, a village whose Indian name was Nacoochee, or *Nagu'tsi* in its Cherokee form. Unfortunately De Soto's narrative does not mention the Indian maiden Chivers was delighted with, although there is a note that a captured Indian queen escaped at that point with three slaves of the Spaniards. The legends would make a tragedy of the queen's death; the narrative says nothing. Chivers of course knew the legend, for he had traveled near the valley to reach the falls of Tuccoa, of which he speaks in glowing terms, [61] and many years later he spoke directly of the valley:

There is a beautiful and fertile valley in Clark County, Georgia, called *Nacoochee, Nakassa,* or *Naguissa* (after the name of a beautiful Indian maiden who was killed there, with the young chief to whom she was betrothed, by her ferociously jealous rival), which signifies *The Beautiful Star.*[62]

William Bartram had passed through the Cherokee village of *Nae[c]oche* in 1776, and noted that it was one of forty-three such villages in the immediate area.[63] Although he does not mention the legend of the valley, he does indicate the mysterious nature of a mound upon which the central Indian council hut had been built, and says that the Cherokees themselves had no memory of its original purpose or builder.[64] Since that time, ethnological inquiries have turned up a variety of historic utensils and instruments as well as a number of human graves, indicating that the artificial mound was at once burial ground, and, for successive generations, living quarters.[65]

The legends surrounding this prehistoric mound in its pleasant, lonely valley attracted Chivers' attention and he gave the name of the valley a symbolic value; at one point he traces its origin back to the Hebrew *Nachash,* signifying Lucifer, "or the *Morning Star* —that is, THE BEAUTIFUL STAR."[66] Thus the symbolism which is obvious as the reader pursues the title poem becomes clearer. Chivers uses Lucifer not as a fallen angel but as an angel of heaven, temporarily restricted to the earth; there is no sense of eternal sin about the maiden Nacoochee.

Dedicated to Chivers' mother, *Nacoochee* includes the first of a series of comparatively lengthy Prefaces devoted to the art of poetry. "Poetry is that crystal river of the soul which runs through all the avenues of life, and after purifying the affections of the heart, empties itself into the Sea of God."[67] So the Preface begins, and throughout its several pages Chivers sustains this tone of serious contemplation. It was his first public utterance on the theory of poetry, and it shows that the Transcendentalists as well as the English Romantics had contributed to his theory. Even at this early date Chivers is certain of the nature of divine inspiration and that the prime end of all poetry is the expression of Divine Beauty.[68]

Toward the conclusion of the Preface Chivers in part explains his meaning with regard to the symbolism of "Nacoochee":

> The word Nacoochee, in the Indian language, signifies beautiful star. There is a lake, or a collection of water, between the Oakmulgee and Flint rivers, in Georgia. . . . The Creek Indians believed that in the centre of this lake there is an island of such extraordinary beauty, that if they could only possess it, they would immediately be made happy. They believe that it is inhabited by the most beautiful of all God's creatures . . . some say that when they approach that Eden of terrestrial bliss, the island continues to move on from them. . . .[69]

Further elaboration of the symbolism is hardly necessary. Chivers continues to say that the present poem is only the first canto of a longer work which "will be published, if proper, at some future day."[70] The time never arrived for the continuation of the title poem, although its substance was used and developed in *Atlanta* (1853), Chivers' final volume of poetry.

It would be interesting to know how well *Nacoochee* sold in 1837, if at all. There are a number of copies extant today, and one bears pencilled corrections in Chivers' hand, all of a minor nature.[71] Printed in New York, unlike his earlier books, it possibly achieved wider circulation than they did, although there is no known review of the volume. Chivers was acting the part of the practising poet when he prepared the contents of *Nacoochee*, conscious of his style and subject matter. He chose some nine poems which he had published previously, either in *The Path of Sorrow, Conrad and Eudora*, or in magazines and refined them for publication in this collection. The changes from the 1834 volume are significant; every one of the six poems revised from this work has been compressed and cut down for *Nacoochee*, either by omitting repetitious or unrelated stanzas, or by pruning some of the extremes of emotion. Where the lyrics of *Conrad and Eudora* read almost as though they had been disinterred from his files to complete a book whose main concern is the title tragedy, *Nacoochee* appears as a much more carefully rounded and balanced work. It is perhaps indicative of the pains Chivers took over this volume that fifteen poems from it were republished, either in original or revised form, in later years.

That this volume reached the hands of various literary figures can be shown with considerable ease. James Russell Lowell, still distant from Chivers' quiet movements about the South and Philadelphia and New York, received a copy of *Nacoochee* from the author, and his copy (now at Harvard) carries marginalia in his own hand. Edgar Allan Poe, whom Chivers had not yet met, but whose name was familiar to Chivers as early as 1835,[72] saw and made use of the title poem in "Ulalume," and so must have seen *Nacoochee* before 1847, when "Ulalume" was first published. Where did Chivers send the volume for review? The local journals in the South which had accepted his fugitive poems surely would be interested in a Chivers collection; but no comment is extant. And residing as he was in and about New York and lower Connecticut, would he not have sent the book to literary friends? If he did, they never published their reactions. I think that the answer to such unexpected silence helps to interpret Chivers and his place in the contemporary literary world.

As we trace the history of his publishing, we will see that Poe was virtually the only important literary figure with whom Chivers had sustained contact, and that the first reviews of Chivers' work appear, as it were, under Poe's instigation. Before he met Poe, and after their friendship had dwindled, Chivers existed on the sub-literary fringes of his contemporary literary world. He moved in paths which are difficult to trace today, precisely because so very few well-known literary men walked them with him. Dedicated to the writing of poetry by his own desires, and determined to express himself in his own terms, Chivers did not fit into the popular and conventional atmosphere which surrounded those who published in magazines and whose names helped sell their work. Later, it is true, his work was accepted quite widely by contemporary journals, but he was seldom a regular and known contributor. And those who did know him, we may imagine, found the confidence with which he judged his own poetry and that of others somehow disconcerting amid such otherwise complete anonymity. Chivers said, "I have had mighty dreams in my life,"[73] and we may agree, for the dreams are recorded in his poetry, but they are seldom evident in the few known details of his life.

But, like all men who have something to say, Chivers did find a literary audience; scattered as it was over the decades, it still includes several of the masters of English poetry, and a few of the popular poets of our language. For example, there existed on a library card in Columbia University's files the name Joyce Kilmer, who was recorded as having borrowed *Nacoochee*.[74] What inspired the young student to inquire after Chivers cannot even be surmised.

Furthermore, there is strong evidence that William Butler Yeats knew *Nacoochee;* "The Lake Isle of Innisfree" concludes,

> I hear lake water lapping with low sounds
> by the shore;
> While I stand on the roadway, or on the pave-
> ments gray,
> I hear it in the deep heart's core.   [11. 10-12]

Yeats' theme is the search for peace in the midst of confusion and distraction. Chivers' theme in "Nacoochee" is the search for beauty and peace on an ideal island, and one of his stanzas contains an image startlingly like Yeats':

> his heart's deep core
> Sank into that deep sea whose ripples had
> no shore!   [11. 224-225]

The concept of the ideal island, located far in the romantic distance appears climactically in Chivers' *Atlanta* (1853), and the slow movement of water seems typical of him. If Yeats did not see Chivers' poem, then perhaps the similarity may stand as coincidence, but it seems probable that the Irish poet did read Chivers, for Chivers was, as we shall see, the first poet to attempt to utilize the dramatic possibilities of the Irish legend of Deirdre, in which Yeats was of course interested.

Such were the first six years of Chivers' publishing career. They are particularly crowded ones, for within this boundary Chivers published three volumes of poetry, several magazine pieces, and a theological pamphlet. Beginning with a personal theme so intimate as to make the poetry seem sublimation, Chivers continued to expand his talents by practice with conventional subjects and forms in "Songs of the Heart," and finally produced the first of the volumes which seem close to his mature poetry. In 1837 he was twenty-eight years old, had been separated from his first wife for ten years, and was about to marry a second time.[75] Financed by his father, he was able to spend his time traveling through the West and strolling through the cities of the mid-Atlantic seaboard, never finding it necessary to practice the medical art he had learned at Transylvania.

I suggest that such a record is a distinctly unusual one, and not alone for its record of achievement. While it is interesting that a young man with no literary heritage in his family, brought up in a small Georgia town founded only four years before his birth, and the graduate of a distant medical school, should venture to thrust himself on the literary scene, an equally valid subject for contemplation is the silence which greeted his arrival. The absence of records concerning his movements is no less unusual than the abundance of those movements themselves.

Chivers apparently met his second wife, Harriette Hutchins Hunt, while in Springfield, Massachusetts, having some books bound. The Hunt family was well known in the region, and the appearance of the young Southern poet surely brought considerable comment. Their marriage took place in New York, on November 21, 1837;[76] the temptation is to believe he may have eloped with the eighteen-year-old girl, whom all remember as strikingly beautiful.

Her presence must have brought understanding as well as love, for just as their marriage marks the end of Chivers' period of literary apprenticeship, so it must have afforded the sympathy Chivers so much needed. No one who remembers Chivers suggests that he was an easy man to live with; the strong will, the complete confidence in his own judgment, and the quick and often excessive emotional response, all evident in his early poetry, surely demanded from Harriette worship and devotion which never questioned. The misery, despair, and anger produced by his first marriage might now fade and be absorbed by his present happiness and by the beginning of his long chase after some sort of public recognition; Chivers was artist enough to need encouragement despite his confidence in his own powers. It remained for the 1840's to provide him with the opportunity to secure that acclaim.

The publication of *Nacoochee* in the fall of 1837 was only one of Chivers' literary labors at the time. While his talents for lyric poetry were developing, as *Nacoochee* testifies, he was still interested in dramatic verse, and the Sharp-Beauchamp case still intrigued him. He began revisions of *Conrad and Eudora*, sharpening the dialogue and establishing a firmer control over his rhetoric. While the revised play was not published until 1851, he was ready for a professional opinion of the text by March of 1838, when he wrote to E. S. Connor, asking for his criticism. Connor was an actor-manager of considerable reputation in America, particularly in Philadelphia, where he managed the Arch Street Theatre.

Dear Sir,—As I have been often delighted with your personation of various characters, if you will call over to the North American Hotel this evening, I will present you with a new Tragedy, entitled Leoni, or, the Orphan of Venice, founded upon fact. As the Author intended "Alvino" for yourself, he would like very much to have you read it, and see how you like it. My private friends have spoken in such flattering terms of it, I feel disposed to let you pass your judgment upon it. As I visit the Theatre at all times when there are good plays, and patronize every thing that tends to enervate the faculties, and strengthen the character, you will favour me with a visit, and see what you think of the Play.[77]

Mr. Connor certainly could have offered precise criticism; for six months before, the woman who was later to be his wife, Catherine Mary Sanford Barnes, a moderately well-known actress and playwright, had written and produced *Octavia Bragaldi; or, The Confession,* the first drama on the Beauchamp murder actually offered on the stage. Chivers' play reads better than Miss Barnes', but she was wise enough in the ways of the theatre to turn the Frankfort, Kentucky, tragedy into a tangled melodrama of fifteenth century Milan. It held the stage until as late as 1854.

Mr. Connor apparently did not see Chivers' play at this time, for in another letter to Connor on May 28, 1851, Chivers again recommends *Leoni* to him, including in his letter the text of the first act, with more to follow. Perhaps Chivers had been inspired by the performance of Miss Barnes' play, which he may well have seen, to rewrite *Conrad and Eudora;* if so, the rewriting was done between November, 1837, and March, 1838.

· 27

A month after Chivers wrote to Connor in 1838, his beloved mother died. He was in the North, presumably introducing his new wife to the nomadic literary life which she would lead with him for twenty years, when the news came. A series of poems place the date of her death and Chivers' trip South for the funeral in the beginning of April, 1838,[78] although the dedication page of *Songs of Sorrow,* whose Preface bears a date of October 18, 1837, is inscribed to his mother as "One in Heaven." Either Chivers added the information about his mother's death to the dedication of *Songs of Sorrow* after he had dated the Preface, or dated the poems on his mother's death a year after that death actually occurred; the former supposition seems the more probable.

His mother's death and his new marriage drew him away from poetry temporarily, for 1838 saw the publication of only two poems. But the following year was one of the more prolific of his career, as he published twenty-eight pieces, all of which he had written during the year. He had returned from his mother's funeral before June of 1838,[79] and he and his wife lived in New York City and Middletown, Connecticut, from 1838 until the summer of 1842, when a series of poems indicates that they moved to Georgia, at least for two or three years. Chivers was to live more and more in the North, settling later for some time in New Haven, and moving intermittently to New York, Philadelphia, and Boston. The reason for his move to Middletown is not known, but he quickly became familiar with William D. Starr, the editor of Middletown's *Sentinel and Witness,* a weekly journal of literature and general intelligence; his first poem in that paper appeared in June of 1839, presumably not long after he took up residence there.[80] The *Sentinel and Witness* accepted thirteen of the twenty-eight new pieces he published in 1839, an indication both of its friendship toward Chivers and of one of his most characteristic habits of publication.

Chivers sent his poems to an extremely wide variety of magazines, some of which turned them down curtly, while others saw the poetry the pieces contained, and published him. Once he had achieved a place in a magazine's columns, he sent them all he could.[81] That poetry which he sent the *Sentinel and Witness* is more mature than his previous work, and contains a number as good as "My Spirit's Bride," a poem which has the control that suggests Keats' influence on his work.

Her form was shadowless—
A being of pure light, who made all things
Around the shadow of her loveliness,
Like an embodied sun, whose radiance flings
A darkness on the surface of clear streams,
Around the center of his focal'd beams.

.   .   .   .

As the stars of night
Are Jewels of Eternity, all hung
Around the brow of God, so they were bright,
And from my heart, around which they were strung,
Looked on the mirror of my soul's deep sea,
And saw themselves reflected burningly.[82]

Contemporary topics of national interest were beginning to interest him too. He may have been seeking to please his increasing magazine audience, or he may simply have been writing as he wished. On October 23, 1839, the students of Wesleyan University heard an address on proposed plans for a seminary in Florida in honor of Major Francis Langhorne Dade, whose death four years before at the hands of the Seminole Indians had set the match to the Seminole Indian War. Three weeks later, Chivers published "The Grave of Dade," offered as an extract from a manuscript poem (not extant), which raised the Army major to the ranks of the nation's great heroes.[83] Death for the sake of liberty always brought Chivers to his feet; he was not simply taking advantage of local sentiment on the subject, but restating a favorite theme.

As long as Chivers could identify himself personally with the occasional subject he was writing on, he could produce poetry. But such personal identification was necessary, and he would have made a wretched occasional poet in the neo-classic sense, where the poet is expected to produce without the slightest element of personal motivation. In all Chivers' poems concerned with local, contemporary subjects, there is always evidence that he had allowed himself to become emotionally involved with the subject. The "Wreck of the Home" is a case in point. The disaster of the steam packet *Home* in October of 1839, a tragedy in which some ninety-five passengers were drowned, echoed widely in the nation's newspapers. Chivers wrote his poem soon afterwards, and it seems a typically occasional poem until we realize that it was only the

· 29

first in a series on the wrath and power of the sea, a subject which apparently always attracted him.[84] Once his imagination had been caught, he could write of that which he had not participated in directly, and the result of this ability is a series of "occasional" poems, occasional only in that they ostensibly concern themselves with specific contemporary detail, while Chivers' real interest lies in his reaction to the occasion rather than the occasion itself.

One of the many poems published in the *Sentinel and Witness,* "Virtue," seems to suggest his wife's first pregnancy, and the intensity of his emotion as he speaks of the beauty in her eyes indicates something of the happiness he had found with Harriette Hunt.[85] Their first child, Allegra Florence, was born on June 9, 1839,[86] probably in Middletown. Chivers' joy at her birth is wholly clear from comments in his poetry and letters; he had seen her in a vision long before her birth,[87] and her presence filled him with joy.

The prose articles which Chivers contributed to the *Sentinel and Witness* during 1839 vary in subject and success. The first, "On the Use of Tobacco,"[88] is an attack upon an article from the previous week's *Sentinel and Witness* describing the beneficial effects of that weed on the human voice. Chivers' objections are couched in medical terms throughout, although the logic hardly seems inevitable. Chivers abstained from both tobacco and liquor, and here attacks both as injurious to the body's normal functions.

The second prose piece, "Frogology,"[89] has no particular object of satire in mind, although it does take general swipes at mankind's certainty that it, alone, is immortal, by "proving" that the frog, of all living creatures, will outlast the day of judgment. Chivers pauses to ridicule animal magnetism, and offers a list of various seemingly esoteric sciences, the study of which can hardly benefit mankind. One of the items on this list is "Conchology," and since Poe's *Conchologist's First Book* had appeared only a few months earlier, perhaps Chivers was including his friend-to-be in his satire. All these sciences, Chivers implies, require and get deep study; but who has ever investigated that most fascinating of subjects, the Physiology of Frogs! His attempt does not come off completely, but the piece is gently amusing. In connection with his later interest in the way in which pure sound, as distinct from denotative language, may be used in poetry, it is interesting to note that he says, only half facetiously, that the concert from a pond of frogs at dusk may teach great knowledge of "the Poetry of Sound."[90] Although he had not yet formalized his later investigations into theory, his interest is obvious.

That Chivers was wise to restrict his talents to poetry rather than to the genre of the short prose sketch is proven by the two which appeared in the *Sentinel and Witness,* "The Resting Place" and "A Mother's Love."[91] The first attempts, with comparative success, to conjure up the horrors of the Day of Judgment, and to achieve his effect Chivers depends wholly upon explanatory statement. The second is an apostrophe on the greatness of a mother's love, unselfish, springing from the soul. As is often the case with his general philosophic or emotional statements, he concludes the pieces by reference to his own life and emotions, here to his own mother, who had died about six months previously.

Chivers' name was circulating among the literary journals by this time, both as subscriber and contributor. When Poe prepared his Prospectus of the *Penn Magazine* in the spring of 1840, he included Chivers' name. He had seen his verses before this date, but had had no occasion to communicate with him. Chivers replied in July, saying that he had been touring the Hudson, and offering encouragement and advice concerning the magazine.

It was the beginning of an eight-year friendship, a friendship which included Chivers' evasive answers to Poe's requests for financial assistance as well as Chivers' offer to open his home in Georgia to him. Their relationship will be considered in detail later,[92] but here it is necessary to note that Poe's letters and essentially friendly criticism of the poems which Chivers sent to him helped to stir the lesser poet on toward literary maturity. Before 1840, although he had published a number of volumes of poetry and a large collection of fugitive poems, Chivers was not widely known. But almost as though Poe's letters and finally his offer of a partnership in his magazine had acted as a catalyst, Chivers began to move in his poetry with added power and sureness. The arrival of the Prospectus of the *Penn Magazine* that day in 1840 was not an explosive or climactic one, for Chivers had already begun his finer work in the pages of the magazines the year before, but it does stand as a sort of symbol, one which Chivers himself may have recognized. Throughout his career, and despite the wide circulation which his verses achieved, Chivers himself remained on the fringes of the literary world; the general absence of contemporary critical comment on his work and the long neglect in which it has lain are testimony enough to his twilight existence. Surely his name was familiar, eventually, to the major figures of the time, but one suspects that he himself never achieved the warmth of companionship and friendly interchange of ideas or criticism which he might have expected. An extremist in almost everything he did, he would be known, at least by reputation, to editors and authors of the 1840's and 1850's but the extreme character of his emotional nature and the complete outward assurance with which he conducted himself both in his poetry and in what little is known of his public life, would prevent easy friendships and social or literary moderation. His attempts at prose satire have suggested one cardinal point in his character, his lack of a sense of humor, and that lack surely kept him at a distance from the literati of the time. Poe, on the other hand, for reasons of his own as well as for a subtle understanding of the similarity of their natures, was willing to continue his correspondence with Chivers. We may imagine the delight with which the Georgia poet received literary intelligence from the well-known editor; indeed, his own letters to Poe are full of a desire to discuss literary matters, both theoretical and practical. Poe was to be Chivers' one real source of entrance into the professional literary world, and although correspondence ceased eight years later, the initial impetus Chivers received from Poe's attentions, scattered and incomplete though they were, helped a good deal toward urging him to fuller poetic expression.

That Chivers seldom or never lost confidence in himself is shown by an exchange of insults with the editor of the *Connecticut Herald,* Thomas G. Woodward. Chivers published a sketch on John Newland Maffitt, at that time chaplain of the House of Representatives, and long a controversial Methodist minister. His career had been everywhere surrounded by rumors of scandal concerning his personal conduct and the possibly heretical nature of his beliefs. He delivered his *Oration* before the literary societies of Wesleyan University in 1841, and after listening to his rhetorical, florid prose style, Chivers had been inspired to write in praise of Maffitt, and to describe Maffitt's libellers as "the vituperative serpents of the earth, who waylay the good, biting them on their heels, to free their hissing tongues of a satiety of poison."[93] The editor of the *Connecticut Herald* replied to this identification in terms hardly complimentary, and Chivers answered, warning that he was "striking at thunder with a long pole."[94] In the next issue of the *Sentinel and Witness,* which Chivers had been using to conduct his attack, he concluded the affair with an article entitled "Awful Death," purporting to be a sorrowful announcement of the death of Woodward "from spontaneous combustion":

For a long time previous to his death, he had been under great mental excitement, caused, as he expressed himself, by *"striking at thunder with a long pole,"* during a fishing excursion. . . . The lightning having struck him in the coronal region of the head, where all the moral faculties are situated, ran down the spinal marrow, and, passing out, laid the *fundamental* principles of his whig constitution bare! A long time previous to his death, he made no use whatsoever of his sympathetic nerve—it being entirely paralyzed.[95]

The coarse nature of his attack, and the essentially brutal components of his comparisons, throw light on a part of Chivers' nature which does not show in his poetry. Sure of the correctness of his own opinions, he would tolerate no contradiction. Whenever objection was made, he struck out as though deeply injured. The product of a sensitive nature, perhaps, these attacks were nevertheless unfortunate and often unjustified. They are reminiscent of the destructive admonitions Chivers himself had received early in his career concerning *The Constitution of Man,* and are representative of a period in our literary history which did not depend upon subtlety in the expression of its opinions. Personalities were always subject to attack, and Chivers provided a unique figure to unfriendly editors. Tempting them by the extremeness of his statements, he replied to their attacks in terms which only reiterate the extreme nature of all of his reactions.

The rigidity of mind which this inability to accept corrective comments testifies to is another possible explanation of why we hear so little of Chivers in the records of the men of letters of his day. His reaction to Woodward's comments is symptomatic of the manner in which he met virtually every controversial subject. Seldom temperate, he voiced his beliefs in a manner so decisive and insistent as to preclude friendly discussion or argument. Less adamant minds would simply ignore him, for he was not to be argued with. Even his poetry shows something of this quality, for there is as much assurance and certainty in his heavenward flights as there is in his expressions of opinion. It is fortunate that the unpleasant side of Chivers' assurance is kept out of his poetry.

It is hardly surprising that this outburst ended Chivers' publishing in the *Sentinel and Witness*. Although literary quarrels and learned disputes might increase a paper's circulation, and although Chivers had been one of their most consistent contributors since 1839, he was no longer welcome, or so it would seem. He remained in Middletown until June of 1842, however, dating a long series of poems from there.

The years of the 1840's preceding the publication of Chivers' fourth volume of poetry, *The Lost Pleiad,* in 1845, saw him switch his place of publication but not diminish his output to any considerable degree. Five publications in 1842 and twelve in 1843 mark his preparation for his next volume of poetry.[96] Almost everything he published in magazine form during these years he later collected, and several of his most successful poems in *Virginalia* (1853), a volume representative of his later work, first appeared at this time. Chivers was now a careful, determined worker at the art of poetry; he had gradually gained more and more control over his form and his technique.

The Lost Pleiad; and Other Poems appeared some time after July 18, 1845, the date of the "Prefatory Apologue." Printed by Edward O. Jenkins of 114 Nassau Street in New York, the volume contains sixty-eight poems, all but one of which is dated. The dates of composition extend from June, 1836, to December, 1844, and twenty of the poems in the book had appeared in magazines during the five years preceding their book publication. Generally, the poems which have been published previously are concerned with the multiple tragedies of the death of his four children in 1842 and 1843. The whole volume has a deeply elegiac tone, and Chivers seems to have selected his most depressing poems for inclusion here; one of Chivers' daughters recalls that Harriette chose the poems herself.

There is no particularly startling advance in technique or form in this volume; it is almost as though he avoided choosing from among his published or manuscript poems any which show experiment or innovation. And since the majority of his experimenting was done in poems whose theme expresses delight and joy in the presence of heaven or the heavenly, it is clear why *The Lost Pleiad* is almost entirely conventional. Much of the subject matter was too close to him for him to achieve anything of the aesthetic distance necessary to create poetry. His stride is calmer and more certain, however. There are hints, too, that he had been working to expand his grasp; for the first time he includes sonnets among his other lyrics. Their variety of scheme is sometimes startling, and it may be that through the exact form demanded by the sonnet he was trying to obtain some of the detachment from grief that he needed.

To the modern reader, *The Lost Pleiad* seems an unsuccessful book, for overt displays of grief are no longer aesthetically acceptable. But melancholia was a disease of the age, and Chivers had it no worse than hundreds of others, and indeed had more cause than most. On the eighteenth of October, 1842, his first daughter, Allegra Florence, died after a shockingly short illness.[97] As a doctor, Chivers was deeply troubled by his inability to save his daughter. Her birth had brought him great happiness, and even before her death he had come to regard her as a heavenly presence.[98] She inspired him to write a number of poems on her heavenly beauty, the most notorious of which is "To Allegra Florence in Heaven,"[99] a poem whose tenth stanza, comparing Chivers' distressed heart to a broken egg, is often misrepresented as being typical of his work. While this simile is not characteristic of Chivers, his inability to restrain his emotion in those poems descriptive of death brings them perilously close to extremely bad poetry; the title poem of *The Lost Pleiad* is replete with the most Gothic of detail describing her death agony.

And while the memory of her death was still fierce in his mind, three other children died in the first four months of 1843, as a tragic Bible record testifies.[100] In the face of this catastrophe, Chivers may be forgiven some of the excesses of grief contained in *The Lost Pleiad*.

From a series of poems published in the *Sentinel and Witness* in 1841 it is evident that Chivers had begun to collect poems for book publication long before *The Lost Pleiad* was conceived. Five poems published variously from August through October of 1841 carry as subtitle "From 'Woodland Melodies'" or a close variant.[101] One is even more specific in stating its source: "From a volume of Manuscript Poems, entitled 'Woodland Melodies.'"[102]

Three of these poems appeared in *The Lost Pleiad*. If they are identified as from an earlier, incomplete collection, whose subject matter presumably would approximate its title of "Woodland Melodies," then the variations from the major theme of *The Lost Pleiad,* an elegiac one, may be understood. Apparently Chivers' composition of the "Woodland Melodies" poems was interrupted and eventually halted by Allegra Florence's death in 1842. When his three other children died the next year, he was completely unable to continue this volume. Inspired as always by his personal emotions, he wrote poems expressive of his state of mind at that time. When he prepared *The Lost Pleiad* in 1845, he simply included the "Woodland Melodies" poems, possibly to provide a certain variety from the theme of death. It seems certain also that a number of the lighter poems of *The Lost Pleiad,*[103] which had not been anywhere published as from "Woodland Melodies," were originally in that manuscript collection as well as those published in the *Sentinel and Witness* as such.

The majority of poems in the volume, excluding the title poem, which is some eight pages long, are extremely short lyrics. Despite the personal sorrow Chivers felt, there is no real fire of emotional reaction here. Perhaps the conventional and artificial frameworks which he constructs about a number of the poems in the volume, formulae which often remove the impression of sincerity necessary to render his grief effective poetry, offered the only method by which he could control that grief. Despite the apparent paradox, it seems that Chivers' emotion was so great that he could only modulate it into poetry by choosing conventional situations through which his emotion infrequently shines. For example, "Sonnet.—The Grave" (p. 24) offers a commonplace statement as theme: man's eventual end is the grave, where all pain and grief are forgotten. Only when he speaks in such standard terms as these can he control his grief. Like *The Path of Sorrow,* this is basically a personal volume of poetry, although its personal nature is hidden behind just such conventionalities as that above, and like that volume also it presents Chivers attempting to discover the correct vehicle for his own inward and overwhelming emotion. *The Lost Pleiad* adopts the strict form of the sonnet and conventional literary situations to cushion Chivers himself from the sharpness of his grief. Occasionally he succeeds in utilizing the protection afforded; "The Soul's Destiny" (pp. 16-17) is a valid example of the moderation he could achieve.

The Lost Pleiad brought the first reviews Chivers had ever received on a volume of poetry, and a good part of this response was due to Poe, who reviewed the volume favorably in the *Broadway Journal* and promised to direct Chivers' increasing fame.[104] Poe's review was quoted in several outlying journals,[105] and may possibly have influenced William Gilmore Simms to modify somewhat his generally unfavorable review in the *Southern Patriot*, for he noticed *The Lost Pleiad* a second time, in more complimentary terms, two weeks after Poe's favorable comment.[106] In a manuscript in the Chivers Collection, Chivers replied to Simms' strictures, and most of his objections seem sensibly motivated, unlike his usual reaction to criticism:

[Simms] says that *"Man ought not to complain!"* Why not? Did he ever lose a child? Whence does he derive this Stoicism?

. . . .

Man must speak or die. He was created to speak. Speech is an outlet for the diffusion of the pangs of his heart. It is by complaining that many ills are borne which would be otherwise insufferable. . . . Therefore, let man speak, for the Angels in Heaven are listening to hear.

. . . .

So, our sorrows for the dead are only audible expressions of a silent desire within which cannot be repressed. It is a mournful prayer to God, in which we not only tell of our sorrows, but implore a deliverance from them. This deliverance we implore when we ask Him to permit us to be all that we imagine of the dead.[107]

Except for the connotations of the word "complain," the body of Chivers' essay seems an honest interpretation of the pressures which moved him to express himself. What he offers as explanation is couched in theological terms; in psychoanalytical terms, his publication of his sorrows would be called sublimation.

The reviewer of the *Southern and Western Monthly Magazine* wrote the most discerning of all the criticisms of the book, although even he failed to understand one important element in Chivers' character. Excerpts from his review indicate both personal acquaintance with Chivers and a careful reading of the text:

We have long known Dr. Chivers . . . as a man of real talent, and very delicate fancy. He possesses a poetic ardor sufficiently fervid, and a singularly marked command of language. But he should have been caught young, and well-bitted, and subjected to the severest training. He is perverse and willful, and his muse labors under the worst of all misfortunes . . . she is particularly monotonous.

Chivers would indeed have expressed himself differently had he been trained to control his genius early in life; yet such training might well have curbed his imagination to mediocrity.

His judgment fails him in the choice of topics, and fails him because of the unmanageable excess of egotism which pervades his mental structure. Of course we employ the word egotism in no offensive, or *personal* sense, but simply in regard to the intellectual and moral organization of the writer. . . . It is the obtrusive aspect which rises up utterly to deny the reader the privilege of that sympathy, which it is the purpose of the author to provoke. . . . He allows the man constantly to interfere with and thwart the objects of the poet. . . .

The poet and his personality may intrude upon his poetry when such intrusion presents complete sincerity of attitude. In his later work, Chivers, as both man and poet, is ever more present, and the integrity and sincerity of his reactions carry the reader along with him. The obtrusion is objectionable in many poems of *The Lost Pleiad* where the artificial frameworks which Chivers found necessary to control his grief reduce this impression of sincerity.

Now, while we admit the frequent fancy, and the occasional grace and felicity of thought and diction, we certainly cannot do more. . . . The monotonous tenor of his strains impairs very much the just claims of Dr. Chivers to the respect of his reader. His skill in versification, his fluency of expression, the delicacy of his tastes, the *spirituelle* in his fancy—these are all, under the just direction of the judgment, elements of success of the poet. It is a willfulness that perverts their use, and mocks continually the yielding sympathies of the reader. Indeed, he will not be read. . . . His ingenuity or invention—perhaps, we should be more correct to say, his imagination, seems feeble and deficient and this may account for the ascendancy of his egotism. But for this deficiency, he would *go more out of himself,* and acquire the necessary variety, in the consideration of other characters and subjects. His *objectivity,* now kept in subjection by his simple individuality, might then expand and grow.[108]

There are just praises of Chivers' technical abilities in this criticism, and the tone of the whole indicates the reviewer's sincerity. Yet—and perhaps this lay at the bottom of many failures to understand Chivers—he cannot but believe that as a poet Chivers would profit from trying to "go more out of himself."

Perhaps this refers solely to the elegiac theme of *The Lost Pleiad*. If so, it is then symptomatic of the essential basis of Chivers' writing and of its occasional success or failure. For Chivers could never "forget" himself; all but a few completely artificial and unsuccessful poems concern themselves with the first person, explicitly or implicitly. His is a personal poetry, constructed entirely out of his own personal reactions to situations and interested in those reactions rather than in the situations. The reviewer was asking something which was manifestly impossible to a man constituted as Chivers was, although later, in his own way, he did "go more out of himself," but hardly in the direction here suggested. Increasingly, as his work matures, does he rise out of himself toward the ideal world of Heaven in his poetry; yet such a rise is as much inward as it is upward; so basically Chivers could not comply with this criticism.

But in any case the reviewer considered Chivers' work seriously and in detail. It was the first time such appraisals had been rendered, and the attention he received was in large part due to Poe's interest. Ironically, the elegiac subject matter so dominant here is not wholly typical of Chivers, and yet he has come down to the twentieth century as a writer of poems about dead children. Although he was overjoyed to have his book generally well accepted, or at least carefully criticized,[109] it is in a sense unfortunate that public attention could not have been caught earlier, by, let us say, *Nacoochee*. That, at least, would not have left the first impression of monotony and repetition which *The Lost Pleiad* did. Chivers wrote to Simms, years later, "I kept locked up for seven years, and gave only a few friends my Lost Pleiad."[110] Is it not possible that Chivers himself understood the atypical character of this book? He was anxious for public attention, as are most poets, yet he did not wish to be known only by *The Lost Pleiad,* which, I believe, is scarcely less intimate (thanks to the orthodox formulas he uses in which to express himself) than *The Path of Sorrow.*

Poe's presence marks this period in Chivers' literary career. From 1840 to 1845, centering around the latter date, their correspondence was comparatively constant. Chivers sent a variety of poems to Poe for criticism, an action which further indicates the seriousness with which he regarded his calling as a poet, and occasionally Poe replied in encouraging terms. Stimulated by this literary companionship, between the publication of *Nacoochee* in 1837 and *The Lost Pleiad* in 1845, Chivers had over fifty poems accepted by a large variety of magazines, and revised much of the undue rhetoric from *Conrad and Eudora*. His literary activity may have been even wider, for Poe mentioned an article entitled the "Luciferian Revelation" which Chivers had sent him, saying he found "a 1000 glorious thoughts"[111] in it. Unfortunately, no manuscript or printed text is known, but when taken with the rest of Chivers' literary productions, it helps to suggest something of the intensity of his activity. These years of the mid-1840's seem to have been happy ones for Chivers; perhaps he had been successful in achieving sublimation of his grief in *The Lost Pleiad*. At the end of 1845 he was in Georgia, and wrote to Poe:

I acknowledge to you, frankly, that I have been in Paradise ever since I returned home. It is Paradise all about here where my wife is. I dream mighty dreams in her presence sometimes. I will tell you one of them some of these days. Her footsteps pave the world with happiness. . . .[112]

Happy in his marriage, his name appearing in the literary journals with a pleasant regularity, Chivers could return to the South very nearly a contented man.

1846-1850

Chivers had been in New York in 1845 to get *The Lost Pleiad* published. He had talked, presumably for long periods, with the one important literary figure he knew well, and these conversations he had with Poe must have helped to spur him on to greater literary activity, although no period of his literary career can be called unproductive.

From the time of the publication of *The Lost Pleiad* in 1845 until the appearance of *Eonchs of Ruby* in the late fall of 1850, Chivers published over one hundred separate poems. Some of these were revisions of earlier work; the overwhelming majority were new compositions. Stimulated by the attention which he had received from his 1845 volume, he continued to write and to find interested publishers. His poems appeared in *Graham's Magazine*, the *Ladies' National Magazine*, *Peterson's Magazine*, the *Christian Index* (of Penfield, Georgia), the *Southern Literary Gazette*, *Holden's Dollar Magazine*, the *Literary Union*, the *Western Lit-*

erary Messenger, the *Knickerbocker*—in short, editors of reputable magazines generally were quite pleased to include his work. The contact with Poe had fired his maturing powers so that he might write on a wider range of subjects, and this increased literary effort is marked by a variety of interest. Lyrics of love, hymns, evocations of Heaven, poetic homilies, and oratorical jubilations in praise of liberty are dated from these years. Where he had had a single, personal theme in *The Lost Pleiad,* he now ranged further abroad in his subject matter yet managed to retain the personal quality which marks his better work.

Chivers had gone South after his visit with Poe in 1845, and he remained there for almost five years, although his wife occasionally wrote to friends that her husband was away too much on business. Presumably his trips, while possibly numerous, were not extended, for almost all of his poetry is dated from his estate in Washington, Georgia, called variously "Oaky Grove," "Oak Grove," and "Villa Allegra," the last after his fondly remembered daughter. It would seem that Chivers had found happiness for himself during this time. His comment to Poe in 1845 about the joy his wife's presence brings him is typical of the tone of many of his poems. *The Lost Pleiad* seems to have sublimated whatever grief overburdened him, and although there are melancholy notes occasionally,[113] most of his poems now ring with his vision of Heaven.

This theme of the glory and joy of Heaven had appeared as early as *Nacoochee* (1837) in such a poem as "The Soaring Swan" (pp. 36-40), and the magazine poems of the years before Allegra Florence's death in October of 1842 show some signs of Chivers' gradual move toward evocation of the divine. "The Song of Seralim," one of Chivers' more successful interpretations of the beauty of heavenly voices, is dated from April of 1842,[114] and "The Heavenly Vision" appeared in June of that year.[115] But it is difficult to find poems of such an exultant tone this early. These two poems, which seem typical of his later ability to conjure up an emotional and joyous view of Heaven, come in the months just before Allegra Florence's death, perhaps indicating that the spirit had come upon him at that time. But her passing and the subsequent tragedy of her brother's and sisters' deaths in 1843 left Chivers with little to inspire him. Grief was his theme, and he collected most of his expression of it into *The Lost Pleiad.*

However, the years following its publication saw an increase in the use of that tone and subject matter which are but incidentally evident in 1842. Death was still a usable subject, but when he spoke his tone was calmer, more accepting, less personally overwhelmed by sorrow. He was now even more obviously a religious poet, but his theological beliefs were seldom contained in homilies; more often he attempted to carry his reader up with him to an emotional awareness of the beauty of Heaven.

Chivers' own personality was deeply bound up in his poetry; his personal circumstances directed the movement of his poetry. The frustration in his earlier years in the face of public silence when his work appeared, coupled with the later loss of his children, had brought on despair, and *The Lost Pleiad*. But no man can forever support such torment and such neglect; so Chivers turned to his spiritual beliefs, turned inward, to find a world in which he could delight. And when Chivers was delighted, when his emotions were joy-filled, he could write good poetry.

Virtually all of the poems published between 1845 and 1850 were gathered into *Eonchs of Ruby,* to which we shall turn presently. But these poems do not represent all of Chivers' efforts of these years. Although by nature and by desire a poet, he spent a good part of his time in these busy years writing prose, either in essay form or as further letters to the journal in Athens, Georgia, which always welcomed his writing, the *Georgia Citizen*. His prose is often as metaphorical as his poetry, and frequently the opinions expressed in prose are considerably more severe than the emotions of his poetry. We have seen that he attacked James Hall of the *Western Monthly Magazine* in violent terms; soon it will be obvious that that same streak of vindictiveness is still present.

But the first evidence of his interest in prose expression is *Search after Truth; or A New Revelation of the Psycho-Physiological Nature of Man*. Printed by Cobb & Yallalee of New York in 1848, *Search after Truth* is Chivers' attempt to explain, in a Socratic dialogue between Politian, the questioner, and the Seer, the basic relationships between man and God. Politian asks a series of germinal questions which the Seer answers in terms which indicate that Chivers could reason with some clarity when he wished to. Chivers' character as well as his poetry would lead the reader to expect little more than emotional enthusiasm; actually the pamphlet is characterized by a careful attention to logic. His religious leanings were strong, he had seen visions during his youth as well as a vision of his daughter before her birth, and his nature was essentially an emotional one. Yet *Search after Truth* presents that emotion under reasoned control, and it is obvious that Chivers is striving hard to convince his reader by processes of argument which are almost Puritan in their precision, once certain postulates are granted. The essay is less interesting as an interpretation of the meaning of existence than as a view of Chivers, the logician, a side of his nature not immediately evident in his poetry or in his magazine prose.

The inspiration of this essay lies close to Chivers' personal experiences and reactions, as does the inspiration for everything he wrote. Having suffered extreme grief during the years of his children's deaths, and having finally risen from such sorrow to a fuller understanding of his always-firm belief in the eternal presence of God, he determined to codify his hitherto undefined religious beliefs; the result is as much a reaffirmation of what he had felt intuitively and emotionally as it is an explication of a religious system to which his readers might subscribe.

The primary purposes of *Search after Truth* are to provide logical proof of the existence of the soul, both in its present state as part of the two-fold composition of man's being and in its Angelic form as an extension of the thought and love of God, and to describe the "probationary" nature of man's life on earth preparatory to his assumption of his divine and immortal position after death. The essay succeeds less well in this attempt than it does in explaining several of Chivers' beliefs and assumptions as found in his poetry.

When Chivers explains his belief in the immortality of the soul and in the divinity of man, he is in part at least explaining his own poetic theory; the two are very closely allied, the second depending upon the first.

Man is the reason of God—the highest expression of God's Ideal of the Beautiful in the creation. It is by realizing here on earth in its fullest extent, the two fold object—*spiritual* and *natural*—of his creation, that he can assimilate himself to the Angels in Heaven. As Man is the incarnation of God's reason in the world, it is impossible for him to exercise his natural faculties in harmony with the manifold beauties of the visible creation, without experiencing some of those ineffable thrills of delight which He himself felt in giving birth to them. . . .

. . . .

Through the vista of the clear-shining future, the already couched eyes of the Prophetic soul can see the lightning-glimmering of the jasper-walled and many-gated City of pure gold of the Living God.

It is only by living in harmony with all things, that Man can understand the expression of God's Beautiful in the world. It is only by having his eyes couched that he can look, as the High Priest of Nature, from the star-lighted Sanctuary of this world into the Angel-lighted Arcana of Heaven.[116]

By considering himself a Seer, and feeling sure that his eyes were "couched,"[117] Chivers might realize fully God's design of the Ideal of the Beautiful. And much of the exultation which is obvious in the poetry of this mature period can be explained by just the terms Chivers has used here. In expressing himself in his poetry, in creating the Divinely Beautiful, Chivers was raised to joy by his own sense of power and by his delight in achieving this ultimate of beauty. Thus when he said that it was the business of poetry to express the Divine as it appears in the Beautiful he was aligning his theory of poetry with his theological belief; both were based upon an emotional identification which Chivers felt with his God. Specific elements of his poetic theory may be found in *Search after Truth*. For example, while Chivers denies Locke's theory of sensation, he actually comes very close to accepting it (or transcending it) when he makes his distinction between the soul's ability to receive knowledge in its earthly and in its heavenly state. In Paradise knowledge will be assimilated independently of the sensory organs, but while on earth all organs are capable of receiving education, are "susceptible of being perfected from birth until death."[118] Furthermore, and here he takes Locke's theory and puts it to his own uses, he believed "that all our [earthly] sensations, whether of pain or pleasure, are really thoughts themselves."[119] In the context in which these statements are found in *Search after Truth*, they are descriptive of the differences between the soul's existence on earth and in heaven; when they are utilized in the Preface to *Memoralia* (1853), his sixth volume of poetry, they serve as the basis for his poetic theory as it has reference to the use of sensory images.

The close tie between Chivers' theological and aesthetic thinking which such a transfer indicates may be elaborated even further to include autobiographical detail. In all probability concerned by the extremes of joy and sorrow which his life had exhibited, and aware that his greatest release from earthly pain came in moments of poetic inspiration, Chivers interpreted this pain as the soul's inability to receive the "melodious impressions" emanating from Heaven while in an earthly state. His description of the comfort afforded by a belief in the immortality of the soul explains in large part his motivation in evoking Heaven in his poetry:

A belief in the immortality of the soul, through the exercise of which we are led to expect a future state of existence, where it shall possess all the pleasures of which it is capable, and for which it continually yearns while in this life, is the only incentive that a man can have, under certain circumstances, to make him desire to live, and fulfil the office which God has assigned him, as a rational creature, while in this world.[120]

The sincerity of tone and strength of conviction evident in such a statement, as well as the definite reference to his own sorrows, suggests that *Search after Truth* was indeed a codification of the emotions and desires which Chivers himself experienced. As theological argument, it can be refuted; as a personal explication of his own motivations it helps explain the close connection between his religious belief and his poetic theory.

Chivers' religious beliefs were quite obviously based upon actual mystical experience he had had himself. Seldom content with theory unsupported by personal acquaintance, Chivers could not have written *Search after Truth* unless his own life had provided proof that there were indeed phenomena which wholly material or physical causes could not explain.

Andrew Jackson Davis, perhaps the most famous clairvoyant of the 1840's and 1850's, had published in 1847 his *Principles of Nature,* dictated over a period of two years while Davis was in a state of trance.[121] His volume, which was rapidly taken up, pro and con, by the wide audience interested in the processes of mesmerism, was an attempt to explain the basis of human life and the universe. His primary insistence was upon the existence of a life other than the physical, and upon the possibility of communication between the two by visionary experience. The whole country was alive to mesmerism, and Chivers, with his deeply emotional sensory reactions, must have turned to this latest proof of the existence of something beyond the physical world with great joy. He had already realized that he could write his finest poetry in contemplation of such another world, and with the advent of public reception of mesmerism he could feel that others besides himself had become aware of those things not commonly known to the world of physical phenomena.

Davis' views achieved their widest circulation through *The Univercoelum, or Spiritual Philosopher,* the first periodical devoted to Spiritualism, edited by Samuel Byron Brittan, himself deeply interested in Davis. Later Brittan became a faith healer after he himself had undergone a psychic experience. Chivers subscribed to the magazine in September, 1848, not long after he had published *Search after Truth.* Brittan welcomed him:

Among those who have been attracted to the New Philosophy, we are permitted to record the name of Dr. Thomas H. Chivers, Washington, Georgia.

Dr. Chivers is gifted with enlightened views and popular talent, and we are happy to number him among our regular contributors . . . he proposes to furnish a series of Spiritual Songs. . . .[122]

Chivers wrote a letter to the editor of the magazine complimenting him on the value of his undertaking:

[*The Univercoelum*] is certainly the fulfillment of that demand which lives immortal in the soul, for a perfect revealment not only of the beauties of external Nature, but of the wonderful wisdom of God, which has long existed in the world. It was a wise saying of Coleridge, the myriad-minded, that we should never declare a truth to the mind of any man who is not prepared to receive it . . . be cautious how you throw pearls to swine. . . . There are some truths which can only be known to the *Sacred Few*—those who have been anointed and set apart by the wisdom of God for the regeneration of the world. The reception of the Univercoelum . . . will be cherished by me as an Angel-visitant from the unseen world.[123]

Chivers was serious in such assurance; he would indeed take very seriously the purport of psychic revelation, and he did send a series of poems, and three prose pieces, before the magazine concluded in 1849. One of these prose articles is the description of his earliest visionary experience and contains also the details of his vision of Allegra Florence eight years before her birth.[124] Another was a recasting of an earlier article on Shelley; Chivers adjusted his comments so that Shelley is particularly the poet of divine truth.[125] His final article, entitled "Orphic Truths," analyzes man as a microcosm of the universe, both being subject to heaven's divine plan.[126] What Chivers had to say about man's divinity and the majesty of the visionary emotion was not out of place in such a magazine, and after it ceased publication, Chivers sought out others of the same nature.[127]

But he would not extend his belief in psychic phenomena to include some of the more extreme claims which mediums throughout the country were mouthing. When he heard that spirits were being commanded to move furniture and dictate poems, he rebelled. Nor would he completely accept the popular fondness for mesmerism; he concludes his final word on such "spiritual" manifestations by saying that "They are noises made at several places, in the *New England States,* by what a certain set of folks call *'Spiritual Agents.'* "[128] Whatever was representative of true spiritual manifestation, divorced from the physical or material world, Chivers could understand and participate in. But when popular opinion picked up the subtleties of psychic phenomena and made them exhibitions, Chivers refused to go along.

While Chivers was constantly interested in the processes and elements of his subconscious world of psychic experience, a world which appears very often in his poetry of this period, he was also beginning a three-year effort as literary correspondent to the *Georgia Citizen.* He had discussed the possibility of contributing a series of letters to both the *Southern Sentinel* (of Columbus, Georgia) and the *Albany Patriot* (of Albany, Georgia), but apparently found the *Citizen* more to his liking. There Chivers published three series of letters: "The Valley of Diamonds," from June 14th to October 20th, 1850; "Letters from New York," from September 20, 1850, to April 19, 1851; and "Letters from the North," from April 26, 1851, to March 24, 1854, a succession which was extended by a new series of eight letters, continuing until November 17, 1854. Taken together, there are sixty-eight, a not inconsiderable effort for a practicing poet.

The first two series, which we may discuss here, are concerned with everything of literary, social, or national importance which attracted Chivers' attention. Slavery issues, popular concerts, lectures, reviews of contemporary books, Biblical stories, and homiletic parables are jumbled together. The letters are basically a literary grab-bag, the loose format of which allows Chivers to wander as he chooses.

Always he is confident of his own judgment; there is no hesitation, seldom a qualified remark. All is superlative; much is declamatory. Something of the coarseness of tone noted in his response to literary criticisms of his own work appears here also, particularly when he is referring to the North's opinion of slavery or to the abolitionists. Much of what he says is designed for local consumption in Georgia, and is spoken as though his readers knew him well, as indeed they must have soon, and were willing to accept his judgment. Occasionally he is consciously cultural, providing discussions of current issues or subjects which surely added a certain sophisticated tone to the *Georgia Citizen*. Moving about on the edges of the literary circles of New York, New Haven, and Boston, Chivers reported what he heard and read as though he himself had been an important part of each occasion. One wonders, sometimes, whether the residents of the literary spotlight were conscious of the close and frequently biased scrutiny to which the Georgia poet was subjecting them. There is a singular absence of comment from the literati in their published journals or letters about the strange doctor-poet who moved among them. The supposition that Chivers remained somehow on the outside of all contemporary literary gatherings grows stronger as the geography of the circumstances comes clear. Chivers, wending his way throughout the North, moved solely by his own desires, might spend the day amid the social and literary world of New York, recording his impressions and reactions carefully, to return to his rooms at evening and write to friendly listeners in the South. His is the report of a foreign correspondent, one who is trying to explain and interpret his present surroundings to his own country, aware that they know little of the country he resides in. Such a situation often produces more than a little pathos, for Chivers so obviously had his heart set upon becoming a member of the world he spent his time describing. Boston, for example, impressed him as the one city where a cultured man might find learned and refined companionship. Yet while Chivers spent so much of his life in the North on the fringes of its society, and grieved privately over the South's seeming inability to provide an atmosphere receptive to culture, he never became any kind of an expatriate nor lost his sense of identification with the South.

The scope of his activities must indeed have been large. He was surely enjoying himself as he examined the world about him, despite his distance from it. In one letter he has received a shipment of steel engravings from London, and among them is one of Hiram Powers' famous statue of the Greek slave; his criticism of the statue is obviously the result of careful consideration. As always, he examined Powers' art in terms of whether or not it has succeeded in approaching Divine Beauty, and makes use of his physician's knowledge of anatomy to criticize the figure. His main objection is that since Powers was probably attempting to produce the most beautiful of physical bodies, he should have "Idealized the Human—merged the mortal into the Angel."[129] Art, be it expressed in stone or in language, should transcend the immediate and actual, seeking the Ideal.

Chivers was interested in a new type-revolving machine, and describes it quite professionally;[130] he himself had invented a machine to simplify the spinning and twisting of silk,[131] and so had both a professional planter's and a publishing poet's interest in mechanical matters.

Furthermore, he finds that all the shopkeepers of New York are thieves, primarily intent on cheating him. Yet surely the sight of his intense figure inquiring about the price of an article must have given more than one clerk considerable pause! New York City itself impressed him, he says, as a city of sin; for the edification, and no doubt delight, of his Georgia readers, he adds,

I intend to tear the obnoxious and flaunting robes of scarlet from the tapering shoulders of this beautiful Lady of Babylon, and present her to the world naked in infamy, God giving me grace to withstand her wily temptations. Sometimes she smells as sweet as if she had just returned from wallowing on a bed of spices. But it is the perfume which Eve took with her out of Paradise after the fall—it is fragrant, but redolent with the memory of a lost world![132]

Despite such temptations as he found about him, one of which was the ballet, he was genuinely delighted by the musical offerings of the city. When Jenny Lind arrived in New York in September, 1850, having been brought here by P. T. Barnum after great success in Europe, Chivers was on hand to record the excitement. She was "the noblest of all God's creatures," but the public which greeted her displeased Chivers:

Jenny Lind is here, and the whole city is upside down on account of her. It is like the tower of Babel while suffering under the wrath of Heaven. It was a wise saying of the Greeks that, *those whom the Gods wish to destroy, they first make mad!* If going mad be the preliminary for destruction, this city will certainly be destroyed, for every man in it is a Midas....[133]

To publicize Miss Lind's arrival, Barnum had sponsored a poetry contest for a song which she might sing as a greeting to America. Bayard Taylor eventually won the award of $200 out of a field of some seven hundred poems. Chivers himself may have submitted a poem. At any rate he did publish one in the *Waverly Magazine* when she arrived in Boston.[134]

Jenny Lind was not the only songstress who intrigued Chivers. Teresa Parodi drew almost as much acclaim from him as Miss Lind had done, and his criticisms of her concerts are detailed and reasonable.[135]

The variety of Chivers' comments is considerable; he realized he had no strict format to follow, and allowed his interests to wander. The picture obtained from the various elements of his letters is of a highly critical columnist engaged in a rather exhausting round of the day's available concerts, recitals, and lectures. That Chivers still had time to write poetry while he was so employed seems remarkable.

He was, after all, a Southerner, and undoubtedly there must have been uncomfortable moments over the subject of slavery. Frequently he remarks wryly that the North had a poor opinion of Southern intelligence and virtue, and his reaction to such slurs must have been quick and sharp. Yet he kept sectionalism completely out of his poetry, and said at one point that he believed satire's province was not poetry but prose.[136] Presumably he felt the same way about such temporal matters as the increasing sectionalism in America. The passage of the Fugitive Slave Law in 1850 was fiercely debated in the public press, and the English abolitionist George Thompson returned to America the same year. Largely responsible for the enactment of anti-slavery laws in the British Empire, he had come in 1834 to agitate for similar reforms here. He was now greeted on the one hand as a martyr for the cause of freedom, and on the other as an agent of the British designing to undermine the United States. Chivers held the latter view, and many of his comments on Thompson are violent in the extreme. Fearful of what British influence might do, Chivers said, "The States are like man and wife—they only quarrel for the pleasure of making friends again. Let but another interfere between them, and they will all become the avengers of the dastardly insult."[137]

In the same vein, Chivers attacked Horace Greeley, editor of the *New York Tribune,* and George Ripley, literary critic of that paper, for their support of abolitionist causes. Ripley was prejudiced, Chivers said, by his "primeval propinquity, to the pestilential shores of a frog pond."[138] Chivers believed Ripley had written the *Tribune's* uncomplimentary review of *Eonchs of Ruby.*[139]

His first remarks on Greeley were friendly enough. Greeley had referred to Southerners, in an ironic tone, as "The Chivalry," and Chivers would set him right:

Greeley, from what I can learn, is a man of some good points; but he sadly disfigures his face, when he "screws himself up to the sticking point" of calling the South "The Chivalry." The truth is, I am and ever have been, at a loss to know what *he can mean* by it. Does he say it in *jest,* or in *ridicule?* Does he mean that the South is *not* chivalrous, and that he merely calls her so because it is an *understood thing,* that she *is not!* Why, if this be the meaning of the man, he is making the most arrogant goose of himself. . . . Surely, Horace Greeley is not such a hypocrite as this![140]

A month after this Chivers had learned Greeley's true inclinations, and his attack upon him, while it shows something of the fervor with which the question of slavery was being debated everywhere, is also interesting as an example of what Chivers' criticism often degenerated to when his emotions were roused. In his poetry, he transmitted his strength of feeling to conjure up Heaven, but in his magazine prose he seldom rises.

Here [in the North] are a set of traitors, who make slaves of *white women,* and pretend to be horror-stricken at the idea of selling a nigger. Is *this "conscience"?* Here are a set of cowards, who drive the widow and the orphan into the basest poverty here at the North, and have the *free nigger impudence* to talk about the slavery of the South! Yet, Horace Greeley is the ringleader of this set of scoundrels. I can show you beautiful young women in this city, who are compelled to work from eight o'clock in the morning until six o'clock in the evening, harder than I ever saw any negro woman work in the South. . . . Go with me to Lowell, and I will show you beautiful girls prostituted to the basest of uses. Yet, these liars call these miserable creatures *free.* Instead of setting the *white slaves* of the North free, they make use of the most roguish and unlawful means to liberate the very property they once sold to us.[141]

Chivers, himself a slave-owner, believed in the institution of slavery, clearly enough. As he continues in this particular letter, it becomes obvious that he is wholly sincere in his belief that the North was the most sinful section of the country he had ever visited. Slavery in the South meant, to Chivers, a long established business venture; in the North, the area which told him he was without conscience in keeping the slaves it had sold him, he saw everything from the slave-labor of the Lowell mills to the fiercely-competitive streets of New York City. But let him describe it:

I lived in this city seven years, and before God, during the whole of that time, I never met with a single gentleman—that is, I scarcely saw a single person—who did not either smoke, chew tobacco or drink whiskey. . . . They do not love a man here for his God-given genius. They have no respect for anything that is heavenly—but love him *wholly* and *solely* for the gaudy, gilded and hollow trappings which the devil has cast around him. Every man here is an Aaron, who cheats the beautiful women out of their gold ear rings, melts them up into a Midas-eared calf, and then falls down and worships it. The only God they worship here is Mammon—a colossal statue ten thousand cubits high, whose head is copper, whose lips are brass, whose legs are iron, whose feet are clay, and whose body is beset with jewels and fine gold.[142]

In this and various other articles on slavery and the North's reaction to it, Chivers retains his view that slavery and the management of it are the South's personal concern. With his entire fortune subject to the outcome of the national debate over the slavery issue, any doubt he may ever have felt corncerning the moral and ethical rightness of slavery was quelled. The intensity of emotional reaction which moved him to thunderous spiritual evocations in his poetry had its equal and opposite effect in his prose, particularly when his subject was slavery. Just as he could rise to mystical heights in poetry, so could he descend a similar distance beneath moderation in his prose, to the point where his attacks upon abolition views become almost hysterical. Part of this violence must surely have stemmed from his position as a Southern plantation owner residing in the North, an area in which he could point out evils he believed worse than any fault which might exist in the institution of slavery.

It is to his great credit that the antipathy he felt toward certain elements of the Northern population was kept out of his poetry. The realm of his verse was not that of temporal disputes, and there is no hint of either the approaching Civil War or the so-called Old South romanticism in his poetry. It is in no way sectional.

These letters to Georgia further suggest something of the variety and number of Chivers' activities. His references to literary figures are generally in the way of incidental criticisms inspired by comment with which he does not agree. Chivers was not an effective literary critic, and often what he says seems to us uninspired or fallacious; but it was invariably said with intense conviction. Many of the points of controversy which he raises provide a fascinating view of the practical literary world of the 1840's and 1850's as it actually existed and not as it now appears in literary histories.

One of his first literary criticisms concerns James Gates Percival, then a well-known and respected poet. Chivers found an old number of the *Philadelphia American and Gazette* in which Percival's poem "Anapestic"[143] had been praised as successfully imitative of the manner of the Greek elegiac poet Tyrtaeus and appropriate to a patriotic elegy.[144] But Chivers cried, "What glory can any man receive from being the 'imitator' of another?"[145] After having noted Percival's failure to arrange his syllables so that they "read themselves," that is, read easily and naturally, and having regretted his inability to utilize the caesural pause to good effect, Chivers turned from Percival to what he believed the real point of objection:

These remarks are not made to detract, in the least, from the well-earned reputation of Dr. Percival,—who ought to be admired only for his profound erudition,—but to refute that self-complacency which arrogates to itself the ability to see that in a man which he never saw in himself.[146]

As he was to do only a few months later in the more important context of Poe's work, Chivers here objected not to the inadequacy of the poetry at hand, but to the inability of contemporary criticism to judge accurately. Praising an author for an effect or technique which the author himself has not sought for or experimented with impressed Chivers as a distortion of fact. Judge an author by his success in what he is attempting, Chivers insisted,

·53

not by arbitrary standards. And while Chivers' acknowledgment of Percival's erudition appears condescending, his objection that critics failed to consider the author's intention arose from personal experience, experience which was to be reinforced by the reception of his next volume of poetry, *Eonchs of Ruby*.

John Greenleaf Whitter, Chivers claimed, exhibited something of this failure in judgment, if in a different context:

> Whittier, the Quaker Poet, is sounding the praises of Fredrika Bremer, whom he calls the *"Swan of Abo."* This is a very good name for her, provided we deny vocality to the Swan—as I believe she does not sing. But does not any poet make an arrant *goose* of himself, to throw away his time in singing the praises of foreign Birds, when there are so many of more heavenly plumage at home?[147]

Chivers agreed with Whittier that America must develop its own subject matter; on his trip to the West in the early 1830's Chivers had stared in fascination at the Indian burial mounds, much as Whittier had, and now he wondered at Whittier's praise of a foreign author. Not necessarily narrow in his outlook, Chivers nevertheless was acutely conscious of America's need for her own voice and melody.

The following month Chivers had read P. J. Bailey's long poem "Festus"; in his review of the work he defined the ideal of poetry:

> No poem can last, as a whole, which does not appeal, in its artistic perfection, to the well-attuned perceptions of the soul of the *truly critical* Reader. [The] peculiar idiosyncrasy [of "Festus"] is *misdirected ambition*. A Poem is no place for the teaching of Hegelian Metaphysics—the peculiar province of Poetry being the creation of beauty.[148]

The same letter contains praise of Mrs. Caroline Lee Hentz, and an attack, similar in kind to that concerning Percival, on the Rev. George Gilfillan, who had published a "Literary Portrait" of Emerson. While praising Emerson implicitly, Chivers is more interested in puncturing the Rev. Gilfillan's analogies regarding him:

> Mr. Gilfillan . . . says that, in coming down from his Mystic Altitudes among men, "Emerson reminds us of Rip Van Winkle descending the Katskill Mountains, from his sleep of a hundred years. . . ." Did anybody ever hear the like. . . . Is there any resemblance between Rip Van Winkle and Mr. Emerson? Did Irving intend Rip to be the *Ideal* Prophecy of

the *Real* Emerson . . . there *is no resemblance*—any more than there is between Bottom the Weaver and General George Washington.

. . . .

Then, again, how can any man be, *"apart altogether from his verse, the truest Poet America has ever produced"*? How can Mr. Gilfillan *know* this? . . . A Poet *cannot* be known *as such*, "apart" from the manifestations of his being—he *must have* an identity. How can any man *"stay at home"* with his *"own soul,"* and become, *at the same time*, intimately acquainted with the *"rugged soil"* of old external Nature? How can anybody—even Mr. Ralph Waldo Emerson—"stand still" on the "rugged soil" of old Massachusetts, and wait for the far-off coming of the Divine Harmonies, and be *at the very same time*, "winging his way through the high and liquid air."

. . . .

What does he mean . . . by saying that "In spite of the penumbra of prejudice against American verse, more fugitive floating Poetry of real merit exists in its literature than in almost any other"? . . . Does he not *know* that America has produced the best Lyrical Poetry of any land under the sun?[149]

America has never lacked for defenders; Chivers will permit no compromising reflection upon her literature. Emerson here seems more a means to an end than the principal subject, although elsewhere Chivers expresses his admiration for him in specific terms.

A week later Chivers made his first public comparison between Poe's "Raven" and his own "To Allegra Florence in Heaven." A writer of the *Literary Union* praised "The Raven" as one of a series of poems whose style "has never before been known."[150] Insisting that Poe had true genius, Chivers regretted "that the authors of such criticism betray . . . a deplorable ignorance of the current poetical literature of the Day."[151] That is, an alert critic would have seen Chivers' own poem as it appeared in 1843 and recognized the basis of the style of "The Raven."[152] The matter of the similarity between "The Raven" and "To Allegra Florence in Heaven" will be reviewed at length in another chapter, but here it may be pointed out that for some time Chivers had been alert to similarities between his own work and that of other poets. In this letter he cited a poem by J. W. Hanson, one by Phoebe Carey, both published in 1849, and several by unknown authors as early as 1845.[153] Hanson's "To My Angel Daughter" resembles Chivers' "To Allegra Florence in Heaven" quite exactly:

Now a sister have the Angels,
Chanting all their grand Evangels!
Sweetest 'mong the star-crowned sisters
    Is the Angel, Florence May!
With her songs of braided sweetness,
Her white wings of light-like fleetness,
And her joys in full completeness,
    In that world of Upper Day.
Sweetest of the white-robed sisters
    Sings and worships Florence May![154]

The resemblances between this poem and Chivers' work, even to the diction, are strong; those of the other poems he quotes are less obvious. Poe was one of a series of authors whose work Chivers believed had been preceded by certain of his own poems of a notably similar style. The comment on Poe's "Raven" is thus found among a number of literary comments in this number of "The Valley of Diamonds," and Chivers does not cite the similarity in outraged terms at all; he is definite in his tone, yet not obnoxiously so.

Contemporary American authors appear incidentally throughout a number of these articles, and occasionally he referred to English writings. Robert Burns delighted Chivers, particularly as an example of the true love of freedom he felt was growing even in England; but that country was beset by tradition-bound "Tories," who would not recognize the presence of a new freedom-loving spirit among men:

Talk to them about the Divine Ante-diluvian Traditions! when they refuse to see the Post-Messianic Truths, and to hear their sublime golden thunders, ten thousand times ten thousand more musical than the Sinai-intonations, with all their beautiful accompaniment of diamond-lightings! Poor, pitiful Devils! you may loose from your iron leash, and set on with your Screech-owl cries, your big Hell-dogs, but you will never hunt this Son of Day back into Chaos again.[155]

Chivers would permit no one to belittle America's literature, but he himself seldom felt restraint, and his criticisms frequently veer close to invective of a hardly corrective sort. Chivers had warned Poe about "tomahawking" minor writers,[156] fearing that he would so cripple hesitant genius that it would be unable to rise in a future attempt. Quite possibly this comment, written in 1840, was inspired by the harsh treatment Chivers himself had received at the hands of the *Western Monthly Magazine* after his *The Constitution of Man* had appeared. Evidently, however, Chivers saw little wrong in pointing out the errors of established and mature American writers. Nathaniel Parker Willis was a favorite target. An extremely popular poet of the time and editor of a series of magazines, Willis was in certain ways one of the controlling literary men of the 1850's. His opinions were sought and his judgment carefully studied; his poetry sold very well indeed. Today he seems more than a little affected, and his verse seldom rises from mediocrity. Exactly why Chivers set out after Willis is not known, but the literary columns of the day suggest that he was not alone in his dislike of the co-editor of the *Home Journal*.

No man can put his finger on a single poem by N. P. Willis, which would authorize him to call him by the sacred name of Poet. His style has an airy *fantasqueness* about it which would lead one, unacquainted with the *true* Art of Poetry, to suppose that he possessed something of the divine *afflatus;* but this is only a manifestation of his extreme artificiality. . . . His rhythm is not his own, but borrowed from others. Had he possessed any originality, he would have invested it in a rhythm of his own. . . . There is nothing in his Poetry to raise it above a perfect platitude, but the *mere expression.*

. . . .

There is, in *all* his writings, an artificiality which betrays an euthanasia not at all to be lamented—and a dilletantesqueness in curtain-lifting which is truly of the Brazen-nose Age, and greatly to be deplored. There is nothing of that sylphlike urbanity of goatism [*sic*] about them which characterizes the Poetry of Moore—but an Oriental baboonism and Nymphomania supremely disgusting. . . .[157]

Chivers' charges of Willis' obscenity must have been based on literary gossip rather than his writings, and in a later article Chivers took note in a disgusted tone of Willis' suit against Edwin Forrest for assault and battery.[158] Willis' brother had been named as corespondent in a suit Forrest had brought against his wife for infidelity, and Willis in reply had attacked Forrest in his *Home Journal*. Such conduct, innocent or guilty as Willis' may have been, simply proved to Chivers' readers what he had been telling them all along. New York was a city of sin and corruption, and a weak man should stay out of it. Chivers himself, apparently able to resist the temptations which he clearly recognized were present, moved amid all such confusion, recording and judging.

William Cullen Bryant is badly misrepresented by Chivers. The Southern poet cannot forget Bryant's abolitionist views, and he distorts a series of comments Bryant made on the songs of the Southern Negro to read as though Bryant were ridiculing them. "Thanatopsis" is Bryant's only real poetry, Chivers declared, and that he believed Bryant had plagiarized from a Spanish original.[159] No indication of Chivers' source for his charge of plagiarism has been found, and it may be dismissed as irrational anger in the face of Northern beliefs concerning slavery.

Throughout these letters Chivers compliments one author and attacks the next, apparently motivated solely by his own personal prejudices, although the fact of his Southern ancestry does postulate all his reactions to abolitionists. As criticism they are occasionally barbed and exact, more often truculent. They are a revelation of Chivers moving in a literary society of which only the top and most vital segments are well-known today. After a survey of this sort the reader cannot but be aware that Chivers was extremely conscious of the details and currents of the contemporary literary world, and tried desperately to associate himself with it by continual critical comment upon it. The world of his poetry seems totally removed from this world, and fortunately his tone here is wholly foreign to his poetry also. Perhaps his appraisal is less valuable as a cross-section of literary and social New York in the 1850's than as a study of Chivers. His irascibility, his changeableness, the heights of emotion to which he could stir himself in prose, are all elements of his true character. That he could contain such limited views as are presented here as well as the scope and sweep of imagination which appear in his poetry is truly remarkable. The explanation of this duality of reaction lies in the nature of the world he describes; this earth incurred little but disapproval, while his visions of Heaven brought shouts of praise.

The literary world Chivers wrote of occasionally gave evidence of understanding this split in Chivers. When Augustine Duganne first published his satirical review of America and her poetry, *Parnassus in Pillory* (1851), he included mention of the Chivers he knew from his poetry:

> Not Orton soars to strike thy highest chord—
> Nor Georgic Chivers, nor Legaré, nor Lord![160]

Four years later a second edition included Chivers as critic, particularly as he charged Poe with plagiarism:

> Not Orton soars to strike the highest chord:
> Not Pike nor Patton—nor Legare nor Lord!
> Not even Chivers, from whose virgin muse
> The graceless Poe stole all that she could loose.
> Unhappy Chivers, whose transcendent lays
> Are out of place in these degenerate days,
> And yet for whom, were half his verses burned,
> A poet's fame the other half had earned,—
> Ah! not from these, or such as these, shall rise
> Immortal song to occidental skies.

Duganne was apparently more perceptive than the majority of his contemporaries, for he saw the essential genius in a considerable body of Chivers' poetry, and recognized what is becoming clear today, that when that body is removed from the failure of the remainder of his verse, a particularly unique and individual poet emerges. In a critical note in the second edition, there is evidence that Duganne saw beneath the criticism Chivers had been writing; perhaps he did not understand the psychological motivation which lay behind Chivers' charges against Poe, but he did know the direction of Chivers' talents:

> Thos. H. Chivers, M.D., of Georgia, has written some good rhymes, but is haunted by dead poets, and passes his life in an insane attempt to prove that Poe gained his reputation by plagiarizing Chivers. Let the doctor leave logic, and try to write poetry, which is more his *forte* than criticism.

We may agree that Chivers' criticism is not always incisive or definitive, yet it is an essential part of his life at the beginning of the 1850's, and it is a fascinating study to watch the manner in which he keeps his attitudes and subjects of his prose apart from his poetry.

Throughout the period in which much of his energy was devoted to these communications to the *Georgia Citizen,* Chivers continued to write poetry. He attempted to prepare a revision of *The Lost Pleiad* (1845), utilizing and enlarging the manuscript collection called *Woodland Melodies.* While he had included a few poems from this collection in *The Lost Pleiad,* he was now apparently determined to change the basic theme of the volume by adding additional poems which would bear out the proposed new title, *Woodland Melodies; or, The Dial of Early Days.* The Preface for the volume is dated April 10, 1850. He intended to include Poe's praise of *The Lost Pleiad,* as the manuscript shows, and the Preface itself indicates that he has not been long from the writing of *Search after Truth,* for several of the essay's metaphors and analogies turn up here.

Whether Chivers would have revised out the following remarks from his Preface when time came for publication is difficult to say, but certainly they are direct from his heart as we have them in manuscript. Perhaps anticipating harsh criticism, he wondered if anyone would ask him why he had been inspired to write these poems. His answer is in terms which are typical of him.

. . . as the Angels in Heaven draw their celestial Rivers of Delight out of the crystalline Light-fountains of God—so did I sing these Songs—these self-revelations of the deepest love and the bitterest sorrow—for the very love of singing.

.   .   .   .

Do not the Flowers love the light? Does not the Sun love to shine? Did not the memory of Eden fill the soul of the first Exile with celestial odor? Just so does my soul love to sing. For what are my songs, but the Memorials of my poet life here on earth?—expressions of my love for the Beautiful—my desires for a Supreme State—my capabilities to enjoy the life of that State—in short, of the influx of the Divine Life of God into my soul?[161]

For all of his exultation as he determines that he has been touched by God, these are lonely words. They sound very much as though he had dwelt upon them privately many times before recording them. Nothing ever came of his desire to rework *The Lost Pleiad;* presumably at least part of his inspiration to make changes in its contents arose from the critic's cry that the volume had but a single theme, a theme which so much reiteration made tiring.

Chivers was more of the contemporary literary world at this time than ever before, and he considered himself both poet, and in a sense, editor, for he had forwarded enough articles to the *Georgia Citizen* to have become familiar to its readers, and, so he believed, proficient in reporting the day's literary and social activities.

With this confidence Chivers prepared a Prospectus for a magazine he hoped to edit, *The Stylus.* It appeared as a broadside toward the close of 1850,[162] and was reprinted in the *Georgia Citi-*

zen on November 9, 1850. Chivers' ambitions had overreached themselves here, for the magazine never appeared, just as Poe's projected *Stylus* remained in manuscript form. One of Chivers' last letters to Poe had offered to establish a magazine in the South for Poe to edit while he lived with Chivers,[163] an offer to which Poe never replied, and now that his friend and literary companion was dead, Chivers reanimated the project. His advertisement has all of the high-flying phraseology typical of Chivers' more extreme moments, and we may be sure that the plan of publishing a magazine had roused Chivers to great enthusiasm:

The subscriber proposes to publish, (to be issued simultaneously in New York, Savannah, Augusta, Macon, Columbus, Atlanta, and Washington) a Monthly Magazine devoted to Polite Literature, Science, and the Fine Arts.

It will be wholly American—entirely original in form and matter—and devoted assiduously to the establishment of a correct Literary Taste in the South.

It will embrace *Essays; Criticisms in Literature* and *Art; Music* and the *Drama; Domestic* and *Foreign Correspondence; Articles* on *Science* and *Medicine; Temperance* and *Morality; Ancient Literature; Retrospective Reviews* of old *English Books;* accurate *Lists* of the *Best New Publications; Personal Accounts* and *Anecdotes* of the *Greatest Literary Men* of *Modern* and *Ancient Times; Tales, Poetry,* and, in fact, every thing that is calculated to inspire the *South* with a love of the *Beautiful* and the *True.*

. . . .

It will be a perfect *Table* of *Adamant* for the *Genius* of the *South*— a golden-voiced *Sibyl* who shall sing sweetly of the *Halcyon Years* to *Come.*

It will embrace not only a perfect Revelation of Man's Life in Time— from his birth to his death—his Physiological as well as his Psychological nature—how, from the Micro-Cosmos he is elevated into the Micro-Uranus—but will give a faithful exposition of all that has ever been unfolded to us through the *Minds* of the *Ages* of his destiny beyond the grave.

It shall be a golden *Museum* around whose Opal Walks shall be ranged on Pedestals of Pearl, the sublimest *Incarnations* of immortal Thought. From the Myrrhine Fabrics which shall ornament its golden tablets shall ascend an Anthosmial redolence as sweet as the odorous incense from the Altar of the Temple of Solomon.

Beautiful Butterflies, Blossoms and Birds shall therein be ensouled, which shall chameleonate, with an ever-varying and multicolored Mosaic, this incense-clouded Pavilion of the Soul. Requiems softer than the honeyed Elegies of Simonides, and Carolings loftier than the lark that sings while soaring to the Gates of Heaven, shall flow out in rivers of selectest melody from this Melphonian Swan among the Reeds.

One wonders what the reaction of Chivers' readers was; surely they must have been startled, and possibly a bit awe-struck, in the face of such vision. Those who knew him realized also that the extremity of his closing paragraphs was not an advertiser's overstatement, but characteristic of Chivers' tone and diction when he was aroused over true beauty or revealed truth.

How far his plans went to provide presses and writers for his magazine is unknown; that he attempted to publish it indicates something of the change that had occurred since his first rather hesitant, if serious, steps in *The Path of Sorrow* (1832). He now can present himself as a literary man acquainted with the ways of the literary world.

As if plans for a magazine were not enough to occupy him, at the end of 1850 he published his fifth volume of poetry, *Eonchs of Ruby, A Gift of Love*. It was published by Spalding & Shepard of New York, and dated 1851, although the copyright, belonging to Chivers, was issued in 1850. Chivers was much better known in 1850 than he ever had been before, particularly since his poetry had been appearing so regularly in the Boston and New York periodicals. Spalding & Shepard allowed their name to be placed on the volume, which indicates a certain confidence in its eventual attraction. However, it is probable that Chivers himself paid in part at least for the printing. This is the best known of his books today, partly because of the unusual and seemingly unintelligible title, and partly because of its regular publication.

Of the forty poems contained in the volume, slightly less than half had appeared during the preceding decade in magazine form. Chivers had added several important poems, particularly the elegy on Poe, "The Vigil in Aiden," and "Avalon," one of his most successful elegies on his children. It is to be presumed that all but a very few of the poems in this volume were composed during the 1840's, and represent his more mature work. *Eonchs of Ruby* contains much of his more unusual diction, and this delight in words often produces effective poetry. The word *eonch* itself was (and is) a puzzle to his readers. Reviewers inquired persistently enough after the volume was published, and Chivers finally answered:

Now for an explanation of the *mysteries* contained in the title of my book—*Eonchs of Ruby*. The word *Eonch* is the same as *Concha Marina* —*Shell of the Sea*. *Eonch* is used instead of *Concha*, merely for its euphony. It is the same as the *Kaur Gaur* of the Hebrews. Ruby signifies, in the language of Correspondence, *Divine Love*. The word *Eonch* is used, as a title, by metonymy, for *Songs*. The meaning of the title is, therefore, apparent—namely, *Songs of Divine Love*. The clouds, I hope, are now dispelled; and the mystery, I presume, evaporates. I hope the day will continue clear.[164]

Chivers' intentions are indeed made clear, and even though his freedom of interpretation may be objected to, his choice seems to have been a reasoned one.

In addition to its unusual diction, *Eonchs of Ruby* contains several of his unique flights to Heaven. "The Chaplet of Cypress" or "Song of Le Verrier"[165] is testimony to his fully developed power to rise from this earth to a view of an eternal, ideal world, a world of which "Avalon" (pp. 49-56) presents perhaps the finest picture. There are few signs of melancholia here; his grief is behind him and his joy and strength are increased.

Yet, all poems considered, *Eonchs of Ruby* is typical of the progress of his work throughout the 1840's rather than of an end-point in his development. *Nacoochee* (1837) was his earliest public collection exhibiting sporadically the strength and fire of imagination which appears so much more obviously here, while *The Lost Pleiad* (1845) may be regarded as the most conventional volume he wrote. *Eonchs* was a necessary and a valuable gathering-up of his talents and accomplishments before he went on to *Virginalia* (1853) and his later magazine work. There is no sharp break at this 1850-1851 date, however; only when *Eonchs* is understood as the result of continued effort throughout the '40's, particularly under the inspiration of Poe's genius, valuable and interesting both for its own content and as that content and form foreshadow Chivers' final work, will the progress of Chivers' genius and talent come clear. The volume contains both his finest, individually-styled poems and his more orthodox work.

The reviewers of 1850 and early 1851 were more impressed by *Eonchs of Ruby* than by any previous volume, a fact which must have delighted Chivers. Augustine Duganne, who was to satirize Chivers gently in his *Parnassus in Pillory*, was generally enthusiastic, although he noted a similarity to Poe which drew a quick and serious reply from Chivers; he is aware of the combination of success and failure which the book contains:

. . . it is an unthankful task to spy out the faults of a book which is more remarkable for its beauties.

. . . .

It is difficult to analyze the order of genius to which Chivers belongs, because he neglects the concentration which might individualize and make it palpable. From his harp proceed master-strains which seem struck out often in a sort of Pythonic delirium.[166]

Whitaker's Magazine began with a particular prejudice and found it hard to get rid of. Their criticism of "Avalon" must have infuriated the deeply-religious Chivers, who knew perfectly well that his mysticism was personal, but could not understand why that might invalidate it.

In the poem of "Avalon" . . . are some few exquisite passages, but it is marred and disfigured throughout by . . . defects . . . and is, in many parts, so utterly incomprehensible and provokingly affected, that feelings of admiration, created by the development of poetic beauty, are lost in disgust at the insipid, unmeaning mysticism of crowded epithets, and unnatural, incongruous conceptions. His aptness at coining words, is frequently displayed, and his frequent and irreverent mention of the Deity, inexcusable and profane. This last named fault is one of far greater magnitude than any which deforms his work, and deserves most unqualified censure. . . .[167]

Surely it was misrepresentation of this sort which drove Chivers to his sharp attacks on contemporary criticism, and made him doubt the worth of any but his own viewpoint. It was blindness and ignorance which Chivers (in a none-too-humble fashion) found fault with. When the same critic, who quotes his Bible in this same review of *Eonchs,* objects to Chivers' refrain "In the valley of the pausing of the moon" (from "Avalon"), by saying "We have yet to learn that the moon ever pauses, and if so, where,"[168] Chivers may indeed be permitted extremes of rejoinder.

Perhaps the essential point of such a review is to prove Poe right when he demanded *criticism* and not favoritism or prejudice, a sentiment which Chivers praised. Had Chivers been able to profit from intelligent and precise critical appraisals of his work, his maturity would have arrived more quickly, and the minor errors and failures of taste which rufflle many of his poems would have been quickly smoothed away. But it was the nature of an essentially amateurish age which failed to understand what Chivers was trying to do; neither sophisticated nor unselfconscious, American criticism before the Civil War seldom stimulated the country's writers. More often the criticism broke or overinflated the less strong.

The American Whig Review did not bother to attempt criticism, It simply laughed:

The publication of this book is one of those extraordinary things which men will sometimes do, and for the doing of which no mortal man can give anything approaching to a reason. It would make a fitting dessert for a heavy dinner of "America Discovered."[169]

Other reviewers came more to the point and praised Chivers for his originality of style and form,[170] and Mrs. Edith Lindsey, in the *Georgia Citizen,* eulogized the Georgia poet in resounding terms, praising particularly the elegies, and quoting at length from various other reviews, all of which were favorable.[171] A second *Georgia Citizen* review five months later was equally favorable, and its author, Jedediah Hunt, Jr., a firm friend of the poet's, praised Chivers in language very much like Chivers' own.[172]

Throughout these reactions Chivers kept up a steady flow of letters to the *Georgia Citizen* and of poems to various other magazines. His energy was endless, apparently, and it steadily becomes more and more obvious that Chivers was extremely serious about the business of being a poet. He devoted his full attention to it, and the testimony of his poems throughout these years is one of growing competency and individuality, despite the general failure of the literary world to do more than silently accept his poetry for magazine publication and criticize it more for what it attempted than for its success in that attempt when it appeared in book form.

1851-1858

Eonchs of Ruby had created a satisfying stir upon publication, an interest motivated partly by the intrinsic value of the poetry in the collection and partly because of the similarity of many of the poems to Poe's work; "Letters from New York" concluded in April of 1854, but modulated easily into a long series of various towns and cities in New England, "Letters from the North";[173]

and Chivers continued to find a place for his poetry in the better magazines. He was at last a known figure, at least by name, and his poetry now drew more critical attention than ever before. He still thought himself capable of editing a literary journal, and even considered the purchase of one. His prose articles, alone, were sufficient to keep him busy; although not so important to him as was his poetry, one imagines, yet they served to establish his position as an observer of the literary scene.

Chivers' letters to the *Georgia Citizen* had begun as "The Valley of Diamonds" in June of 1850. They continued, under varying titles, for four years, during which time Chivers moved erratically and as he wished over the New England states, staying during 1851 and 1852 at the Tontine Hotel in New Haven, moving to Boston in 1853, and settling for a few months in 1854 in Mt. Vernon, just into the country from New York City. By February of 1855 Chivers had returned to Georgia, and his poems show places of composition from a variety of locales about the state. Had Chivers not returned to the South at Christmas of 1854 we may presume that he would have continued his communications to the *Georgia Citizen* without signs of fatigue. When he did return to Georgia it was to leave the North for the last time. His stay in Mt. Vernon until early December of 1854 marks the last time any of his compositions were dated from above the Mason-Dixon Line. Chivers was a professional author in the 1850's, able to live comfortably as he wished from private income, traveling for the sake of his own pleasure, and responsible to no one for anything. This freedom gives a certain lack of direction to his prose articles, but taken together the many squibs, essays, and paragraphs he sent to the *Georgia Citizen* make fascinating reading. That Chivers should continue to send his letters regularly when he is in no way obligated indicates something of his contant desire to affirm his literary vocation.

The content of this section of his letters is much like that of the earlier; Chivers takes his reader on a tour of the literary affairs of the day, and makes his own pronouncements. He often reviewed books, and paused once to notice that the third installment of Melville's *Israel Potter* (in *Putnam's Magazine,* September, 1854), "is a very poor imitation, in logic as well as plot, of articles on like subjects, published in Blackwood's Magazine." [174]

He described the city of New Haven at length, and dwelt particularly on the Tontine Hotel, at which he was staying. Apparently the Hotel accommodated more or less permanent guests, and was of itself a community. Inspired by the beauty of some resident maiden, Chivers wrote "The Belles of Tontine":

> So, within this stately Palace,
> Called the Tontine, kept by Allis,
> Standing Eastward of the Eden of the Green—
> Dwells the one with eyes of azure,
> Melting in her soul of pleasure,
> Shedding love-light, without measure,
> On her lovers in Tontine—
> All agreeing she is Belle of this Tontine—
> Cynosure of all the lesser lights that twinkle in Tontine.[175]

New Haven's architecture is praised, and Chivers walked down the street to attend Yale's 151st Commencement exercises, despite the fact that his first reference to the college concluded, "Old Yale looks very ancient—pretty much like an old man, who has more soul in his body than that body will be able long to bear."[176] The commencement itself pleased him, and he was inspired by the academic procession:

Thursday was a glorious day for the Commencement. The Corporation, the Alumni and the Students formed a very imposing procession as they marched into the Centre Church. It was, indeed, a living stream of vivacious young manhood, bearing upon its undulating bosom the merchandise of high hopes and lofty aspirations. A more beautiful sight than an army of intellectual young men going up to receive their crowns of glory from the grateful hands of the great high Priest of their long-loved Alma Mater cannot be imagined by the soul of man.[177]

Although the final metaphor may be a bit pagan in its connotations, Chivers was sincere in his praise; education, he continued to say, was a "diadem of beauty," and those who possess it "will walk the earth as the *true* Sons of God."[178] One wonders what the students of that graduating class had thought of Chivers, a publishing and consciously professional poet, who lived not far from their campus. Surely he must have cut an odd figure, impressive but certainly not conventional in his statements. Attracted by the dignity of the procession, Chivers attended a meeting of the Yale chapter of Phi Beta Kappa, and there was shocked by the poor delivery of the class oration, and even further disturbed by the

· 67

quality of the class poem, "The Pilgrim Fathers": "The Theme, itself, one would think, was enough to have brought blood out of a turnip...."[179]

Chivers became almost intimate at times in these letters, speaking tenderly of the sight of a beautiful young child, or again of the beauty of autumn foliage, or of the Aurora Borealis as it appeared in New Haven. One is constantly tempted to wonder what it was that Chivers' readers in Georgia came to expect of the occasional letters in their paper. Certainly it was not a rounded, complete picture of social or literary activity; there are almost no names present in the articles except when Chivers attacks a particular author, and lectures and musicals which he attends are described in general, almost theoretical terms rather than precisely analyzed. In all probability the *Georgia Citizen* readers looked forward to these communications as much for the view they afforded of the Georgia poet himself as for the intelligence about Northern affairs.

He attended a concert by Ole Bull, a violinist of considerable contemporary fame, who impressed Chivers greatly: "Not only is he great as a Demiurgos of the beautiful—as a mediator between the actual and the ideal—but he is a true revelator of the fantasque moresqueness of the Mysteries of the Nibelungen Land." That Chivers occasionally achieved a certain playfulness in his prose is clearly shown as he continues:

The grand overture of Martha, by Flotow, as performed by the Germania Band, possessed some pathetic, as well as stirring passages; but, upon the whole, contained too much of the
Corybantine Brass
Of an all-fired Jackass,
to suit me. The truth is, in the expression of the beautiful, through the pathetic, there is no need of any Donkey at all.

I am willing to acknowledge that it was on the mouse-colored back of a Donkey that our Savior rode with such triumphant gentleness into Jerusalem; but we have no evidence that he ever brayed on that occasion. Donkies are good in their places. When mixed with the blood of a horse, they make good mules—and this is all that can be said in favor of them.

The variety of description which his readers might expect is indicated by that upon the Germania Band and the following upon Alfred Jael, a pianist who appeared with Ole Bull.

The music, as Alfred Jael touched the keys of the Piano, seemed to run down out of his soul and crystallize itself into rhythmical alternations of pure Rubies and Diamonds on the ends of his fingers—whereas, it hung drippingly on those of Strakosch, like prismy stalactites from the canopy of the enchanted Caverns of the Nymphs.[180]

When Chivers was in Hartford he stopped at the Wadsworth Athenaeum, where he looked through Dr. Robbins' collection of Americana. The items which most fascinated him were a pine chest which had traveled to America on the Mayflower, and had been the property of Elder Brewster, "the old black-looking Dinner-pot of Miles Standish, the Hero-Captain of New England," and the tavern sign of General Israel Putnam.[181] Any variety of subjects might come before the *Georgia Citizen* reader.

One topic which drew immediate response from Chivers was that of slavery; sincerely and often violently opposed to abolition, and convinced that the institution of Negro slavery was not only economically necessary to the South but also divinely ordained, Chivers could see little justice or truth in any Northern appeal to abolish the Fugitive Slave Law or the Missouri Compromise. His expression on this subject is likely to be as extreme as anything he ever wrote, but certainly he was not alone in objecting strenuously to Harriet Beecher Stowe's best-seller, *Uncle Tom's Cabin* (1852). It sold so well that Chivers hardly had time to object before the whole public was aware of the book; so Chivers spoke against the book dealers who stocked it, and praised one bookman with Southern sympathies for refusing to sell it.[182] Later, he called it a "filthy" book, and contrasted it with what he believed an infinitely more accurate picture of the South and slavery, Ellwood Fisher's *Lecture on the North and South* (Cincinnati, 1849). While Chivers' high feelings may be seen as sectionalism, they also are another instance of the extreme qualities of his emotional response. Yet as a Southerner living in the North, he could not but be conscious of the growing sectional controversy, and his defense of his native land surely was as violent and thorough in his conversations as it was in his letters.

His firm defense of slavery presents one particularly interesting sidelight. While he believed in certain of the views of the Transcendentalists, it is obvious that he did not follow them in their attack on slavery, although he never spoke against them by name. The only two literary men whose names are particularly well-known today whom Chivers attacked were Lowell and Whittier, and then only in passing.[183] His targets for attack were the more noisy of the abolitionist clergymen, and of course Horace Greeley of the *New York Tribune*. His editorials had roused Chivers to call him an "agitator" and to claim, metaphorically, that he flew a flag of "agitation" above the *Tribune* building. Despite his objections,

it still remains flapping its iron sides in the odoriferous breezes of delectable Flunky-dom to the no-little delectation of the thin-skinned Loafers who puff and blow about the Abolition Wigwam in a repercussive thundering, somewhat resembling the crackling of the corybantine brass of Hell.[184]

Chivers' views on slavery present only one real problem to the student of his poetry: how did Chivers combine his belief in the perfectibility of man and in man's divine nature with his equally firm stand on the ethical rightness of slavery? While no clear answer can be given, by analogy this dichotomy becomes somewhat less perplexing when it is recalled that Chivers' local, contemporary views are kept out of his poetry, that his poetry always deals with a world at the remove of romantic distance or the filter of his own mind. Just as Chivers seldom allowed satire or criticism to appear in his verse, so he excluded any hint of sectionalism. And while this does not fully explain his attitude toward slavery as contrasted with his belief in man's divinity, it does suggest that Chivers had managed to partition his mind, as it were. One might consider practical, everyday problems of life, national or private, at one moment, and then switch to the more elemental forces of poetic inspiration in the next. There was never any overlapping of the two.

His fixed views on slavery certainly did not recommend him to the more popular literary figures of the day. In 1854 he had been in Boston for about a year, and surely he had associated with some one or two of the Cambridge circle. The absence of any formal comment about Chivers' poetry from, let us say, Longfellow or Lowell, may in part be explained by his opinions on slavery. Yet in 1852 G. K. Dickinson, an actor of considerable contemporary fame and a friend of Chivers', planned to introduce him to Longfellow, already having spoken to the latter about Chivers' interest in the theatre.[185] One suspects that the meeting, if it took place, may have been an uncomfortable one, for surely no two poets were ever further apart in their poetic practices, or, indeed, in their personalities. Lowell, as has been noted, knew Chivers' poetry, and read it aloud to his classes as "the shell of Shelley."[186] The letters which Lowell is said to have exchanged with Chivers have not been found, and it is difficult to imagine their content.

One wonders just what Chivers did when he was in Boston. The city was the seat of America's literary efforts, and Chivers found himself diametrically opposed to the views of the directors of those efforts over the most popular issue of the time. He could attend concerts and listen to lectures, as he gives evidence of having done, but was he actually introduced to the Harvard circle? Did he ever go out to Concord? He says nothing of any such visits in his letters from Boston, and yet he must have been known by the Concord and Cambridge literati, for the Boston magazines accepted several of his more extreme and more successful poems. Apparently Chivers stayed at the Central Hotel in Boston, and there is evidence of several trips to Lowell; nowhere is there indication that he became part of Boston's literary life. His accusations against Poe, a name not particularly well liked in Boston, thanks to Poe's attacks on Longfellow, had appeared in the *Waverly Magazine* in 1853, not long after he had arrived in Boston, and that magazine was widely enough read to bring Chivers' name to the critical audience of Cambridge. Yet no published comments on Chivers from his Boston audience exist, despite the fact that Lowell, for example, had received at least three of Chivers' books as complimentary copies.

Yet for all the failure of a really critical audience to respond to his work, in the opening months of 1853 Chivers published three volumes of poetry. In January of that year Chivers had written to obtain several hundred copies of *Eonchs of Ruby* from the binder's, for he wished to have "the misprinted poems taken out and new sheets printed and inserted." The result of this was *Memoralia; or, Phials of Amber Full of the Tears of Love, A Gift for the Beautiful,* published by Lippincott, Grambo & Co., in Philadelphia. The "misprinted poems" referred to only one poem, actually, "The Vigil in Aiden" (an elegy on Poe), the first poem in *Eonchs of Ruby*. Exactly why "The Vigil in Aiden" was omitted is not clear; Simms had implied it copied Poe, to which Chivers had explained that it was "founded upon Poe himself,"[187] a statement which close examination of the poem bears out. Furthermore, Chivers had not yet begun his accusations against Poe (although he had voiced them quietly in the *Georgia Citizen*); so there can be no suggestion that he was trying to avoid comparisons between his work and Poe's which might in turn ruin his charges of plagiarism. The most feasible explanation of his omission of the poem is that "The Vigil in Aiden" had not been well received by the critics. Chivers substituted twenty-six new pages, including the new title, index, and a long Preface; *Memoralia* appeared as a new volume unless the reader was familiar with Chivers' work. He was not alone in this practice of republishing earlier work; the multitudinous gift books of poetry often simply changed title when a new book was demanded. The Preface to Chivers' volume is of considerable interest in a study of his poetic theory, but of the six new poems two had already appeared in magazines. Generally, reviewers considered *Memoralia* along with *Virginalia,* also published at this time, rather than alloting it separate criticism.

Virginalia; or, Songs of My Summer Nights. A Gift of Love for the Beautiful, also published by Lippincott, Grambo, was the main publication of 1853. Where *Memoralia* was little more than a new edition of an older volume, only five of *Virginalia's* one hundred and four poems had been collected before. But almost half of the poems had reached the pages of the magazines during the preceding years.

The variety of technique and subject matter which is included in *Virginalia* suggests what I believe to be the true nature of the volume. Chivers had been published with increasing frequency during the last half of the 1840's, and this increase continued through the next ten years; *Virginalia* represents the best of these magazine publications up to the time of its issue. One feature of the volume is the general continuity of poem length, almost all of the poems averaging about one hundred and fifty lines; heretofore, each of Chivers' volumes had included at least one long poem, a sort of central piece, which usually did not come off as successfully as Chivers might have wished. In *Virginalia* he had settled down to the form which suited his talents best: stanzaic poems utilizing a refrain, depending to a very large extent upon rhythmic and melodic cadence rather than upon developing theme or subject matter. Here he is very much the personal romantic poet, speaking about himself in tones which are at once sincere and individual. Only a few of the poems suffer from incongruity of image or excess of sentiment. His scope includes everything from choric chants, depending largely upon an oratorical tradition for effect, to subtle stanzas almost entirely dependent upon sound rather than sense.

The unique qualities of the volume were generally well perceived by his critics, although one who concealed his identity beneath the signature "American" said only, "What possible motive could have induced the author of the book before us, after having written his verses to publish them, we have no means of knowing. . . ."[188]

It seems that no publication of Chivers' could ever go without at least one carping comment, and this time the *New York Quarterly* voiced what readers of the volume must have considered a uniquely inappropriate introduction:

The quaint conceits of these title-pages are a warning of the affectation and absurdity which nestle within the covers of the present astounding volumes. Such a barrage of pedantry, piety, blasphemy, sensuality, and delirious fancies, has seldom before gained the imprint of a respectable publisher. If the reader can imagine the fusion of the Hebrew Prophets, Solomon's Song, Jacob Behman, Edgar A. Poe, Anacreon, Catullus, Coleridge, and Isaac Watts, into one seething, simmering witch's caldron of abominations, he may form some idea of these fantastic monstrosities . . . the poetry, so called . . . consists of a series of changes on a few magnificent, sonorous epithets, interspersed with wild imaginative flights of the most nondescript character, evidently introduced in a desperate attempt at variety.

.   .   .   .

We must omit the most characteristic passages in the poetry of the "Heaven-inspired" bard. It is hardly fit to bring before decent readers. Such a strange compound of voluptuous passion, mawkish sentimentality, and transcendental, ecstatic piety savors more of the reveries of some oriental monkish mystic, dreaming under the shade of the palm-tree, than of a man in broadcloth and shirt collars belonging to the present keen-eyed generation. But this is not the worst of it. The damning fault of this poetry is its utter want of true feeling. No emotion is too sacred, no experience too private and personal, to be set off with the jingling fineries of phrase, which fall so loosely from the pen of the writer.[189]

Although the "keen-eyed" critic comes perilously close to parodying himself at one point, this review does indicate the shock that

Chivers' poetry induced in unsuspecting magazine editors. Outraged by poetry which did not follow the conventional canons of the day, this editor (and he was hardly alone in his refusal) would not accept poetry dependent upon cadence and music rather than instructive theme and simple verse patterns. While it is true that any volume of Chivers' work contains bad poetry, each volume also includes poems which, while they are apart from the conventional tendencies of writers like Whittier or Longfellow or Lowell, are worthy of close attention.

Jedidiah Hunt, Jr., a correspondent of Poe's and a good friend of Chivers', reviewed *Virginalia* for the *Georgia Citizen,* and his comments help point up the inevitability of the intense objections of the *New York Quarterly* critic.

We are wholly at a loss to satisfactorily determine to what school, the main scope of Dr. Chivers' mind belongs; for, among the peaceful army of our Minstrels his precise correspondent is not found. Had the lamented Poe been spared, Dr. Chivers would have had a companion worthy his rank and station. Their minds seemed to have been cast, originally in one mould. . . . The strains which our more lowly Bards put forth, and which win our best affections, because of their touching tenderness and simple pathos of feeling, find no response, with our author, now under consideration. . . .

. . . .

The period is not distant when Dr. Chivers' style of composition will take and maintain its legitimate position in the qualified estimation of the Student and the matured Scholar. Let the period be sooner or later, he has only to bide his time, by an exercise of submissive, yet unfaltering patience, for which he is eminently distinguished, and there is being completed for him in the Temple of well doing, a niche, where his Genius will be personified by a Parian Statue of Affection—beautiful as it will be merited, and faithful as it will be enduring.[190]

The eulogistic character of this appreciation does not obscure the important point, that Chivers was writing, in his mature work, against the accepted styles of his day. Hunt's belief that he would be accepted if he but had patience has taken just about a hundred years to be borne out.

In light of a controversy which was to break out in its pages within three months of this review, the opinion of the *Waverly Magazine* is interesting:

. . . We were attracted, in the first instance, by the originality of [the poems]—as well in the tone of thought as in the flexible and flowing metre, which expressively adapts itself to every movement of his inspiration. . . . In these poems the reader will find something different from the old canons and old expressions, obeyed and repeated by those poets which the general taste holds in estimation . . . he goes back to those poetic impulses and principles, which existed at the beginning of all poetry, and . . . takes his own pathway by the rarely trodden shores of romantic poetry. Not such romantic poetry as we have adopted and cultivated, after the spirit and tone of the mediaeval times; but a poetry drawing its inspiration from higher sources—from that innate sense of melody and devotion which must have belonged to the first wondering and impressible spirits . . . of the East. Those whose minds are pitched to the tone of a more etherial harmony can alone appreciate properly the verse of Dr. Chivers. . . . But the originality of his style and views may very well arrest attention. . . .

At the first glance, every one must concede to Dr. Chivers the merit of imitating no one. Considering that our literary world is so crowded and deafened . . . by mocking-birds of every bill, we insist that such is a great merit. . . . He writes with passionate emotion; and this, on whatever ground you find it—Greek or Gothic—is the genuine Helicon. . . . He appears to be pouring out his mind in irrepressible soliloquies, that shape themselves in rhythmic cadences. . . .

What you chiefly remark in these lyrics is the fearlessness with which the author gives himself up to his thoughts. . . . In this rapture of composition his mind seems absolutely crowded with imagery poured out in an affluence perfectly prodigal . . . the verses before us prove that the essence of poetry is Passion. For the poet here seems to be all feeling; and her fervor forces you to sympathize with the continual ecstasies of his muse. . . . We, who are a good deal of the tame old school ourselves, can easily understand why the generality of critics might not take cordially to such poetry as this. They are always in a mean. . . .

But change must grow in all things; and Dr. Chivers has given poetry a pronounced new aspect and bias, and turned the streams of Helicon into fresher channels, watering the growth of new flowers, and waking the sound of new echoes in its course.[191]

The review is given at such length because it insists upon two of the most important aspects of Chivers' poetry. The first is the fact that Chivers seems to have been working out of a new strain of poetry, although there are examples of the same exotic diction, heady rhythms, and melodic hypnosis in Poe and several others writing before the Civil War.[192] The second is the critic's assurance that the effect of Chivers' verse is a unique one, free from imitation and wholly dependent upon the nature of his personal reaction to experience.

The personal nature of so much of Chivers' poetry is evident further in his last publication during 1853, *Atlanta: or The True Blessed Island of Poesy, A Paul Epic—In Three Lustra,* which was printed for him at the *Georgia Citizen* office. It appeared in an expurgated text in the *Georgia Citizen* itself in January of that year.[193] The Preface is dated July 18, 1842; since the style of the volume suggests his later work, and since there are no known biographical facts which indicate he might have been working on the text in 1842, either Chivers dated the Preface incorrectly or had conceived the plan of *Atlanta* (which is expounded in the Preface) long before he commenced composition.

The title of the volume itself, like that of *Eonchs of Ruby,* demands explanation. *Atlanta* presumably refers, indirectly at least, to Mount Atlas, in Libya, on whose top the heavens were fabled to rest. *Paul* is in reference to the Apostle, and *Lustra* of course refers to the periods of five years.[194] Atlanta, the earthly contact with heaven, is seen as the source of all poetry. The poet achieves something of the vision of St. Paul, and that vision extends itself over a series of years. *Atlanta* is a single long poem of some thousand lines divided into three cantos, or lustra, and its subject is the search by man for the ideal world, the Terrestrial Eden, symbolized here by a beautiful island on which lives a most beautiful maiden. The poem traces man's progress to the island and explains his final success in finding the ideal in terms of his physical union with the maiden. The temptation to consider the poem autobiographical cannot be permitted, despite the obvious reference to Chivers' final happiness with his second wife. While *Atlanta* will be investigated at length later,[195] it may be noticed here as marking one of the final points of Chivers' publishing career. Simms had advised him only eight months before to "Give up fugitive verse" and "address yourself to labours of length. . . ."[196] While Chivers had fault to find with Simms' advice, it is entirely possible that he considered it seriously; if he had prepared the Preface as early as 1842, he now apparently felt capable of handling the difficult job he had set out in that Preface. There he states that no epic poem has ever delighted the reader in its entirety, but that "beautiful or select passages only" give him delight. Therefore he designed *Atlanta* as a series of images, flowing fast upon one another, consciously attempting to keep to a minimum all passages of exposition explaining movement or theme. On the surface *Atlanta* appears an exotic verse romance. Rightly understood, it is a particularly unique sort of epic poem, the meaning of which lies almost entirely on the symbolic level.

Chivers was anxious that his poem might be critically recognized. He even sent a copy to Horace Greeley of the *Tribune,* whose views on slavery he attacked so violently.[197] He could do so because in his mind, apparently, his verse and his prose belonged in different worlds. The difference in tone between his most characteristic poetry and his critical prose has already been noted; the presentation of *Atlanta* to Greeley was made because of exactly the same distinction. There is no record, unfortunately, of any response from Greeley.

Actually, there was only one critical response to the volume; possibly editors felt that their reviews of *Memoralia* and *Virginalia* had done Chivers' talents justice enough. But the *Southern Literary Messenger* spoke of *Atlanta* for over two pages,[198] and their tone is another indication that criticism frequently failed of being either objective or reasoned.

Beginning with amused comment on both the title and the lapse of time between the date of composition of the Preface and its publication, the reviewer parodies the verse romance of the poem, a feat particularly easy to accomplish since Chivers was content to warp that narrative wherever his symbolism demanded a different tack. Throughout the review Chivers is given no credit at all, and *Atlanta* is regarded as a mighty joke, perpetrated by a crazed mind which did not, the reviewer implies, itself understand what it was writing. The most frustrating criticism which can be offered to a writer is that, after all, what he has written was simply not worth writing.

Fortunately the *Southern Literary Messenger's* opinion of Chivers' value did not at once discourage him. 1853 had seen the publication of three volumes of poetry; 1852 through 1854 saw Chivers compose a number of his finer experiments on the nature of rhythm and sound, particularly his "Chinese Serenade"[199] and "The Roll of Fame,"[200] and, all told, after 1852 he published forty poems before his death in 1858. That after 1853 virtually every one of these poems was published in the one paper which remained faithful to Chivers throughout his publishing career, the *Georgia Citizen,* suggests something of the sudden drop in his popularity. The poems themselves are generally just as competent as earlier work, and several, as I have suggested, are vitally interesting as attempts to broaden the limits of poetic technique.

But in August and September of 1853 Chivers became involved in the worst literary controversy of his life; the public reaction to the part he played in it was such as to prevent any further popularity with any reputable journal; it was not so much what Chivers said, in the beginning, as the way he said it. Just as he insisted, fiercely and dogmatically, upon minor issues in the past, here, in his attack upon Poe and in his certainty that Poe had plagiarized elements of "The Raven" from his, Chivers', works, he speaks in an almost pathological tone of outraged virtue and truth. A more objective mind would have presented the case and allowed reasoned argument to follow. Chivers could never be objective in considering his own work.

Chivers' published comments on plagiarisms from his own poetry began in July of 1850, when he disagreed with a contemporary critic about the originality of Poe's style; in a rather quiet tone he said that actually "The Raven" had been derived from "To Allegra Florence in Heaven" (*LP*, pp. 15-16) and from "Lament on the Death of My Mother" (*LP*, pp. 20-21).[201] Then he listed five later poems by as many poets which he believed had been inspired by his "To Allegra Florence in Heaven" and not by Poe's more famous poem. These five poems vary considerably in their success and in their authorship; one Chivers believed had been written by Poe himself ("The Departed," *Broadway Journal,* July 12, 1845); one was by an unknown "Stranger" ("Autumn," *Southern Literary Messenger,* XI, 649-650, November, 1845); one was by John Wesley Hanson, a Universalist minister and poet ("To My Angel Daughter," *Boston Museum,* I, 313, March 17, 1849); one was by Phoebe Carey ("Dirge," *National Era,* III, 98, June 21, 1849); and one poem was from *Blackwood's* ("The Stormy Sea," LXI, 91, January, 1847, by "Delta" [David Macbeth Moir]). Each of these poems is closer to Chivers' form than Poe's, except that of J. W. Hanson, which follows a favorite Chivers theme. The point is not so much whether or not these particular poets were inspired by Chivers' work, ("To Allegra Florence in Heaven" had appeared in *The Lost Pleiad,* his first volume to achieve national prominence), although Chivers makes a rather good case of that belief, as it is the terms in which he expresses his belief. He is not outraged, nor is he indignant; he even notes that "The Departed" and Phoebe Carey's "Dirge" have a certain pleasing beauty about them. Furthermore, he is as much pleased over the fact that the style of these poems is now being used in America as he is in his belief that he, rather than Poe, began this style. He believed that the one mark of distinction which American poetry might hope for to set it above English work was the fact of its originality of style. If Chivers had never gone further in his discussion of the sources of Poe's "Raven" or of other imitations of his work, no critic would find fault with him for long.

But after such a temperate beginning, Chivers' pride began to work more strongly, and his statements take on the nature of an obsession rather than a belief, of pathological anger rather than reasonable self-interest.

Chivers' sensitivity to possible plagiarism combined with his deep respect for Poe's work when he learned that Mrs. Lydia M. Tenney had published a spirit "Message from Edgar A. Poe,"[202] and he objected quickly:

> In the first place, Poe never wrote any such Poetry as this—therefore, could not have dictated it to Mrs. Lydia H. Tenney. She was therefore, never an amanuensis of his—nor does she possess the least aptitude in her mind to be so. In the second place, Poe would never dictate, from a SUPERIOR SPHERE, to a mind in *this,* or *inferior* one that of which he was not the *original*—particularly in an ungrammatical language—as is the case with the last line. . . .[203]

Chivers was annoyed because the editor of the *Spirit Messenger* had presented Mrs. Tenney's poem in all seriousness as Poe's; such poor poetry is an insult to his memory, said Chivers. He then continued to object that a poem entitled "Mary O'Shane," which Mrs. Tenney had said was dictated by the spirit of McDonald Clarke,[204] was "a plagiarism—the rhythm having been stolen from a Poem [of mine] entitled *'The Moon of Mobile.'* " With this comment it begins to come clear that Chivers understood the rhythm of "To Allegra Florence in Heaven" (trochaic tetrameter, catalectic) to be the element which made the poem original. Thereafter, he might expect any poems which utilized this meter, and it is a comparatively rare one, had been influenced by his work.

Up until this point Chivers' statements have been sensibly and quietly phrased and motivated. When he accused J. W. Hanson of having plagiarized from him again, however, a certain obsessive note is present. Chivers saw Hanson's poem "The Stars"[205] and quoted several stanzas in proof that the "original" of the poem was his own "Apollo." Hanson wrote:

> Are the stars a flock of lambkins,
>   Which graze, when the sun's clear light
> Has gone, in the blue fields of Heaven,
>   Their shepherdess the Night?   (11. 1-4)

Chivers' poem begins:

> What are stars, but hieroglyphics of God's glory writ
>   in lightning
> On the wide-folded pages of the azure scroll above. . . .[206]

The obvious inferiority of Hanson's lyric is what concerns him who would understand Chivers rather than the fact that the next year Hanson announced that the poem was actually a translation from the German.[207] Other than a metaphor which concerns itself with interpretations of the stars in the sky, the two sets of lines have little in common; yet Chivers was driven to notice this similarity and publish his belief that Hanson had taken the poem from his work. Surely there was something more than simple certainty that his style and theme were the originals which moved Chivers. Once committed to examining the magazines for poetry which seemed similar to his own, Chivers lost whatever critical judgment he may have had. It became impossible for him to examine a poem which had a theme similar to one he had used (which of course does not constitute plagiarism), or which had been written in a rhythm or meter he felt was his own, without assuming influence.[208]

Yet he was not completely unreasonable. Only six months before he was to accuse Poe again of having borrowed from his work for "The Raven," he defended him stoutly and at length from the charge of having plagiarized "To One in Paradise" from Tennyson.[209]

His own charges against Poe had appeared in a moderate tone in the *Georgia Citizen;* he enlarged and intensified them when he wrote a series of articles for the *Waverly Magazine* of Boston in 1853. The content of his charges will be examined later, but a review of the progress of this literary debate will provide further elaboration of our knowledge of the change which came over Chivers when he wrote of plagiarism of any sort. No longer able to present what were apparently quite reasonable beliefs in any but the most exasperating and violent of statements, Chivers here indulged all his powers of invective and distortion in an attempt to prove his point.

His principal claims were offered in the "Origin of Poe's Raven," which appeared on July 30, 1853, over the signature of "Fiat Justitia."[210] It later became obvious to Moses A. Dow, the editor of the *Waverly*, that Chivers' fine hand was at work, but only gradually did Fiat Justitia's opponents realize Chivers' presence. In this article, Chivers is put forward as the true originator of the style of Poe's "Raven," part of the claim resting on Fiat Justitia's belief that Chivers had supplied the "never-more" refrain of "The Raven" and had been the first to use a trochaic rhythm for elegiac verse.

This drew a reply from Henry S. Cornwell, himself a poet, who produced an earlier use of "nevermore" and objected to Chivers' claim about trochaics.[211] One who signed himself only "J. J. P." also attacked Chivers, deducing that Chivers must be a Northerner, and thus have been inspired to attack Poe, a Southerner.[212] No one, apparently, would even consider the possible truth of Chivers' accusations. Enraged, Chivers replied, again via Fiat Justitia, in ineffective and distorting prose. The sample given below is in large part typical of his methods of argument in these counter-attacking articles, and even this short quotation is enough to suggest something of the failure of his critical sense. Throughout he quoted excerpts from Cornwell's essay, attempting to refute them, but never considering the basic question of his own truthfulness.

He very pertinently affirms—manifesting, at the same time, a truly marvelous intuition into his own wonderful psychology—"We may be *thickheaded,* but really, we cannot perceive by what kind of reasoning the writer comes to such a quick conclusion."

Who doubts it? Who ever doubted it? Who will ever doubt it? Nobody—as nobody ought to be better acquainted with the *thickness* of his skull than he is himself. The truth is, this is the very reason why he cannot *"perceive"* it. But is it not really wonderful that this man has sagacity enough to know that he is treading on hallowed ground—in short, entering, with unhallowed feet, into the uninviting door of a forbidden threshold?

• 81

He says, "But an examination of the simple item of *punctuation* we think sufficient to show the lameness of his arguments here, without going a step further." But why? Why does he *think* so? Does he not *know* it? If he *does not,* why talk about *thinking* it? Thinking will not do—particularly when this thinking has to come through such a *"thick"* skull.[213]

The dodging and quibbling which Chivers depends upon here is hardly persuasive. It is the result of that same violence of temper which we have seen before, and which, once out of control, could deform the facts of Chivers' case so badly as to obscure them. The debate continued through September and into October, Chivers adopting a second pseudonym, "Felix Forresti," to write in defence of "Fiat Justitia."[214] Two other participants entered the argument soon, one making satiric reference to Chivers, the other pleading for something much needed in the debate, a degree of impartiality and objectivity.

If Poe gained "notoriety" by choosing to imitate a particular style which he evidently *admired,* it is undoubtedly proper that the *inventor* of that style should receive the benefits arising from the invention. But if Poe wrote for the "Broadway Journal" in *praise* of Chivers' poems, and afterwards frequently imitated his style, probably he intended no *deception,* but merely followed the dictates of his own taste. . . .[215]

But as dispassionate a voice as this was soon lost in the uproar, even though S. Herbert Lancey, a contributing editor of the *Waverly,* who thought well of Chivers' case but deplored his presentation, sentiments with which today's reader may concur, reminded all that Poe himself had made unsubstantiated charges of plagiarism, particularly against Longfellow. He concluded, " 'tis better to let the dead rest, nor seek to mar their fame."[216] This Chivers could not do. He had committed himself and there was no obvious retreat without the admission of defeat.

Yet his final article in the *Waverly Magazine* suggests that he was trying to control his temper. He at last turned to a direct analysis of the poems under dispute and attempted with fair success to prove their similarity. It must have shocked his readers, who knew Fiat Justitia only as a vindictive contributor to the *Waverly Magazine,* to hear him announce that he was gathering material for a biography of Poe. He said, a "lucid exposition of all the manifold resemblances between the two poems" would there be offered;[217] much of the fascination of this remark lies in the fact that the manuscript of Chivers' *Life of Poe* contains only the most incidental reference to either of the two poems under consideration here, Poe's "Raven" and Chivers' "To Allegra Florence in Heaven." That manuscript contains little but praise for Poe's poetic abilities. The animus which at first seems apparent from the series of articles in the *Waverly* is actually a deceptive result of the fact of controversy itself. We have seen how Chivers found it impossible to accept contradiction or correction; his unrestrained and illogical extremes in these articles are the result of similar emotional pressures.

Chivers could not forbear explaining one further circumstance in this last article. The *Philosophy of Composition,* he said, was written as a *"concession article"* after Chivers "had accused him of having derived ["The Raven"], soul and body,"[218] from "To Allegra Florence in Heaven." Such a statement means that Chivers had actually spoken to Poe about the fact of plagiarism. Other than this single reference, however, there is no indication that either poet felt any guilt or nervousness over the similarity of their styles. Chivers' charge should be dismissed as a further product of the distortion of his critical sense.

Moses A. Dow put an end to the controversy on October 29, 1853, by announcing that no further debate would be published in the *Waverly Magazine;* he also took time to reprimand the participants for the violence of their charges, particularly as represented by further manuscripts which he had before him but would not publish.[219] A summary of Chivers' attacks indicates that other than his first article, the "Origin of Poe's Raven" (August 30, 1853), and his final published statement, "Poe's Plagiarisms" (October 1, 1853), the substance of his remarks had been addressed against those who had attacked him, usually in terms which are as unconvincing as they are unpleasant. However, as a later chapter will attempt to show, the articles beginning and ending the controversy do contain comparisons and similarities which demand exact analysis.

Seen in the light of the other literary controversies in which Chivers was involved, the *Waverly* feud assumes its correct perspective. Chivers could not control himself in the face of contradiction of any sort, particularly when it involved assertions concerning his much-admired friend Poe. Having lost all objectivity, Chivers departed from the factual presentation which might well have convinced his readers. Our tendency is therefore to confuse his wild statements in the face of attack with the more ordered logical prose of those articles which concern themselves with Poe alone and forbear reference to secondary figures like Cornwell. Taken in its entirety, this controversy shows something which the rest of Chivers' prose might have led us to expect, the suspension of critical judgment and insight before accusation, a tendency which comes close to destroying his valid points of argument. Yet when these points are removed from the emotional and confused atmosphere of this controversy, and seen analytically, the basis of his claims will prove, I believe, to have been sound.

Two further instances of literary controversy will prove even more conclusively how uncritical and even unethical Chivers could be before the onslaughts of his emotional reaction. In July, 1853, just before the Poe controversy began, a poem entitled "Anna's Grave," by J. R. Snead, Esq., appeared in the *Waverly Magazine*.[220] Snead was a fellow-townsman of Chivers, a business acquaintance and a good friend, and had sent a poem on the death of his wife to Chivers, who replied.

I received your letter, enclosing the Poem. . . . Some of the lines were pretty and manifest a fine taste for the Art of Poetry; but, on the whole, the Poem was rather imperfectly made out. Of course I do not say this in a critical sense, but as a hint to you to do better next time. You will understand what I mean when you see the version which I have given of it, as published in the *Waverley Magazine*—now on its way to you. I have retained only a few of your lines. . . . As the poem has been entirely *re*written by me, of course I did not over-reach your request in publishing it with your name. As it is now published, it is a perfect Gem. . . .[221]

Apparently Snead had requested Chivers to examine the poem, but not to publish it. Chivers' action in revising and publishing the poem is not to be questioned, but he republished it in *Dodge's Literary Museum* on July 15, 1854, under his own name.[222] This discrepancy was detected within a week, and Ossian E. Dodge, the editor, requested publicly that Messrs. Snead and Chivers explain the apparent plagiarism. J. Starr Holloway, who had apparently been following the *Waverly* controversy, wrote to say that, althought Snead and Chivers might be the same person, "as Dr. Chivers is suspected of a variety of soubriquets, (*Fiat Justitia,* for instance),"[223] he doubted it very much. Chivers replied promptly to Dodge and, with his usual disregard of moderation, claimed that the poem was his own, and that he had used a pseudonym in publishing it in the *Waverly* because he thought so poorly of that magazine after the manner in which it had handled the Poe controversy: "I disinterred it from that rotten sepulchre [the *Waverly*], wherein the divinest things would be rendered wholly mortal, to enjoy its present immortality in the fame-bestowing pyramid of American Letters [*Dodge's Literary Museum*]—for how could I let it rot in such a grave?"[224] Strangely enough Chivers' assertions had the desired effect, for soon Moses A. Dow, editor of the *Waverly*, not only admitted that Dr. Chivers had originally given them the poem, but also affirmed that he had always believed it to be Chivers'.[225] Dow also included in that issue a letter from Mrs. Jane E. Locke, a comparatively popular poetess of the day, who had known Poe in various connections, particularly as she introduced him at Lowell when he gave his lecture on "The Poetic Principle."[226] Her letter stands as important testimony in clarifying Poe's opinion of Chivers. The matter of "Anna's Grave" was debated for several more issues of each magazine, finally evolving into a fight between them. Mrs. Locke's letter had apparently been prompted first by the Poe controversy of the preceding year, and finally by the Snead charges of 1854.

... from a personal acquaintance with [Dr. Chivers], whom I know to have been a warm friend and admirer of Mr. Poe, I am surprised that he could admit an accusation of the kind to blot the literary fame of the greatest genius America can boast, making claim though it does for the greater originality and power of his pen. And I may say, from a long personal acquaintance with the former, (E.A.P.,) . . . I am convinced there could have been no such thing as plagiarist in the character of the man.

. . . .

On turning over Dr. Chivers' published volumes, there are, in truth, some of the most beautifully original and wildly plaintive passages, full of richness and melody, and not unlike in vividness to the conceptions of Poe, yet easily accounted for, perhaps, without a denial to either of originality. At all events, private letters from the great poet [Poe] assure me that he was in very truth an admirer of his powers, also, and placed as high an appreciation on the passages . . . as I have. And who did not wither under *his* criticism might be free to stand forever.[227]

Other than a letter from Mrs. Clemm to Chivers, concerning Poe's appreciation of his poetry, this is the only evidence extant of Poe's privately-expressed admiration for Chivers' poetry. The admission of Poe's admiration, however, did not deter Chivers from replying to Mrs. Locke by repeating many of Fiat Justitia's arguments, if in a wholly different and polite tone.[228]

Snead had been forgotten in the heat of the argument, and was not referred to again. Mrs. Locke's letter helped to establish Chivers as one whose poetry Poe had admired, but Mrs. Locke would not admit Chivers' beliefs concerning Poe's plagiarism, and so he accepted her compliments yet insisted that she understand the validity of his arguments about "The Raven." Chivers was unable to compromise his beliefs in the face of what should have been regarded as obviously sincere help from Mrs. Locke; mild as he had been four years before when he first stated his beliefs, he was now convinced beyond all change.

A final instance of Chivers' hypersensitivity regarding plagiarism involves Longfellow and the controversy which arose soon after the publication of "Hiawatha" regarding that poem's possible derivation from the Finnish epic, "Kalevala."[229] Chivers followed the controversy with considerable interest, probably drawn by the claims of originality in meter. Besides, Poe himself had accused Longfellow of plagiarism years before. Chivers outdid any other accuser; his articles are the most violent possible example of what his originally mild-enough comments on the subject of plagiarism have degenerated to. Longfellow's poem was not derived from the "Kalevala" at all, but from an astounding variety and selection of Chivers' own poems. It would be fruitless to analyze at length the details of his charges, for he chose parallel lines from "The Vigil in Aiden" (EofR), "The Mighty Dead" (EofR), "Isadore" (EofR), "Lord Uther's Lament for Ella" (EofR), and even from Atlanta. His quotations were not only taken out of context, they were rearranged, so that a six line quotation, for example, may contain lines from a variety of stanzas, or even from several poems. By and large, when Chivers took passages from his own work and placed them next to excerpts from "Hiawatha," whatever similarity is apparent exists in rhythm. "Hiawatha" is written in trochaic tetrameter, and all of Chivers' quotations from his own work are in the same meter; wherever he could discover a poem utilizing something like the tetrameter catalectic trochaics of "To Allegra Florence in Heaven," he found evidence of plagiarism.

A variety of critics and journals had taken up the charges that "Hiawatha" had its origin in the Finnish epic. Chivers replied in tones which are characteristic of the whole article:

> Now, what will the Editor of the Tribune say to this? What will that old Buzzard, mis-named the New York Review, say to this? What will the Editor of Putnam say to this? What will his Critic—the gentleman who had his last "Thanksgiving Dinner spoiled" by a new Apician morsel, called Spanish Trochaic—say to this?—What will all the other Succotash-eating thieves of the Land of Thanksgiving say to this? Do they not owe me everlasting thanks for thus enlightening their benighted minds on the enchanting topics of literary larceny? Verily, I think they do.[230]

The frustration and violence of emotion which are evident in such an ill-judged statement are typical of all of Chivers' final prose work. He had become so involved with his own desires and past performances that he could no longer speak critically. His attack on Longfellow is not much worse than others which were made at the time, but it is the endpoint of a long series of literary controversies in which Chivers became involved. Completely unable to restrain himself, he departed from any moderation or considered statement so far as to very nearly ruin his literary reputation; it would be difficult for any but the most objective of contemporary literary critics to have viewed any of Chivers' work calmly after such a misrepresented attack as was Chivers' upon Longfellow. Understandable only in terms of the sense of frustration built up by long years of comparative oblivion, a frustration which was violently increased by the failure of his public to see the valid facts in his charges against Poe, this attack on Longfellow is an unpleasant conclusion to his discussions of literary matters. It is well to remember that the emotive powers here represented in a most unfortunate manner are refined and transmuted in his poetry. The split between Chivers the essayist and critic and Chivers the poet is surely pathetically evident now. The only connection between these two elements of Chivers' personality is the strength of imagination and emotion present in each. Fastened to a sublime subject, this strength could produce effective poetry; held down by the prosaic and mundane, it drove Chivers to fantastic and pathological extremes of self-indulgence and egoism.

Chivers last major poetic effort was inspired, for once, by his fellow citizens in Washington, Georgia. They determined to ask their resident-poet to prepare a eulogy for the Fourth of July celebration in 1856. Chivers found himself too ill to deliver the poem as they had wished him to, and instead had it printed by C. R. Hanleiter & Co., Printers, of Atlanta, Georgia. The pamphlet's title reads, *Birth-Day Song of Liberty. A Paean of Glory for the Heroes of Freedom.* Its twenty-nine long stanzas would have made a long day's reading, but it remains an interesting example of Chivers' method of working with the oratorical tradition.[231]

Chivers had moved permanently to the South in early 1855; he remained in Washington, Georgia, until the fall of 1856, when for unknown reasons he moved to Decatur. He no longer expected to find publication outlets in reputable Northern magazines after the *Waverly* controversy in 1853, followed as it was by his involvement with J. R. Snead, and although he continued to compose and publish poetry, his main outlet was the faithful *Georgia Citizen.* The poetry of these last years still reflects something of the strength and power of his early experiments in the 1850's, yet does not alter the judgment that *Virginalia* (1853) probably represents his major effort.

In 1856 he was honored in quite an unexpected manner, as Oglethorpe Medical College, of Savannah, elected him Professor of Physiology and Pathology. Such an election suggests that he had been active in the medical world during his long publishing career, but there is no evidence to support such a supposition. And three essays he contributed to the *Oglethorpe Medical and Surgical Journal*,[232] after he had sensibly decided against accepting their offer of a professorship, testify to his amateur status.

One final literary attempt remained to be completed before his death in 1858. The Irish fable of Deirdre, a legend which had caught his attention as early as 1845, when he found a reference to it in the footnotes of Thomas Moore's *Irish Melodies,* was just the sort of fantasy which would delight and inspire him. Moore's footnote had directed him to the first volume of the *Transactions of the Gaelic Society of Dublin* (1809), where he found a literal rendering of the legend by Theophilus O'Flanagan. Chivers stays close to the original in his dramatic version of the tale, entitled *The Sons of Usna: A Tragi-Apotheosis, in Five Acts,* which he had printed by C. Sherman & Son, Printers, of Philadelphia. He had apparently had the finished play by him for some four years, for a letter to the editor of the *Georgia Citizen,* written just before he left the North for the last time, indicates that he then had a completed play ready for publication,[233] and the Preface to this play is dated from Mt. Vernon, New York, on November 7, 1854.

The Sons of Usna is the first dramatic use of the legend. It suggests that Chivers was working toward something closer to acting dialogue and movement than is present in his earlier plays. The blank verse rises at times to the heights of his best poetry, but often the metaphysical speculations which Chivers added to the narrative plot carry his poetry to correspondingly extreme depths. The confusing effect the combination of verse melodrama and theological questioning must have had upon the play's readers is indicated by the single review it received, of course in the *Georgia Citizen:* "In [Dr. Chivers] we may be pretty confident of meeting with three things of no small moment:—ingenuity and acumen of thought . . . the finer spirit of learning,—and breadth of view. . . . Language is vital in his hands. His style might be described as metaphysical. . . ."[234] *The Sons of Usna* might impress its readers even though it would never reach a stage.

In a sense, what happened to *The Sons of Usna* had been occurring throughout Chivers' life; readers were impressed, often confused, and when confused frequently antagonistic. Not an author to whom anyone might be indifferent, Chivers surged through fifty years of American thought and expression without ever finding a firm area in which he might settle as a known, respected, and popular poet. Never content with half-measures, he shocked and upset those readers who were able to see his genius, and annoyed and disgusted those who believed him mad or incomprehensible. When he died in the early morning hours of December 19, 1858, after a short illness, his wife noted that his final words were, "All is perfect peace with me."[235] Surely that was the first time he had been at peace during his extremely active life.

While the full extent of his genius will become evident only after we have analyzed the literary background out of which he wrote as well as the subject matter and technique that genius utilized, any study which failed to encompass the intensity of his literary activity would be misleading. As has become evident, much of Chivers' energy was loosed into prose channels, and his letters to the *Georgia Citizen,* as well as his erratic movement through the literary world of mid-century America, must be understood as being just as much representative of him as are his poetic evocations of heaven.

These letters, and the literary interests from which they sprang, as much as the variety and number of his collections of poetry, illuminate a facet of Chivers' personality which motivated him throughout life. Once he had found that the literary world was the one in which he could best express himself, as evidently he did in his first volume of poetry in 1832, he set about tutoring himself in the ways and methods of a professional man of letters. His resulting failure to find either critical audience or helpful literary companionship so worked upon him that his last years were clouded darkly by charges of irresponsible accusation and literary feuds unpleasant to read of today, unpleasant largely because Chivers usually appears in the wrong. The critic is frustrated by his knowledge that Chivers' poetry deserved the attention it did not receive, at the same time that he realizes that much of the cause of this silence arose from Chivers' demanding attitude toward the audience which should have received him. This paradox is especially apparent in the *Waverly Magazine* feud; the intensity of Chivers' desire to receive something of the acclaim he deserved, an intensity of emotion which produced much of his best poetry, automatically destroyed all chances of his obtaining it. That Chivers' inability to solve the problem thus presented drove him back to isolation on his Georgia estate we have just seen; that the critic must separate Chivers' poetry from its author's tempestuous desire to defend and praise it is immediately obvious when that poetry is analyzed.

In a sense, Chivers' career is one of contemporary failure and final success. His desire to establish himself as a prominent man of letters, for reasons which vary from the personal and egotistical to the spiritual, was never fulfilled. His need as well as his desire to express himself in poetry, a need created by the transcendent side of the same reasons which operated in moving him to attempt a career as a literary professional, was in its turn fulfilled almost as completely as he himself insisted it ought to be, a fact which should become clear in the succeeding chapters.

Chapter Two

∽ Literary Influences

To call the years at the middle of the nineteenth century in America a Renaissance demands that several distinctions be made. Emerson, Thoreau, Hawthorne, Melville, and Whitman today offer confirmation of the statement; but in 1855 the American reading public would scarcely have testified to their greatness. Emerson, the lecturer, was heard, yet but half understood beyond Concord; "The Custom House" introduction to *The Scarlet Letter* many thought "more piquant than anything in the book" and perhaps 6,000 copies were sold in two years, after which sales dwindled;[1] although only sixty copies of *Moby Dick* remained after the Harper's warehouse fire, a second edition was not called for until 1863 and Melville rightly feared he would be remembered as the author of "Typee, Piddledee, etc.";[2] Thoreau's *Walden* never touched the contemporary "lives of quiet desperation" it was designed to change; and Whitman could not sell the thousand-odd copies of *Leaves of Grass* even though it had the same ornate binding as *Fern Leaves from Fanny's Portfolio,* which was still going strong in 1855 after an original sale in 1853 of 70,000 copies.

Such a record of failure to react to what are considered today the staple items in the nineteenth century Renaissance does not mean that there was no literary activity, nor that that activity lacked an audience. By 1835 there were sixty-five daily newspapers published in America; eight years after the first Lyceum was founded in 1826 there were over 3,000 such groups, well-attended and highly respected; and the American reception of Scott's novels and Byron's verse romances would have saved the financial life of the former and increased the fortune of the latter had copyright laws demanded payment of royalties to authors residing outside the United States. Americans were hungry for "culture," and the story of the English Romantics in America is a record of publishers trying to supply the public demands. Scott, Byron, Campbell, and Moore took their turns on the shelves of bookstores from Cambridge and Philadelphia to Louisville and Charleston. By the middle of the century several characteristics of the American audience stood clear; it was a feminine audience, for the male segment of the population was busy with material success; it was an audience self-conscious of America's youth and inexperience in the world of culture, and one which demanded written explication of the facts of prosperity, goodness, and adventure which its country displayed so variously. It was also a family audience, and periodicals such as *Arthur's Home Gazette, A Journal of Pure Reading* had wide success.

Mr. James D. Hart, in his informative and entertaining *The Popular Book*, has studied the literary taste of America during these years, and his conclusions prepare the way for an understanding of the background out of which Thomas Holley Chivers came and of the audience which necessarily greeted his work. English romanticism, in Scott's and Moore's terms, found a prepared ground:

The impulses that made the public ready for romanticism . . . were more than literary. Romanticism's philosophic concepts, emphasizing idealism, imagination, boundlessness, and greater personal freedom, may have been theories unknown to average American readers, but they were what many experienced first hand, whether as individualists in the East's nascent capitalistic enterprise, or as pioneers on the westward-moving frontier.[3]

After all, the colors of the American landscape, whether geographic or atmospheric, were vivid and sometimes loud. Men did seem larger than life-size when the westward travelers reported from the Mississippi; the view from Nob Hill might well approximate that from Darien's peak; and when the news came back from Sutter's sawmill, it only confirmed what a man with vision might well have suspected.

While America's physical destiny lay clear and open before many, others saw inward frontiers which, they believed, might be investigated with equal profit and success. Phrenology provided Whitman with an analysis of his character and some curious diction for his poetry. Mesmerism was greeted with wild excitement; A. J. Davis dictated the *Principles of Nature* while in a trance,[4] and proclaimed that the inner workings of man and the universe might be understood through visionary experience. The psychic boundaries, so it seemed, were disappearing as rapidly as were the geographical.

Such an account fosters the view that indeed the middle years of the nineteenth century were a Renaissance, a Renaissance of a particular kind in which the public participated fully. That this public overlooked the major literary expressions of the period is not surprising, for the expression they chose was so much clearer, so much simpler, and so much more in keeping with the evidence they saw about them than the ambiguous views of an Ishmael or the anarchistic analogies of a Thoreau.

Thomas Holley Chivers was both typical and atypical of this public. He was a product of its extremes and its delights, for he too saw visions and believed America the New Jerusalem, and his poetry could come only from a setting which combined sentimentality, self-confidence, and a belief in manifest destiny. Yet, as his isolation, his failure to find literary companionship, and his pathological charges of plagiarism testify, he was also distinct from it.

An analysis of the literary influences on Chivers' work will help to point out both these characteristics, for Chivers reacted with the rest of the country to certain of the English Romantics, while he went beyond most of them in his appreciation of others, notably Shelley and Keats. In *Eonchs of Ruby* he speaks of a "Philomelian Eclecticist of Song,"[5] and the name, in certain respects, may be applied to Chivers himself, for his work shows the influence and at times the phrasing of Byron, Keats, Shelley, and Tennyson, while there are less obvious and sometimes momentary echoes of Young, Pollok, Campbell, Moore, and Elizabeth Browning. In his delight in these poets he was not far afield from the popular favorites of the magazines and reprints, although his use of them is peculiar to his own genius, and his early fondness for Shelley cannot be widely reproduced in American poetry.

It is in the areas in which he departs from the standard imitation of the English Romantics that he succeeds best, particularly in his experiments with rhythm and in his often startling diction. But his early reading in Scott and Byron prepared the way for the later and more pronounced influences upon him, and once his literary taste and character had been fertilized, as it were, by such vigorous exponents of romanticism as these, he was able to

react to Shelley, for example, because Shelley suited his temperament, because he testified, in positive expression, that the poetic
areas Chivers found most compatible and which fitted in with his
emotional response had been probed before; Shelley might serve
as a guide. Chivers is a clear product of what I have outlined as
the nineteenth century's public Renaissance and his value to
American literature is found in his own individual use of the
creative atmosphere he found about him. And though there are
strong currents of influence obvious in his work, he managed to
translate that influence into an expression which is peculiarly his
own; despite his vigorous denial that the "moment" must coincide
with the "man" to produce individual artistic creation, his poetry
is both the product of America in the middle 1800's and of his
own emotional and literary bent.

Once the influence upon Chivers has been outlined, much of his
translation of this influence into unique terms, Chiversian terms,
can be indicated by a study of his typical theme and form. Here
again Chivers is a typical magazine poet and yet his own master.
He could exult over Jenny Lind's soprano or shroud himself in
often genuine grief at the death of a daughter; he could write a
Birth-Day Song of Liberty to be declaimed at a Georgia Fourth of
July celebration or use the heroics of the Alamo for a *deus ex
machina* in a tale of love betrayed. And by line or by stanza he
sometimes succeeded remarkably well in these attempts; but his
own imprint was on the work when he evoked Heaven or felt the
majesty of the Mississippi. Chivers' readers have come to remember the tumbling, sometimes strangled trochees of his rhythmic
chants to the vastness of the universe, and the lilting cadences
dedicated to the beauty of a Lily Adair or a Rosalie Lee.

MINOR INFLUENCES

The few pieces of argumentative verse which Chivers wrote do
not indicate that he partook of the Neo-Classical understanding
of how logical and detailed didacticism may be translated into
poetry. He did not often refer to the Augustans, and with his conception of poetry as that which evokes higher truth in terms of
the beautiful, any poetry of his which shows didacticism is a vio-
lation of his creed.

He speaks once of Pope; the "Essay on Man" is "a perfectly

prosaic Theme" and it is obvious to Chivers that "Pope was no Poet," nor, he adds, was Cowper.[6] Chivers' disassociation of himself from neo-classicism is not wholly theoretical; surely he had sampled the older English poets in his youthful reading. No home with any pretense of a library could have been without one of the forty-five editions of the "Essay on Man" published in America between 1747 and 1799.[7] His dislike of the Augustans must have been founded upon actual association with them as much as upon theoretical disapproval of their poetic beliefs. Yet beyond the single reference to Pope, and standard comments on Shakespeare and Milton, he rarely turned from the Romantics to indicate he had read in the older body of English expression; once, surprisingly enough, he refers to Lyly's *Campaspe*, whose author was "one of the sweetest singers that ever raised his clarion voice to the gates of God."[8] It may well have been Lyly's diction which intrigued Chivers. Normally, however, Chivers wrote of and for the present, as that present offered inspiration for paeans to America, views of Heaven, or expressions of personal tragedy and grief.

We know from his own comments that Chivers long admired Edward Young; thirteen of his poems use quotations from him as mottoes, and Chivers included him in his catalogue of dead patriots and poets in "The Mighty Dead," noting that he was "Religion's Cicero."[9] In his admiration for that pensive poet's *Night Thoughts* Chivers was not alone; along with Blair's *The Grave* and the finer, more delicate work of Gray, it prepared the way for the feminine audience of the 1800's, and the number of editions each of these works went through in America indicates that the melancholy urge was as firmly established here as it was in England.

The didacticism of *Night Thoughts* surely encouraged such poems of Chivers' as "What is Life!" and "What is Death!", published in his first volume, *The Path of Sorrow* (1832); they establish the orthodox Christian view of this life as a pathway to the next, an interpretation which Young repeats again and again to his infidel Lorenzo. Later, in "A Longing to Know," Chivers discusses, in verse which is carefully controlled and in places polished, "the dark veil which keeps the soul below Pavilioned from Eternity."[10] He concludes that there are set limits to man's knowledge, suggesting that he had assimilated more of Pope's "Essay on Man" than he realized. Normally Chivers would not pause to argue or discuss; his assurance is usually so great that he can readily transport himself beyond that veil; such a poem as "Sophia" (*V*, pp. 94-95) combines an essentially Augustan element of analysis with a more typical Chiversian shout of worship.[11]

But Young provided more than an example of palatable didacticism; the melancholy which overhangs *Night Thoughts* found a sympathetic audience in Chivers after the multiple tragedy of his children's deaths in the 1840's. *The Lost Pleiad* (1845) makes greater use of *Night Thoughts* as mottoes than any other volume, and the title poem of the volume, macabre in its Gothic detail of the death agony, continues Chivers' belief that death opens the way to new life.

> For all pure joy is but the same
> As grief—they differ but in name.
> For grief is joy above the height
> Of that sad joy we call delight.
> And thus, in grieving, we express
> That our deep joy is in excess.
> Thus joy, for Love, becomes so deep,
> It turns to grief, which makes us weep.
> This grief, expressive of our love,
> Is like that joy they feel above—
> That holy joy which fills the sight
> With tears of infinite delight;
> That joy above which joy below
> Doth ape by rising into wo.[12]

Such an expression of melancholy rationalized into joy surely bespeaks the eighteenth century; the Gothicism of the death detail is far more vivid than anything Young undertook, however. It is in the personal aspect of "The Lost Pleiad" and of many of the other elegies on his children that Chivers' poetry departs from Young's essentially philosophic work. Young shares with Chivers a delight in the heavenward glance and the exclamatory statement, but his purpose is a didactic one connected only tenuously with personal tragedy or grief. Chivers was seldom a preacher, and when he does preach, it is in the tones of an evangelist rather than of a speaker who wishes to convince through reason.

Surprisingly, Young's diction, in his less controlled moments, seems close to Chivers'; "adamant," "amaranthine," "ambrosial," and "cerulean," words familiar to Chivers' readers, perhaps seem to be more typical of Elizabeth Browning than Edward Young, but in the Ninth Night particularly, "The Consolation," Young celebrates the Judgment Day in phrases which indicate something of where Chivers may have learned his delight in evocative description.

> I see! I feel it!
> All nature, like an earthquake, trembling round!
> All deities, like summer's swarms, on wing!
> All basking in the full meridian blaze!
> I see the Judge enthroned! the flaming guard!
> The volume open'd! open'd every heart![13]

The excitement which Young attempts to generate is perhaps dampened by his didactic purpose; Chivers' diction and imagery are more vivid:

> when the Lord of life
> And glory shall appear, arrayed in robes
> Of righteousness, with one foot on the neck
> Of Death, the other on the mouth of hell,
> And drawn by steeds of lightning down the aisles
> Of constellated glory—there shall come
> Ten thousand whirlwinds from the sea of God!
> And with the mighty eloquence of winds,
> That sweep the wild illimitable waste
> Of unfenced prairie, where the exiled tones
> Of ocean gather up in prayer to God;
> And where the grisly darkness of the woods
> Sends out the tempests to the azure hills,
> And from the frowning solitudes are torn
> The sinuous tendons of the giant oaks—
> Shall join the hallelujah of the storms. . . .[14]

While Robert Pollok provided much of the imagery for this poem, here Chivers has elaborated Young's explanations into detailed imagery suggesting visionary experience.

Young was among those authors whom Chivers read early in his life.[15] He provided Chivers with a refrain for "Avalon," one of his better poems, and Chivers' transformation of Young's "Or bid the moon, as with her journey tired, /In Ajalon's soft, flowery vale repose"[16] into an effective refrain is typical of his development of Young's imagery:

> For thou didst tread with fire-ensandaled feet,
>   Star-crowned, forgiven,
> The burning diapason of the stars so sweet,
>   To God in Heaven!
> And, walking on the sapphire-paven street,
> Didst take upon the highest Sill thy seat—
> Waiting in glory there my soul to meet,
>   When I am lying
>   Beside the beautiful undying
>   In the Valley of the pausing of the Moon,
>   Oh! Avalon! my son! my son![17]

Young's Christian orthodoxy appealed to the youthful Chivers, as did certain of his metaphors and the more evocative elements of his diction; when the 1840's brought the death of four children, it was but a matter of memory to recall the consolations and the reassurances of *Night Thoughts,* and Chivers could neglect the didacticism for the emotion.

The Reverend Robert Pollok (1798-1827), a Presbyterian minister of deeply emotional if orthodox faith, published as his major effort *The Course of Time* (1827), an epic poem describing the Day of final Judgment. While his interest clearly lay more with the theology than with the poetry, several of his phrases excited Chivers' far more powerful imagination. Pollok is one of the earliest obvious influences on Chivers' poetry; virtually all of the traceable borrowings from *The Course of Time* occur before 1840.[18] And, just as in the case of Edward Young's influence upon him, it was neither the theology nor the plan of the whole poem which delighted Chivers. Reading carefully, he seized upon images and details, and turned them to his own, individual ends. Chivers' power to create a vivid image is seldom more obvious than in his use of *The Course of Time.* Pollok writes:

> Sun! glorying in thy strength from age to age,
> So long observant of thy hour, put on
> Thy weeds of woe, and tell the moon to weep;
> .   .   .   .
> Tell men and women, tell the new-born child,
> And every eye that sees, to come, and see
> Thee set behind Eternity; for thou
> Shalt go to bed to-night, and ne'er awake.
> Stars! walking on the pavement of the sky—
> Out sentinels of heaven! watching the earth,

> Cease dancing now; your lamps are growing dim;
> Your graves are dug among the dismal clouds;
> And angels are assembling round your bier.[19]

When Chivers took this scene his larger mind and the pictorial quality of his imagination transformed it into effective poetry:

> Time is appalled! the moon is struck with fear!
> And palsy rains decrepitude on earth!
> For, faithful to his summons, he prepares,
> With all his rich magnificence of stars,
> And with his glorious pageantry of spheres,
> To see the mighty martyrdom of Death!
> And at the funeral of the corpse of Time
> Behold the angels dig his grave in chaos!

Continuing, Chivers describes the moon at this final moment:

> For she has found her grave-clothes in the clouds!
> And frightened at the widowhood of earth,
> She wanders blindfold from her wonted path,
> And, wailing for her ocean-lord, she puts
> On Sack cloth for the dying sun, and sets
> Behind Eternity to rise no more![20]

While Chivers would probably have agreed with much of Pollok's orthodoxy, just as he extended Pollok's images until they seem to make supernatural movements visible, so he would have become heretical in the face of strict Presbyterian limits. The epic form would not appeal to him, of course; the imaginative power required to animate such a scene as that just quoted could not be sustained for long.

Had Chivers not realized early in his life that his bent was not toward narrative or epic poetry, he might have reacted more obviously to the combined poetic assaults of Scott, Campbell, and Moore. The popularity of these three poets among the reading public of America was wide and lasted for some time. Scott made the largest mark, and his romances were standard reading up until the Civil War. In the South, he was the poet of chivalry and the middle ages, and the tournaments conducted in the South in the 1840's are a unique regression of our cultural history.[21] Chivers never speaks of him, nor does he attempt to reproduce the backward-looking romanticism of his poetry. Thomas Campbell pleased Chivers more, apparently. His lines describing the fall of Poland in 1794 (in his *The Pleasures of Hope*), despite the gallant efforts of her defender, Thaddeus Kosciusko, are the source of Chivers' "Kosciusko's Resignation,"[22] a poem in which Chivers successfully combines a rhythmic anapestic meter with a theme, that of the divinity of freedom and liberty, which was later to be one of his favorites.

The wide-spread popularity of Moore's *Lalla Rookh* presents an interesting example of Chivers' adaptation of materials essentially unsuited to his genius; Moore's orientalism never appears in Chivers. He avoided it just as he had avoided Scott's evocation of the middle ages. Furthermore, his theory of poetry, as suggested before, did not permit lengthy narrative poems. Echoing Poe, he said,

It is . . . clear that no poem of any considerable length, from the very nature of the revelations subsisting between the power of the soul to receive, and the impressions to be made, can be pleasing . . . for any length of Time. . . . This is the reason why Lyrical Poetry always has been, and always will be, pleasing to the soul.[23]

Yet he might make use of the exotic diction for which Moore provided explanations so conveniently in his footnotes; "To Thekla" depends for effect upon such place names as "Oman" and "Yeman," both of which have their origin in Moore's footnotes.[24] A more important use of these voluminous notes occurs in "To Allegra,"[25] published in 1839, where he quotes number 293: " 'The angel Israfil, who has the most melodious voice of all God's creatures.'—*Sale.*" Poe altered this phrase for use in his "Israfel," incorrectly attributing it to the *Koran;* Chivers spells the angel's name after Poe, not Moore, with an *e,* and given the similarity between Chivers' "The Song of Seralim," a poem which makes use of Poe's later rephrasing of the note, and Poe's "Israfel," this first reference to the name Israfel becomes vital in establishing a case for Chivers' independent discovery and use of the name.[26] The facts that the two poems by Chivers which utilize Moore's researches both appeared in 1839, and that his first use of a quotation from *Lalla Rookh* as a motto was published the same year, suggest that year as the one in which he first examined the long romance thoroughly.

There were other uses Chivers might make of *Lalla Rookh*. Chivers had seen visions early in his life, and presumably his belief in their validity was soon established; so when he read that the prophet Azim died happily because

> His soul had seen a Vision, while he slept;
> She, for whose spirit he pray'd and wept
> So many years, had come to him, all drest
> In angel smiles, and told him she was blest![27]

such an occurrence might seem to him one not only of literary value but of spiritual truth. And in 1842, when "The Heavenly Vision" was first published, it contained the refrain, "She came from Heaven to tell me she was blest."[28] Chivers worked on the poem for some ten years, and when it finally reappeared in *Virginalia,* Moore's line had become a typical Chiversian image:

> The hyaline wavelets of her voice of love
> Rose on the soundless ether-sea's calm breast;
> Amid the interstarry realms above,
> To God in Heaven, telling me she was blest.[29]

When such a transformation occurs in a particular image, surely the transformer has made it wholly his own; Moore's atmosphere of exoticism has long since been lost, and the image has become an integral part of another scene.

As a lyric poet Chivers might be expected to react more obviously to Moore's *Irish Melodies,* a collection which held public taste in America for some years; a number of these songs are still sung today. The first magazine publication of Chivers' poetry that has been found, "Lines on Parting, Dedicated to the Ladies,"[30] is designed to be sung to the tune of one of the more popular songs of *Irish Melodies,* "Come, Rest in This Bosom." Chivers used the same source again, years later, in his "Song of Love of Bella."[31]

In the same collection Moore included "The Song of Fionnuala," following it with a long note explaining that it was based on an Irish legend of a woman transformed into a swan and condemned to wander over Ireland until the ringing of the first mass bell, at the arrival of Christianity, at which time she would ascend into Heaven. The exotic name, the unique scene, the ascent to Heaven would all appeal to Chivers; Moore's rendering of the legend presents Fionnuala's voice, questioning when her release will come. Chivers answers the question and describes the occurrence:

Beside an island in an inland sea,
A virgin Swan came, in the time of spring,
Her Heaven-revealing, dying song to sing!
Veiled in the night's divine tranquility,
Far in the reeds, where she had come to float,
There rose up from her silver-sounding throat
A whirlwind of cherubic melody,
Which hurricaned the silence of the night,
And rapt with an immortal ecstasy—
(Making them think it day in their delight)—
The birds within the solitudes—when right
To Heaven, transfigured, glorified, she went,
Leaving the world in mute astonishment—
Drowned in the deluge of her agony.[32]

Chivers' greatest discovery in *Irish Melodies* occurred when he read the letter prefixed to the third number of the series. In suggesting that Irish music is perhaps not as ancient in its origin as certain patriots would imply, Moore demurs further that he can love his country "without believing that Irish was the language spoken in Paradise." Whether or not Chivers ever speculated on such a nice theological question, he could not but have been caught by this fanciful reference; Moore's ubiquitous footnote referred him to the *Transactions of the Gaelic Society of Dublin*. From this brief suggestion Chivers found the source of one of his several plays, *The Sons of Usna*. In his introduction to the play, Chivers explained his source for what became the first dramatic use of the Deirdre legend:

A beautiful translation of the ancient dramatic Irish tale, literally rendered from the original Gaelic, entitled, *"Daidra; or, The Lamentable Fate of the Sons of Usnach,* may be found in the . . . Transactions of the Gaelic Society of Dublin, by Theophilus O'Flanagan.

A strange fate for an innocuous footnote! And although such an inspiration may perhaps not stand as literary "influence," it is the most influential effect Moore's extremely popular poetry had upon Chivers. It would seem that he used the Irish poet's poetry more as a reference work than as a source of handy images or situations. It suggests what I believe to be the true explanation of the many literary echoes found in Chivers' poetry; he was consciously a professional poet in his attitude, a poet who read widely, and who was always ready to respond to his own genius.

It has not been particularly apparent in this analysis of momentary influence upon Chivers that he was attracted most strongly by diction and imagery, especially when accompanied by tones indicating deep emotion. Chivers dropped out Moore's oriental settings when he used his imagery, and he failed when he tried to copy Young's ratiocinative qualities as well as his emotional tones; in Elizabeth Browning there was little need to be selective. Her instruction is entirely in the terms of emotional reaction, and her settings are no more than outlines on which she distributes imagery and diction such as delighted Chivers. He dates his sonnet, "On Reading Mrs. Browning's Drama of Exile," September 10, 1845; we know he read Poe's review of this work in the March, 1846, number of *Graham's Magazine*.[33] Perhaps the lyricism of this "drama" actually did strike Chivers as suddenly and furiously as he suggests in his praise of her power:

> Like some great storm-cloud from the troubled ocean,
> Pregnant with lightnings which are born in thunder,
> Waxing like mountains in their Heaven-ward motion,
> Till, by their own strength, they are torn asunder—
> Weeping themselves to death in freshening rain;
> So rose up from thy soul that God-like strain,
> In Miriam-jubilations through the sky,
> Filling the star-gemmed altitudes on high
> With deep, pathetic wailings, full of pain!
> Then, like Apolyon's [*sic*] last sign, when he fell,
> Scented with memories of the Eden-gladness—
> God's mercy following him with wrath to Hell—
> While Angels' tears dropt on him in their sadness;
> So died upon my soul thy song in blissful madness.[34]

Even in his praise of Shelley, whom he admired so highly, Chivers does not write of such overwhelming reaction. *The Drama of Exile*, a narrative poem tracing the first day of Adam's dismissal from Paradise, is interspersed with various songs, those of the Eden Spirits, the Earth Spirits, Gabriel, Invisible Angels, even of the Morning Star to Lucifer, who appears as a strangely pitiable figure. These lyrics were the source of the poem's delight for Chivers. Full of romantic diction and dependent upon indefinite, vast, suggestive imagery, they very much resemble those poems by Chivers which evoke God and the Heavens; most of these were published after he had praised Mrs. Browning, and it seems likely that he was genuinely inspired by her intensity of emotion and lyric strength. Her diction, often using color words and exoticisms such as "empyrean," "evangels," or "hyaline," surely helped Chivers (as Shelley did) to move away from the earlier Byronic influence toward his most typical expression. One example will suffice: Mrs. Browning writes,

> I charge thee by the choral song we sang,
> When up against the white shore of our feet
> The depths of the creation swelled and broke. . . .[35]

This image was used twice by Chivers; he had no difficulty in putting himself in the place of Gabriel, who is the speaker in Mrs. Browning's lines. Such an ability to ascend heavenwards in his poetry, and to view Heaven at close hand, or to chart the upward progress through Milton's chaos, is one effect, I believe, of his having read Mrs. Browning and Shelley. Chivers utilizes Gabriel's statement in an elegy (dated 1846) on his sister's death:

> Up through the hyaline ether-sea
> Star-diademed, in chariot of pure pain,
> Through th' empyreal star-fires radiantly,
> Triumphant over Death in Heaven to reign,
> Thy soul is gone, seeking its Blest Abode,
> Where break the songs of stars against the
> feet of God.[36]

The movement and color of the first lines prepare for the statement of the fourth and fifth lines, and the final Alexandrine makes physical and material the harmonies of song. His indebtedness to Mrs. Browning in no way lessens the success of the image.

Two years after the dating of this poem, Chivers presented his interpretation of Urbain J. J. Leverrier's emotions when, by astronomical calculation, he postulated the existence of the planet Neptune:

> Circling the Cyclic-chorus of the spheres,
> Sphering the Epicycle of his song—
> He sings his anthems, through th' eternal years,
> Outside the orb-paths of th' Empyreal throng.

> Floating in chariot of celestial fire,
> Sphered Heavenward through th' Empyreal Ether-Sea,
> He rays his sphere-tones out unto the choir
> Of God until they fill Eternity.

Tempestuous whirlwinds of deep melody
Dash from his orb-prow on his spheric road—
Rolling in mountain-billows on Heaven's sea
Against the white shore of the feet of God.

Shouting Excelsior to the starry choir
Flooded with rapture, now he Heavenward rolls,
Glinting those golden tones of lightning-fire
Proceeding swiftly from the Angel's souls.[37]

Mrs. Browning's image is still visible, but it has been enlarged and assimilated until it seems a part of a larger image. Without the information supplied by the title, it would be impossible to determine the poem's meaning; given the fact of Leverrier's discovery, however, it becomes an interesting, if not wholly successful, attempt to recreate an inward, emotional exultation. Chivers' dramatic situations are seldom contrived; often he does not state them, but when he does, his poetry, unlike much of Mrs. Browning's, springs directly and often effectively out of the given situation. She helped to provide Chivers with a vocabulary and with an example of a certain kind of image; perhaps it is symbolic of a change in Chivers that she and Shelley helped to bring about a rather extraordinary result; namely, that a poem whose refrain and idea came from Thomas Moore,[38] an earlier image-source, was so revised by Chivers that one critic has called it evidence of Mrs. Browning's or Shelley's influence upon Chivers, Moore having been wholly assimilated.[39]

Such poets as these provide the background against which the more important influences may be analyzed; this background offers certain conclusions, conclusions which further my belief that while Chivers was a rather unusual lyric poet, he was writing at least in part with the general fashion of the times. Yet long narratives were popular before the Civil War, as Longfellow's successes testify, and Chivers was not part of this tradition. The popularity of long verse narratives grew out of America's fondness for the sentimental novel. Such poetry provided form for the expression of America's adventurous spirit and the detail of her half-known landscape; Chivers felt with Bryant and many others that it was a time for national poetry, one which would glorify the New Jerusalem, but he was wise enough to leave to others the creation of it. And in avoiding such a form, he failed to come under any strong influence from those who practised it. Such influence as

· 105

they did exert, usually by diction, image, or concept, has been traced; that tracing outlines a selective poet at work moulding his own expression.

In addition to the narrative poetry so popular in book form, America of the early nineteenth century was also a land of magazine poets; only in rare cases did an author expect remuneration for any poetry which might be so published, a fact which encouraged editors to include incidental lyrics at the bottom of their columns. Such lyrics normally suffer from awkward craftsmanship and sentimentality, and often they are occasional; Chivers' poetry is weakened by faults of structure and of tone, in much the same manner, but he is seldom occasional. Like most of the rest of the magazine poets, Chivers was most at home when he could express his emotions; unlike them, however, he normally presented his expression in an interesting, sometimes unique, manner. It has become obvious from this study of minor influence that he derived his style and themes only partly from the more popular poets of the day. In the following pages I will attempt to show from whom the bases of his inspiration came. And the result of such investigation will indicate, I believe, that while he was deeply conscious of certain literary influences, he managed always so to assimilate such influence that the product is his own.

THE BIBLE

The influence of the Bible on Chivers' style cannot be traced as fully and as directly as one might wish. It is certain that his Baptist upbringing brought him early into contact with the King James Version, and the comparative isolation of his home no doubt fostered his reading of the Bible. If we were able to list the volumes that the young Chivers knew, we would surely find the Bible among them; and given his early happiness, his consciousness of love surrounding him, to which he testifies in his poetry, and the religious cast of his father's household, it is easy to imagine Chivers finding in the Bible not only theological instruction (little of which shows in his verse; it is not Baptist or Methodist: it is personal), but also a sense of identification with the mysteries there unfolded. I doubt that Chivers' understanding of the Bible in his youth was more than an emotional one, one which fostered the mysticism obvious in his poetry. For surely that mysticism was not a sudden light come upon him; had it been such, we may be cer-

tain that Chivers would have told us of it. No, Chivers' religious-
ness is an early and natural product, which, if it eventually soars
beyond conventional belief into conscious and purposeful identification with God, was forced into such wild flights by the warping
effects of his youthful marriage and its resulting scandal.

We have no factual proof of this progress; we can only infer it
from later expression. I would suggest that Chivers' knowledge of
the Bible was an extremely natural and normal one, for its influence would have been more pervasive in his imagery, in his style,
and in the tone he adopts had he later studied it conscientiously
as a source of literary experience. We have enough evidence to
assert his close acquaintance with it; but that evidence is not such
as to indicate that Chivers regarded the Bible as either a literary
source-book or the only theological one, for on the one hand he
does not incorporate Biblical imagery into his poetry as, for example, Shelley or Browning did, and on the other hand his theology,
like his poetic expression, was much too personal a thing to have
been derived from any single source. That he used quotations
from the Bible as mottoes to some thirty-nine of his poems indicates acquaintance; it does not indicate deep literary indebtedness.

And to which of the Testaments would Chivers turn? The
answer may be quickly based on the fact that only on rare occasions does Chivers dwell upon damnation and retribution. His
mind was clearly a New Testament one, one which prophesied
from the fact of the Resurrection. Such is the quality of almost
all of his religious poetry. But, in contradiction stands the fact
that almost every one of the mottoes he uses is from the Old
Testament. It is difficult at first to explain such a discrepancy.
Chivers was not concerned to offer warnings of sinful conduct, and
of the sure punishment to follow. But he was concerned to paint
the character of the Heaven he himself had envisioned; he was
deeply interested in the role of the poet as a prophet. His was the
Orphic interpretation of the poet's duty, and the prophets of the
Old Testament were strong in their promises of Christ's coming.
From them, perhaps, he could gain a strength which he himself
very clearly lacked. There is nothing of the grim power of Isaiah
in any of Chivers' poems, yet it was from this prophet that he
quoted most often. It is a case of subconscious awareness of an
inner lack, and a buttressing against this lack by means of one
who could stand firm and certain.

It is in his first volume, *The Path of Sorrow,* that we find almost all of the definite Biblical influence; it is here particularly that we find the prophetic tone. In later years Chivers had no need to adopt such a tone; but here, at the very beginning of his poetic career, and in a volume devoted largely to a defence of his own conduct in his unsuccessful first marriage, he had great need "To sing a prophecy,—exempt from ire; / And tell the world my heart and soul's desire."[40] And it is just where Chivers fails to curb this "ire" that his tone becomes reminiscent of the Old Testament. In "The Prophet's Dream" Chivers speaks of his future work as poet. He, as poet, has been inspired by God's prophet, and he speaks to reassure himself of his power and inspiration.

> His righteousness and love—all else of worth—
> Shall be unrivalled; and his glory too,
> Shall rest alone, and beam in going forth;
> His soul shall rain affection's pearly dew,
> To inundate his cheeks! and he shall eat
> The manna from the unseen hand of Him,
> Who shall prepare a mansion and a seat,
> Beyond the reach of obloquy and sin!
> And when his days shall end, they shall begin.
> His numbers shall continue still to roll,
> And ope new fountains in the human heart;
> From out the ocean of his mighty soul,—
> Which is not yet the whole—'tis but a part!
> Shall flow a river, and its waves shall roll
> Into the ocean of Eternity!
> Which shall unfold the ire of vindiction's soul,
> Which heaven, earth, and hell, shall see;
> And spirits of Jehovah, with him be.[41]

This is prophetic in tone, but missing from that tone is the power and strength which are so often in evidence in the voices of the Old Testament. Chivers is the prophet, but he is the prophet who is to "act the lyric part." His voice is only indirectly prophesying retribution, for Chivers could not long gaze upon that which was terrifying or evil.

The prophetic poems which seem to have been influenced by the Old Testament are few.[42] The fact that he could adopt such a tone is important not only to show the influence of the Bible upon him, but also to indicate that he did not feel need to resort to intermediaries, as it were; the cherubim and seraphim and even the angels which appear in his poetry are at best vague figures. Chivers was in direct contact with his God and his Heaven, and the way to his Heaven is not populated by the figures of Christian mythology. In fact, Chivers' use of the Bible in his poetry only rarely includes mention of the Biblical prophets or poets themselves. Nor is there any sustained use of symbol or allegory from Biblical sources. It is a comment on Chivers' sense of identification that he can speak of his own trials in the following terms:

> And they shall nail his hands and sinless feet,
> With piercing nails!—and crown his head with thorns!
> And Calvary shall be his lone retreat;
> Succeeded by the resurrection morn!—
> A brilliant star—Aurora dyed in blood!
> Which shall illuminate the trembling earth,
> With crimson light; while tears, in sorrow's flood,
> Shall inundate the land, for godly worth;
> Whose death shall buy him an eternal birth.[43]

The imagery is familiar, but the clear implication that Chivers feels a correspondence between his sufferings and Christ's is a rather startling one, and one which, I think, shows better than anything else in his poetry the extent to which the Bible was a personal document to him. With this evidence in hand, it is understandable why Chivers' Biblical scenes are not populated with allegorical and symbolic figures; Chivers himself was the principal actor in such scenes.

When emotion is strong in Chivers, he often turns to the Bible for imagery and background. In his attempt to resolve his feelings about the wrong done him at his first marriage, he says that

> . . . the great
> Development of his authoritative power,
> Which reigns triumphant and has sate
> As umpire of the world, since that great hour,
> When the mighty heavens rolled her vows throughout
> Revolving blessedness, and swore the day
> That chaos breathed an earth-born light,
> And sat Jehovah's sun on gnomen time
> To point eternal love, that all was right—
> His will be done, and it shall e'er be mine.[44]

Chivers is expressing his own emotion through imagery and situa-

tion taken from the Bible. When he himself feels distressed or
distraught, he sees Heaven troubled too:

> When nature's sun grew dim, and heaven's candles
> Seemed to glimmer on the hoary mount, where
> Heaven's pure viceregent stood abased, by ire
> And indignation of a guilty world,
> And wept in bitterness—so do I weep![45]

He is eager to reassure himself that God is with him:

> . . . hear me, heaven! thou hast made
> Me what I am; and thou hast been to me,
> A righteous father; let me reach my thought
> Above this middle degradation! let
> Me pour my melody to thee, and thee
> Alone; for thou, my Father, hast sustained me
> In all the vast sublimity of grief!
> And can'st thou here escape the tribute which
> I owe, for thy unprecedented love!
> For I am what I am, by thy great law.
> My soul is but a handful of thy love—
> That rectified divinity which rolls
> Within the grasp of thy infinity!
> Which thou hast scattered on the earth, to show
> Thy glory and thy matchless might. And now
> My God! if words, with warmth and gratitude,
> Can adumbrate to thee, my soul! a spark
> Of thine—I humbly sacrifice my life
> Upon the altar of thy love!—then, take
> My vows, my life, my soul, my love, and all
> I claim on earth—my youth has suffered much—
> My fearless soul is drunk to last forever.[46]

The intensity and obvious sincerity of such a passage suggests
that during his younger years Chivers was indeed dedicating himself to his God, and it is clear as we read further in his work that
that sense of identification and dedication which he was creating
here became strong enough for him to turn to other matters in
his later poetry. That is, we do not find such direct appeals to God
(never to Jesus) in the poetry published after *The Path of Sorrow*.
He had succeeded in establishing in his own mind his position as
God's voice, and apparently never felt the need again to reassure
himself of God's presence. The Heaven that appears in his later

110 ·

poems is very much a personal one, and there is no sign of anything but welcome to the soul ascending to it.[47]

The poetic books of the Bible provided Chivers with suggestive
details enough to create that Heaven, but the expression of them
is surely his own; there is the flavor of *Revelation* in the familiar
passage from "The Lost Pleiad":

> While walking with thy snowy feet
> Along the sapphire-paven street
>   Before the jasper-walls above,
> And list'ning to the music sweet
> Of Angels in that heavenly Hymn
> Sung by the lips of Cherubim
> In Paradise, before the fall,
> In glory bright, outshining all
> In that great City of pure gold,
> The Angels talked about of old.[48]

It is entirely possible that Chivers developed his fondness for
repetition from a reading of the Bible. Particularly in the *Psalms*
is there evidence of parallelism, the repetition of certain verses,
and the repetition of first or last lines.[49]

There are, of course, familiar Biblical phrases scattered throughout Chivers' work, usually in a rather orthodox manner. For
example, in "Song to Isadore" we find

> Hear the Golden Gospel thunder
>   Through the world, dear Isadore!
> Tearing Sin's dark throne asunder,
> While the Rock of Ages under
>   Us stands firm forever more.
> Hear the Golden Gospel thunder
>   Through the world, dear Isadore![50]

Such a usage of Biblical phrases does not indicate any real debt;
"Rock of Ages" is common property.

In "Lily Adair" he uses an image from *Kings:*

> From her Paradise-Isles in the ocean,
>   To the beautiful City of On,
> By the millifluent rivers of Goshen,
>   My beautiful Lily is gone!
> In her Chariot of Fire translated,
>   Like Elijah, she passed through the air,

·111

To the City of God golden-gated—
The Home of my Lily Adair——[51]

The only unique thing about such an image is the presence of Chivers' diction, which translates it into something almost entirely his own. But the same image probably serves as inspiration for another passage which is more typically Chiversian, and certainly indicates a deeper assimilation:

Up through the hyaline ether-sea
Star-diademed, in chariot of pure pain,
Through th' empyreal star-fires radiantly,
Triumphant over Death in Heaven to reign,
Thy soul is gone, seeking its Blest Abode,
Where break the songs of stars against the feet of God.[52]

This is true Chivers; the original Biblical image has been changed and condensed, and, perhaps, improved. The "chariot of pure pain" is certainly more aggressive than its original source. It is in instances like this one that Chivers has succeeded in putting his Biblical sources to valid use. Unfortunately, these are few.

The conclusions which seem clear after this review of Chivers and the King James Version indicate that the Bible was an early and an important influence on him. In *The Path of Sorrow* borrowings in the form of phrases, imagery, and situation are frequent enough to show indebtedness. The suggestion that the repetitive structure of the poetic books of the Bible, particularly the *Psalms,* had an influence on Chivers' statement that the refrain "is not only an ornament, but an essence,"[53] and on his consistent practice, seems entirely logical. And it is in this volume that Chivers achieved his sense of identification with Heaven; the prophetic tone here used develops into a confident, certain evocation of Heaven. The tone becomes apocalyptical in Chivers' transport into higher realms.

BYRON

In the 1820's and 1830's in America, almost no sensitive young man was completely unaffected by George Noel Gordon. His personal life, so well known to all in England, was equally notorious across the Atlantic; from the walks of Harvard Yard to the Southern plantation, Childe Harold's cape swung in every melancholy breeze. Chivers was not as badly bitten as some, fortunately; it was not Chivers who invited Byron to America, concluding seriously that

of all the tracts of darkness in our broad land, I suspect that the imagination of Byron would be most peculiarly struck with the DISMAL SWAMP. With what thrilling sensation would his adventurous Fancy tread the chill ooze of its miry soil. . . .[54]

The average reader of Byron's work seized upon a single concept, that of the poet as melancholy wanderer, cast out and despised by society, yet strong in love of freedom and liberty. The scandals surrounding Byron's personal life drew mixed response, from Harriet Beecher Stowe's defence of Byron's wife to sympathetic identifications of the writer with Byron as wronged genius. Chivers belongs in the latter group.

There is no evidence as to when Chivers first read Byron, but it would have been impossible for a young student who wrote poetry while in medical school to have overlooked the English lord for long. In his first volume, *The Path of Sorrow*, Chivers pays tribute enough to Byron; while there is no poem addressed to his first literary master, lines from his work serve as mottoes to six of the eighteen poems, and virtually every poem in the volume bears the imprint of his particular tone and subject matter.

Chivers wrote *The Path of Sorrow*, as the title suggests, out of his own heart-breaking experience with his first marriage. It is possible to reconstruct from the autobiographical material in this volume the outlines of what must have happened. Still young, the product of a happy and sheltering home, he fell in love with his cousin, Frances E. Chivers (daughter of his Uncle Joel), whom he refers to only as "Angeline,"[55] and married her; there are no suggestions that the opening days of their marriage were anything but happy. But soon she left him with their daughter, named for her mother, and Chivers blamed "a fiend, a cursed fiend," for the destruction of their marriage. One manuscript poem contains a note in Chivers' hand indicating that this person was his wife's aunt, Frances Chivers Albert.[56] She had been the wife of his Uncle Thomas Chivers and soon after Thomas' death in 1818 had married into a family named Albert. The reader is given to believe that gossip and slander were the weapons used in ruining Chivers' marriage. In any case, when we understand the relatively rural and cloistered atmosphere of Washington, Georgia (founded in 1805), and remember the disputes which surely occurred among the families of Chivers' eight known aunts and uncles, the intimations of personal scandal involving the son of Colonel Robert Chivers, a respected landholder, and the young girl becomes clear; it was not something that could be kept out of local gossip. And it would be remembered. Chivers' account of the affair, one which is undoubtedly prejudiced in a very human way, shows that he himself was hurt, puzzled, and sometimes quite angry.[57]

The immediate effect of the scandal was Chivers' decision to leave town. His early schooling had been under a local tutor, Mr. Thomas Lacey,[58] and now he ventured into Kentucky to Transylvania University, at which he registered in 1828. The M. D. he obtained was to grace his name above almost every poem he published.

It is a remarkable testament to Byron that in those poems which are mostly autobiographic Chivers uses lines, phrases, and themes which evoke the name of the British poet. Byron's influence on Chivers did not last for any great length of time, for Chivers' sense of identification with Byron was based upon the similarity of his own family troubles to those of Byron's, and once he had put them behind him, he also avoided reference to Byron's poetry. In three poems he speaks directly of Byron. In "Byron's Dying Prayer to Ada," in *Conrad and Eudora* (1834), he drew upon his own experience to present a scene of farewell which the world had heard about long since. It is interesting to note that when Chivers republished the poem, in 1837, he omitted Byron's name and made the whole general with a new title, "The Dying Poet to His Child"; his own sorrow was behind him, and, besides, the editors were growing tired of references to the author of so many easily-imitated poetic romances. In *Eonchs of Ruby*, "The Mighty Dead" was a calling-up of dead patriots, and Byron appears briefly as the apostle of liberty.[59] And in *Virginalia* Chivers republished "Byron," a poem which had originally appeared six years before;[60] here Byron's figure has grown away from that of the melancholy wanderer:

> Archangel-like, he looked in God's own face,
>   Whose features in lakes, mountains he did trace—
> Nature, God's symbol, with unstudied grace,
>   With child-like trust, did he in joy embrace.[61]

It is perhaps too simple an analysis of the problem to say that these three poems, the only ones in which Chivers speaks directly of Byron, represent the various stages of Byron's position in Chivers' mind. His final role as evocator of Nature (amid rather incongruous hints of transcendentalism) came only after he had impressed Chivers as the poet of freedom, and, firstly and most importantly, as the solitary sufferer fleeing before the world's displeasure, strong only in his sense of dedication to his calling.[62]

The validity of Byron's and Chivers' youthful sufferings is a subject which tempts the critic; in Chivers' case we know little beyond his own comments that his home was a happy one until calumny forced him to leave. We cannot judge his case except in the terms he uses, and these are often suspect, if only because they so resemble those of Byron. Whatever our judgment on Chivers' early misfortunes may be, whether self-inflicted or not, Chivers himself quickly saw the parallel between his life and Byron's. In flight, Chivers went to medical school, Byron eventually to the Mediterranean; both found in personal sorrow (sincere or not) the wellspring of poetry. For Chivers it was a method of purgation, a defence against slander which he could not combat in any other terms. And it was to his delight that he found such expression congenial.

He grew out of this sense of identification with Byron soon enough, but the terms of the identification are worthy of comment.

The most obvious example of this parallelism occurs in "The Dream," 316 lines of unrimed verse, built entirely after Byron's poem of the same name. Ten of the stanzas begin "A cloud came o'er the vision of my dream"; six of the nine stanzas in Byron's poem open with "A change came o'er the spirit of my dream." Each poem opens with a quasi-philosophical analysis of the dream-world and each notes the value of the imagination. The theme of each presents the various stages of a love affair, the resulting marriage, and the final infidelity and regret. Professor Damon[63] suggests what may be the important point: that such work is not plagiarism but the conscious identification of one man's fate with another's. This volume was, after all, devoted to a defence of his own position, and if he could suggest that his case paralleled the famous English lord's, the audience might better understand.

"The Minstrel's Valedictory" is also the product of Byron's influence, although less obviously so. It presents Chivers, the

Minstrel, at his moment of departure from the life he has known. He looks forward with some confidence:

> Above the mountain of my soul, I see
> Some future blessings, such as soothe my pangs,—
> Invite my thought beyond the dark blue sea,
> While hope's strong anchor in my heart string hangs—
> Await my call, and friendly bidding me
> Partake of bliss, and smile, and then be free.[64]

But before he goes he will tell again the story of his betrayal; then follow the details with which we are already familiar. He leaves home, wronged by society, but strong in the belief that his cause is just. The figure which emerges from Chivers' lines is that of Childe Harold.[65] And in "The Lament of Youth" there are direct borrowings from *Childe Harold*. Chivers' "I have that within / Me, which shall last till time has laid me low!" [ll. 220-221], began as Byron's "But there is that within me which shall tire / Torture and Time. . . ."[66] And Byron's famous lines "Roll on, thou deep and dark blue Ocean—roll!" are twice used by Chivers.[67] Chivers makes the similarity of their problems more obvious when he asks,

> Have I not been a mock for hell and all
> Her clan? have I not had my bosom torn?
> Did I then falter? and, did I then fall?
> Was I a wreck of love, as soon as born?
> Did I not have the heart-string which first bound
> Me to the world, cut loose from all its ties?
> Hear me, my God! did I not then control
> The interdictor of my love—she dies!
> Oh, my Angeline! answer for thy soul.   [ll. 338-346]

Byron had asked almost the same questions in the fourth Canto of *Childe Harold*.[68] The entire poem might be a further adventure in the career of Byron's other-self.

It is possible that Byron's blank verse had some effect upon Chivers' use of the form. *The Path of Sorrow* contains four longer poems in that meter,[69] and although Chivers returned to blank verse again in *Nacoochee* and *Memoralia*, it is clear enough, from his concentration and comment on rhyming effects, that in his later work he did not find it as suitable as stanzas permitting the use of refrain.

Childe Harold's Spenserian stanzas were used in "The Siege of Vienna," in *The Path of Sorrow* (pp. 72-83), a poem evoking the thoughts of the liberator of Vienna when it was under siege by the Turks in 1683. He never combined his use of Byronic theme with the form in which Byron so effectively expressed that theme. Byron's influence was less technical than thematic, although Chivers did return to the Spenserian stanza in "Nacoochee," a poem which shows no influence of Byron.[70]

In these poems, and in two other lyrics written to his wife,[71] Chivers is following a vogue in which American poetasters and poets indulged themselves for nearly forty years.[72] Chivers, fortunately, outgrew the essentially unhealthy channeling of his own experience through Byron's lines and themes. He is to be forgiven, however, for even this transgression. The confused and sometimes inarticulate wailings which make up the subject matter of *The Path of Sorrow* were products of a terrifying and shocking experience. And as uncomfortable as they sometimes are to read today, they are the beginnings of Chivers' poetic career. Byron, thanks to the publicity given to his own personal scandals, offered reassurance to the Georgia youth that others had experienced his sufferings. It was necessary that they be expressed, and, once expressed, Chivers could forget them. In later years he never speaks of his own early sorrows, and his references to Byron are in terms of the poet who died at Missolonghi and not of the husband of Anne Milbanke.[73]

KEATS

The Galignani edition of the works of Coleridge, Shelley, and Keats was published in Paris in 1829; an unauthorized version, it was banned in England immediately, but copies were imported across the Atlantic—the history of the copyright laws is familiar to all students of nineteenth century literature. Hyder Rollins has expressed serious doubt that more than a few scattered copies of the original editions of Keats' work had reached America, but with the arrival of the 1829 edition, America welcomed the poet with a good deal more acclaim than did his countrymen.[74] Early reprints of the Galignani edition appeared at Philadelphia, one of the centers of interest in Keats, in 1831, 1832, 1835, 1836, and 1837. The thirties apparently saw Keats' fame spread along the seaboard, and George Keats' presence in Louisville helped to carry his name into the Southwest. In contrast, it was not until 1840 that a separate reprint of Keats' work appeared in England. The history of his influence and reputation in America has been thoroughly investigated by Mr. Rollins.

When did Chivers first discover one of these many reprints? It is impossible to tell exactly. He was in Philadelphia in 1834 and again in 1837; Professor Damon notes that this latter date marks the beginning of Keats' influence on Chivers' work, and quotes stanzas from "The Dying Beauty" (*Nacoochee*, pp. 49-51) as an indication of Chivers' maturing craftsmanship under the Keatsian influence.[75] When Chivers printed the poem in the *Christian Index* in 1837, he dated it "N. Y., Oct. 1837." There is no way of telling whether this printing preceded or followed the publication of *Nacoochee*, the Preface to which is dated "September 10, 1837." Presumably he had sent the poem to the magazine and included it in his text at about the same time. In any case, with its New York date-line, it could have been written immediately after Chivers' visit to Philadelphia in 1837; such an assertion would lead one to believe that it was indeed on this 1837 trip that Chivers first saw the Galignani edition, and, presumably, the complete works of Keats. But the title poem of the same volume, "Nacoochee," certainly written before his trip, also shows a certain Keatsian influence. It is a tale of an Indian maiden seeking to escape from her earthly lover; she seeks shelter on an enchanted island, and, at the approach of her suitor, is carried up to Heaven by the Angel of Death, who appears on a white horse. This brief narrative structure is the least important element in the poem; throughout Chivers uses it only as a frame on which to hang the descriptive and evocative elements. That is, he seems to follow Keats' pattern in placing the emphasis upon the decorative qualities of the work and not upon the structure. This was Chivers' first attempt at a longer narrative poem. In both the preceding volumes, *The Path of Sorrow* and *Conrad and Eudora*, his concern had been with shorter forms, particularly the personal lyric, a form in which he could express his emotional concerns following upon his unsuccessful first marriage and his equally emotional attempts at standard love lyrics (see particularly the "Songs of the Heart" section of *Conrad and Eudora*). Neither in these lyrics nor in any of the several poems accepted by magazines do I find

Keatsian elements; they are noticeably lacking in that distinctively sensuous quality which marks Keats' poetry, and their metrical roughness indicates that he had not felt the influence of any craftsman in verse. Furthermore, these lyrics are characterized particularly by a tendency to allow emotion to overflow, to gush forth. Under the stress of his personal tortures, Chivers found Byron a perfectly adaptable model. His feeling that the pattern of his life was following that of the English lord's has already been noted.[76]

In much the same way of negative proof, we may note that all of these earlier poems are concerned with the first person, with Chivers himself. If he, as actor as well as recorder, were not present, there would be no poem; he is writing out of his own experience and has not yet the trick of keeping his own person in the background. We can trace the influence of English Romanticism, yes; but we cannot find evidence of Keats' concern with that artistically and objectively conceived form which makes the emotional content of the poem all the more effective by keeping it under strictest restraint and control.

Since his 1837 volume does show evidence of just such restraint, and since no poem before that date indicates Keatsian influence, I feel it is reasonable to conclude that sometime during the middle years of the 1830's, possibly during his 1834 visit to Philadelphia, Chivers purchased the pirated printing of the Galignani edition. That he had perhaps met with Shelley before this date I will attempt to show,[77] and that he felt a kinship with Coleridge becomes obvious as we study the materials that were his most typical subject matter.[78] Keats' influence becomes obvious at once, in a general manner, and Chivers found the basis for one of his most famous lines in Keats as late as 1853.

It is probable that Chivers understood Keats' ability to keep an aesthetic control over his emotions; but it is certain that Chivers could not achieve that control to any extended degree. Professor Damon offers these stanzas from "The Dying Beauty" as indication of the results of Chivers' study of Keats' artistry:

> She died in meekness, like the noiseless lamb
>   When slain upon the altar by the knife;
> And lay reclining on her couch, so calm
>   That all who saw her said she still had life;
> And like the humming-bird that seeks the bower,

But wings her swiftly from the place away,
Bearing the dew-drop from the fading flower—
Her spirit wandered to the Isle of Day.

She died in softness, like the Dorian flute
When heard melodious on the hills at night—
When every voice but that loved one is mute,
And all the holy heavens above are bright.
And like the rainbow of the sunny skies,
(The dew-drop fillet of the brow of even)
That blends its colors as the evening dies,
Her beauty melted in the light of Heaven.[79]

He is probably speaking of a close friend; but for almost the first time he is content to suggest his own emotion rather than display it. The tendency here shown to build whole stanzas about one or two similes is one which Chivers indulged in often; it may possibly be a result of his acquaintance with Shelley. He republished the poem in *Virginalia* as "Euthanasia" in a shortened and improved form. That he decided to edit the poem indicates his continuing attention to matters of control and intensity. Manuscripts of Chivers' poems indicate that he developed a tendency to examine and revise his poems quite extensively. This habit sometimes led him to re-use phrases, lines, even stanzas of previously published poems. But it also demanded that he attempt to refine his own work, and he frequently turned unbalanced and awkward images into effective poetry. His study of Keats may well have offered the inspiration for such reworking, for enthusiast though he was, Chivers was artist enough to recognize the delicacy and precision of Keats' smooth-flowing suggestiveness.

"Nacoochee" itself shows Keats' influence. As has been pointed out, the story line is almost wholly subordinated to description; as a matter of fact there are serious flaws in the structure. Nacoochee's suitor, Ostenee, is lost from the poem when Chivers turns to stanzas of evocative description of Nacoochee. Chivers lapses into the first person without warning, although in his description he does avoid his old habit of thrusting himself into the foreground. Nacoochee's beauty of form is described in some detail; it is Keats' sense of physical beauty bound up, in typical Chiversian fashion, with spiritual or mythological detail, sometimes in symbolic connections.

But it was not until Chivers wrote *Atlanta,* published in 1853, that he managed to combine suggestiveness with physical, pictorial detail in Keatsian fashion. In "Nacoochee," an essentially poor poem, Chivers was confused between his former, uncontrolled evocation and his delight in suggestive, non-pictorial detail, and a newly-awakened realization of the value of control and of the pictorial quality inherent in detail of a certain variety. But in *Atlanta* he manages to combine a certain amount of control (no longer does he allow the first person to intrude) with detail that is at once suggestive and pictorial; and all this in a poem which takes its comparatively unimportant structure from "Nacoochee."

In describing the sacred island of the earthly Eden he sounds much like Keats:

> The Hills, like some great Caravan encamped,
> At noontide, on the desert of the world—
> Still billows of the World's great terrene sea—
> (As if they were the mighty graves of Gods—
> The rising stepstones to the Deity—
> Bristling with lofty pines, that in the distance looked
> Like mystic moss covering their purple backs—
> Spread out in undulating lines afar—)
> Were deluged with rich radiance, as they lay
> Propping the thunder-clouds of Heaven, beneath
> The golden glory of the springing Sun
> Rising in such Empyreal pomp from out
> The Emerald splendor of the Eastern Sea—
> Flooding, with his great Seraph-splendor, all
> The cavalcade of golden-glory clouds
> That rolled, in lofty mountain-piles, on high,
> Like incense from an Altar up to God—[80]

The attempt to establish vastness is still present, for the Isle seems an oasis in "the desert of the world," but the intimate detail of the "pines" and the rich color imagery suggest Keats. Previously Chivers had not used as many color adjectives as are found here. Of course the whole is made typically Chiversian by his constant attempt to extend any image until it offers a connection with Heaven or to God. If it is suggested that Chivers would not necessarily have been conscious of Keats' work when he wrote this poem (c. 1852) the answer, I think, lies in the fact that *Atlanta* is directly derived from "Nacoochee," which, if my basic assumption of Chivers' discovery of Keats is correctly dated, was written with the experience of his discovery of Keats fresh in his mind.

In the Preface to *Atlanta*, he comments on a statement quoted from Bacon's "Of Beauty," that "There is no exquisite beauty without some strangeness in its proportion." Such a statement might refer the reader to Coleridge; it would never suggest Keats. But Chivers objects to Bacon's theorem:

But this cannot be the truth; that characteristic which makes beauty enchanting is independent of mere "strangeness"—for to the perfectly couched eyes of an illuminated Seer, all things appear beautiful that are *really* so. It is the objective indefiniteness of the charms of any pure beauty, to an uncouched, subjective eye, which makes it appear "strange."

To Chivers' objection to mere "strangeness" Keats would certainly agree; and it is not a great step from Chivers' "really" beautiful to Keats' identification of truth and beauty. It is evident that a series of analogies could be drawn from Chivers' statement,[81] but such evidence does not deny the possibility of Chivers' having been deeply impressed by "Endymion" and "Ode on a Grecian Urn."[82]

Furthermore, in "Endymion" there is a passage which might have come directly from Chivers had he been the earlier poet:

> The rill
> Thou haply mayst delight in, will I fill
> With fairy fishes from the mountain tarn,
> And thou shalt feed them from the squirrel's barn.
> Its bottom will I strew with amber shells,
> And pebbles blue from deep enchanted wells.
> Its sides I'll plant with dew-sweet eglantine,
> And honeysuckles full of clear bee-wine.
> I will entice this crystal rill to trace
> Love's silver name upon the meadow's face.[83]

For a similar appeal, Chivers admired the famous midnight feast depicted in "The Eve of St. Agnes":

> And still she slept an azure-lidded sleep,
> In blanched linen, smooth, and lavender'd,
> While he from forth the closet brought a heap
> Of candied apple, quince, and plum, and gourd;
> With jellies soother than the creamy curd,
> And lucent syrops, tinct with cinnamon;

Manna and dates, in argosy transferr'd
From Fez; and spiced dainties, every one,
From silken Samarcand to cedar'd Lebanon.[84]

Chivers' feast is similar in situation, although the sexes are reversed and there is no such attempt at sensory contrast as makes Keats' poem so effective:

So, when he woke, she fed him with her own
Fair hands, on fruits plucked from the Eden-trees—
On golden, luscious Nect'rines, Apples, Pears,
And Mangoes, yellow Plums, delicious Dates—
Conserve of Roses mixed with Damson Cheese,
And Curd, made of the sugar from the Maple-tree—
Sweeter than Ring-Dove, Turkey, or the Swan,
Or softly macerated flesh of Deer.[85]

The source of these lines is clear enough. Chivers has attempted to achieve the same combination of native and exotic dishes; the inclusion of the American sweet, maple sugar (from the rock maple, of eastern North America), is a nice domesticating of the Eden isle.

Occasionally Chivers depended upon Keats for thematic material. "Isabel," of *Eonchs of Ruby*, tells a tale of separated lovers, kept apart by her false friends, friends whose final move is to tell Isabel that her lover is dead. At this news she dies, only to return on occasion to curse her false friends. Keats' "Isabella" has much the same story-line, although he does not introduce the return from the dead as Chivers does.

Bayard Taylor knew of Chivers' verse, and paused in his *Echo Club*, a series of poetic parodies, to include mention of a stanza from Chivers' "Rosalie Lee," and an image from "Apollo," which he prefaced with the statement that it was "One of the finest images in modern poetry."[86] Taylor quoted the third and sixth lines of the following stanza, changing the first word of line three to "Like," and reversing "of" and "for" in the sixth line:

Like some deep, impetuous river from the fountains
everlasting,
Down the serpentine soft valley of the vistas of all Time,
Over cataracts of adamant uplifted into mountains,
Soared his soul to God in thunder on the wings of thought
sublime.

With the rising golden glory of the sun in ministration,
  Making oceans metropolitan of splendor for the dawn—
  Piling pyramid on pyramid of music for the nations—
  Sings the Angel who sits shining everlasting in the sun,
  For the stars, which are the echoes of the shining of the sun.[87]

In agreeing with Taylor that the image is striking, I take exception to his distortion of the image; such distortion is particularly frustrating to an admirer of Chivers, for even Bartlett uses Taylor's reading of Chivers when it quotes the stanza from "Rosalie Lee," which Taylor printed in an equally distorted fashion.

But perhaps the primary praise for the image should go to Keats, for although Chivers makes it peculiarly his own, Keats' lines from "Hyperion,"

> There must be Gods thrown down, and trumpets blown
> Of triumph calm, and hymns of festival
> Upon the gold clouds metropolitan,   ,
> Voices of soft proclaim, and silver stir
> Of strings in hallow shells . . .[88]

offer the seemingly unique word choice, if in an entirely different context.

Chivers knew his Keats. That he was, consciously or unconsciously, affected by Keats' ability to write restrained, intense poetry I have tried to show. That Chivers learned something of this technique from Keats appears obvious when we note the improvement in his verse after the middle years of the 1830's, when he first read Keats. After that period, the majority of his better poems show a closer attention to physical detail, detail which reflects a certain sensuousness of nature apparently common to both Chivers and Keats. The latter's poetry taught Chivers to theorize that "Poetry consists in Ideality . . . an Ideality of the soul . . . possessed of sinuosity—as well as flexibility of motion. . . ."[89]

In *Conrad and Eudora,* Chivers published "Lord Byron's Dying Prayer to Ada"; it contains reference to Chivers' love for his own dead daughter, and proof of Chivers' belief that a parallel existed between his life and Byron's. He reworked the poem twice; in its first reappearance, as "The Dying Poet," in *Nacoochee,* it begins with a quotation purporting to be *"Keats' Dying Words,"* and is clearly intended as a description of Keats' swift rise to Heaven at death. In a sense this change in the poem is symbolic of Keats' influence on Chivers; he provided Chivers not only with an example of a close-working, suggestive, sensory-minded poet, but also with a corrective to the essentially false and harmful emotional connection Chivers had established with Byron.

Perhaps a close study of Keats' short lyrics, his odes, would have made Chivers a better poet, but his emotional response was apparently to Keats' earlier work, "Endymion" in particular. It must be remembered that Chivers probably tried to comprehend both Shelley and Keats at once, as it were, in the Galignani edition. Shelley suited his lyricism better than Keats.

SHELLEY

Shelley, in his less controlled moments, has been associated with Chivers' love of ecstatic poetic flights. Lowell, to whom Chivers had sent a copy of *Nacoochee*, thought him a "droll illustration of the shell of Shelley";[90] he nevertheless thought enough of Chivers to present three of his volumes, probably complimentary copies, to the Harvard Library. But the sense of Lowell's remark does not indicate the relationship between the two poets, as I shall attempt to show.

No case of literary influence upon Chivers, except perhaps that of Byron, is a simple matter of a poetic device learned, a phrase borrowed, or an inspiration received. Chivers took what he wanted from the English Romantics, but he took it in such a way as to make the surface identification simple and the analysis of the extent of influence difficult; that is, in most cases, what he took he made his own. It is possible to draw up lists of unusual words used by both Shelley and Chivers,[91] but such duplication is not in itself important. What is important is the general quality or cast of such a list; it will indicate that Chivers found in Shelley a poet who had written in terms he himself used to describe his own visions, to indicate his dedication to the poet's prophetic calling, and to deliver himself of his more uncontrolled images of Heaven and this world. In short, the use of such words will indicate a similarity in temperament and quality of mind rather than any particular literary influence.

Chivers presumably saw the body of Shelley's work for the first time[92] when he bought the Galignani edition of Shelley, Keats, and Coleridge, sometime after 1832. In a letter to Poe on July 12,

1842, he mentions an article on "the genius of Shelley," which he had written and which was published two years later in the *Southern Literary Messenger.*[93] It is built largely about superlative adjectives and comparisons with Byron and Moore. "The difference between Byron's poetry and Shelley's," Chivers said in his article, "consists in this, that the breathings of the former are the melancholy outbreaks of a spirit at war, from disappointment, with the world; those of the latter are the pathetic expressions of a soul which panted after an *ideal of intellectual perfection.*" The italics are Chivers', the phrasing suggests Shelley's "Hymn to Intellectual Beauty," and it was in a sense of kinship with such a desire that Chivers always regarded Shelley. As criticism the article is poor stuff; one critic noted it was "nothing but 'a figure of speech.' "[94] But it does serve to show Chivers' attitude. He admired Shelley's skill, but it was the spirit of the man which delighted him; I am sure he would have gone to Ireland with Shelley, in full confidence that the mission would succeed, had chance placed him in England at the right time. He and Shelley, he felt, were true speakers, men who had seen the vision and knew it their duty to announce its content to the world. Unfortunately, it is in the matter of poetic ability that the two differ so widely; Chivers had something of Shelley's far-reaching vision but he had little of the skill necessary to control it. Some of Chivers' poems might be characterized as what Shelley would have been without artistic restraint; had he learned more of Keats' control to combine with his flights he would have been a better, and a different, poet.

Perhaps a poem published in *The Lost Pleiad* explains his sense of identification:

Shelley

The vulgar hated thee, because thy soul
Would stoop not to the vulgar things of earth;
But, eagle-like, spurned all but self-control,
Though proud not of the privilege of birth—
And from the hawks of earth soared gloriously,
On wings of fire, into the heavens on high.
Thy soul was like an ocean, crystal, deep,
Whose bottom is all paved with sands of gold;
Whose thoughts, like sea nymphs, there did ever keep
Strange pastime, ever striving to unfold
Their heavenly charms, while weaving songs for thee,
To clothe thy name in immortality.

Thou didst desire the unadulterate truth,
As one who seeks what may be found, if sought—
The first love of his heart in earliest youth—
Though not amid the realms of mortal thought—
And, soaring far beyond all things, didst bring
Back unto Man the Truths which Angels sing.
As when God said of old, "LET THERE BE LIGHT!"
"AND THERE WAS LIGHT," amid the HALLS OF
    TIME;
So, when thy soul dawned on the world's dark night,
All things grew bright beneath its song sublime,
Till, unto man's high soul such joy was given,
The things of Earth became like things of Heaven.[95]

Chivers, too, was hated by the "vulgar"; they even thought him mad. True to his inner spirit, he too had turned inward to express the "heavenly charms" of his soul. And if today Chivers' version of "the unadulterate truth" seems less than prophetic, it was at least the honest expression of his thought.

He admired Shelley for his unfolding of "Truths which Angels sing"; it becomes clear when we find Shelley's name in "The Mighty Dead"[96] that those Truths should be interpreted to include Shelley's love of liberty. There Shelley is praised in three stanzas as the poet of love and divine liberty, "The ISRAFEL among the Sons of Song."[97] Chivers had found in Byron the same strong love of freedom, and, as Byron's influence faded, Shelley was able to reassure Chivers of the duty of the poet to foster just such liberty as Chivers felt existed in America. There are poems in Chivers' early volumes which express his love of liberty,[98] but his clearest expression of that feeling may be found after his first reading of Shelley, in *Eonchs of Ruby* and *Virginalia;* there is no expression of this theme in *Nacoochee* (1837), or in *The Lost Pleiad* (1845). Shelley was "eminently a great reformer,"[99] working toward the day when men would be free from false, earthly restraint, and Chivers' poems on freedom and liberty announce the coming of that day in tones which are clearly Shelleyan.

And it is perhaps in terms of tone that Shelley's influence on Chivers can best be understood. In those volumes which preceded *Nacoochee,* Chivers does not indulge in any but the most restricted flights, his view is limited to himself and his own problems, and those problems are not such as to incite him to identifications

· 127

with Heaven or elemental forces. He speaks personally. However, even in such a poem as "Nacoochee" there is evidence that Chivers' view is expanding. The poem is the first evidence of a literary vision, that is, one which is created to allow the poet to express his awareness of a contact with something beyond his own physical experience and not immediately connected to personal emotion. Such a vision as is expressed in an article in *The Univercoelum* describing Angels visiting his sickbed[100] is of an entirely different nature from the description of Nacoochee alone on her blessed isle. Here Chivers allows himself to describe the physical details of a terrestrial Eden, and the tone in which they are described has a quality which is new. In such a poem as "The Retrospect," in *The Path of Sorrow,* he speaks in evocative, urgent tones; such tones have been modified and made more ecstatic in "Nacoochee." He is exalted as he describes Nacoochee, carried out of himself until the terms of the description become wild, unlimited by any necessity to relate them to the immediate physical world.

> And her locks were as the dawn
> Of the morning on the sea,
> When the waves are wandering
> To the borders of the free.
> And her language was as deep
> As the earth from heaven above;
> And she sang the moon to sleep
> With an ecstasy of love.[101]

If the critic desires a single word to describe this tone it can be best approximated in *soaring.* In no other single element of his writing does Chivers so much resemble Shelley. One is tempted, for example, to look for parallel passages whenever either poet described the flight of a bird.

> Higher still and higher
> From the earth thou springest
> Like a cloud of fire;
> The blue deep thou wingest,
> And soaring still dost soar, and
> soaring ever singest.[102]

The words seem to be Chivers', but the tone of "To a Skylark" is what marks both the similarity and the difference between the two poets. Shelley, as it were, stands on the earth and watches and listens to the bird; Chivers has no trouble in flying with him to his inevitable destination, Heaven.

> Thou art soaring around the throne of light,
> Bathed in the tingling radiance of the sun
> Whose bright effulgence, gilding thine abyss
> Of burnished glory, scales the heights of heaven!
> For on the velvet vesture of the hills,
> Throned in the fulgence of the hills,
> In desert embrace—bosomed by the groves—
> And where the liquid flowings of the waves
> Woo the enamoured banks—thy home shall be.[103]

In both descriptions there is an urgency of tone coupled with an exalted delight in the beauty represented. The intensity and urgency can be found in Chivers' earlier poems; the exaltation is new, and it is very close to the feeling of the poet who shrieked, and clasped his hands in ecstasy:

> Shouting Excelsior to the starry choir
> Flooded with rapture, now he Heavenward rolls,
> Glinting those golden tones of lightning-fire
> Proceeding swiftly from the Angels' souls.[104]

Chivers on occasion borrowed directly from Shelley, of course. In "Idealon,"[105] Chivers makes use of the heavenly chariot from *Queen Mab,* the vision of the maiden from *Alastor,* and the temple from *The Revolt of Islam,* to offer a favorite theme, the return of a loved one from the dead.

"The Evening Land"[106] begins with a motto from Shelley, and is built about one of the Choruses from *Hellas;* in his refrain Chivers quotes line 1029, "And follow Love's folding-star," and takes his title from the next line, "To the Evening land!" There is a similarity of spirit between the conclusion of *Hellas* and Chivers' poem, Shelley speaking of the birth of a new world and Chivers of love in a land where love may be free and true.

"Una," one of Chivers' most typical and more successful attempts to describe the beauty of a woman in terms which are far from the realistic or the sensuous, contains Shelleyan music and verbal borrowings:

> The air around all warmly musical
> Dissolving, silently, the Heavens above her,

· 129

Like an incarnate Moon majestical—
  As if the soul was music that did move her,
And, Pleiad-like, could bring the Gods from
  Heaven to love her.

· · · · · · · · ·

  A golden stream of purest Poetry
    Flowed from her lips in Pythian inspiration—
  Storming my heart, with its deep melody,
    To love immortal as her jubilation—
  Which ruled my thoughts as God rules the creation.

· · · · · · · · ·

  Then, from their rosy nest in her pure heart,
    Her snow-white, dove-winged thoughts to Heaven
      went soaring—
  Climbing, with unpremeditated Art,
    From star to star, up to the sun, downpouring
  A deluge of deep song with Angel-like adoring.[107]

One of Chivers' more notorious poems, "To Allegra Florence in Heaven," offers a clear example of the most important single technical influence Shelley had on Chivers. Of the eleven stanzas published in *The Lost Pleiad,* eight are built around similes, all but one of which are stanza-long. The remaining three stanzas carry the main details of the theme, his grief at the deathbed of his daughter; it is significant that these three stanzas are the first, seventh, and final stanzas. In other words, Chivers had used this theme, one which affected him deeply, as a frame for a series of comparisons or extensions from the original dramatic situation to a much wider and more inclusive scope. He compares her to a sinking moon, a wind-blown cloud, an angel, a fair flower, and concludes, unfortunately, with a comparison of his grief-stricken heart to an egg which can never be mended. His success with these similes is not the point here; what is important is the similarity between Chivers' technique and Shelley's. In "To a Skylark," for example, of the twelve introductory stanzas, those used to set the scene for Shelley's question, his theme, nine are built upon similes. Perhaps the difference between the two poets lies not only in their respective degrees of success with the use of similes, but also in Shelley's effective and necessary thematic stanzas at the close. Chivers was content to state the theme in scattered stanzas, embroidering it with similes throughout; Shelley united his similes with his theme so that the physical situation of

the poet as he creates the poem is evident and important throughout. In Shelley there is no sense of embroidery; all is functional.

It becomes evident that Chivers did adopt this technique from
Shelley when we realize that before his volume of 1837, he made
little use of the simile; after that date, almost every one of his
poems, particularly those which deal with visionary or mystical
experience, depends upon simile.[108] It may be possible to limit
even further the years of Shelley's major influence. Every one of
the examples mentioned in this study was dated or published
between 1839 and 1845. Virtually every one of the traceable borrowings of word or phrase occurs in a poem written or published
between those two dates, the majority being dated from Middletown, Connecticut, in the first two years of the 1840's.[109] Of course
it is possible to find Shelleyan influence in his later work, particularly in those pieces advocating freedom and liberty, but the first
force of Shelley's effect occurred between the publication of
Nacoochee (whose title poem shows signs of Shelley's lyricism) in
1837 and *The Lost Pleiad* in 1845. This influence—on his tone,
his technique, his subject matter—is most obvious during these
years; the fact that there are not traceable borrowings from Shelley
after this period[110] does not indicate that Chivers fell under another influence, but that he absorbed Shelley's method so well that
many of the pieces which we know as most typically Chiversian
("Rosalie Lee," in *Virginalia,* for example, is built almost entirely
on a series of similes) show only distant evidence of his study of
Shelley.

Julia Power, in her study, "Shelley in America in the Nineteenth Century," concludes that

The poetry of Chivers, however, was not influenced by that of Shelley,
as a careful examination of his verse will show. . . . Poe comes near the
truth when he states that Chivers was not influenced by Shelley or by
any other poet.[111]

I cannot agree that this is a correct analysis. I have given evidence
that Chivers borrowed from Shelley, wrote at length in praise of
him, and changed his style and technique after having read him
for the first time. It is of course true that Chivers does not succeed
in his poetry as well as Shelley does; perhaps it is with a desire
to dissociate the two poets that Miss Power decides that "Chivers should be considered an admirer of Shelley and not an imi-

· 131

tator."[112] One who has studied Chivers' work can agree that he was not an imitator of Shelley, but at the same time insist that the influence was strong, and, for the most part, helpful. It may be argued, with Bayard Taylor, that "Poe finished the ruin of him which Shelley began,"[113] but this demands a postulate which I am not prepared to grant. No poet "ruined" Chivers; yet no poet, and particularly not Shelley, "reformed" him either. Shelley's influence increased certain tendencies which Chivers already had: the intense and uncontrolled expression of inward experience, the extension of personal experience to include the realms of Heaven, and the notion of poet as prophet and liberator.[114] An unknown critic's remark, penciled in Duyckinck's copy of *Memoralia* (in the New York Public Library), that the volume is "Shelley 30%" is a testimonial to its similarity in diction and tone to Shelley, for there are no evidences of direct borrowings. In that volume particularly Chivers combined Shelley's emotional lyricism with his own delight in cadence and rhythm to produce poetry which, in part, at least, justified the concluding lines of the penciled note in *Memoralia*, that the volume was "a d—— sight better concoction than is served up by any contemporary poetaster except A. [lgernon] C. [harles] S. [winburne], W. [illiam] W. [atson], R. [udyard] K. [ipling]."[115]

TENNYSON

Tennyson was not known to more than a scattered few American readers before the almost simultaneous publication of the English and American editions of his 1842 volume of *Poems*. Only a few copies of the 1833 volume reached America, although its contents were much appreciated by the few who saw a copy, and those comments on Tennyson which did appear in America before 1842 are generally favorable.[116]

In the *Georgia Citizen* for August 2, 1850, just before Chivers began his work on Poe, he spoke of an appropriate choice for the now-vacant laureateship; both John Wilson (*Blackwood's* "Christopher North") and Tennyson seemed to him fine candidates, but of the two he preferred Tennyson. Yet Mrs. Browning, "the milk-white Swan of Albion," seemed to him an even better choice.

Tennyson was not unknown to Poe, whose editorial position forced him to read widely in British periodicals, but Poe never quoted or reviewed any of Tennyson's poetry before 1842. After the appearance of this volume, Poe praised the poems for their treatment of beauty, and quoted from Bacon's "Of Beauty" in his appreciation of the "strangeness" of the beauty Tennyson achieved.[117]

It might be expected that Chivers would go along with Poe in his praise, but such is not the case. In a conversation with Poe which he recorded in his *Life of Poe,* after Poe said, " 'I consider him one of the greatest poets that ever lived,' " Chivers replied, " 'My God! Poe! how can you say that? . . . Why, his Poems are as effeminate as a phlegmatic fat baby.' "[118]

Chivers was recording a meeting which had probably occurred in 1845; that, at least, was the date of his first meeting with Poe. Chivers must have examined this statement a number of times during his writing of his *Life of Poe,* a project which began soon after Poe's death and continued until the year before Chivers' own death in 1858.[119] We may conclude that Chivers' opinions, as expressed in the *Life of Poe,* represent considered views. His exclamation that Tennyson's poetry is "effeminate" is an extreme at best. The meaning of that characterization becomes evident from a letter written to Poe shortly after their conversation. Admitting that his judgment may have been too hasty, Chivers praises "The Gardener's Daughter," "Recollections of the Arabian Nights" and "Locksley Hall," but will not forego certain reservations:

He is a lofty imitator of Shelley, without a *tithe* of his force. He possesses fine ideality, but there is too much conventional grotesqueness of abandon, with too *little* artistical skill, in him to be compared with Shelley.[120]

He further revised his opinions of Tennyson's skill (but not of his purpose) in his next letter to Poe: "There is a fine finish—a more elaborate perfection in the Poems of Tennyson than in any Poet that ever lived. Every line is a study."[121] Poe may have persuaded him to re-examine Tennyson's work (although there is no letter extant); but whatever the inspiration Chivers' statement does provide evidence that he studied Tennyson's method and style, carefully separating them from subject matter which (as we shall see) he objected to.

The distinction between Chivers' regard for Tennyson's skill as

· 133

a craftsman and his insistence that Tennyson lacked the "passion" of a great poet is further shown in one of Chivers' analyses of Poe's opinion of contemporary poetry:

[Poe] called Tennyson the greatest of Poets precisely because he is the least like the old Elizabethan Gods—for which very reason I deny him any such praise. He contended that Tennyson produces effects by writing an idiosyncratic Paean. The Elizabethan bards produced their effects by writing something otherwise than a Poem. The Elizabethan bards wrote Gothic Poems; Tennyson, Greek AEidolons. This is the difference between the two. The Elizabethan bards wrote out of the heart; Tennyson out of the brain. The Ink horn which they wore by their sides, was full of the white wine of Heaven; Tennyson's crystal inkstand contains nothing but cold water from the Pierian Spring.[122]

Chivers' comments would seem to indicate that Tennyson's influence upon his work will be found mostly in elements of style and technique; there are surprisingly few instances even of this.[123]

Those instances of similarity which are present all occur after the crucial date 1842. If Chivers knew Tennyson before that, it was not well enough to be influenced by him. Nor is there any Tennysonian echo in *The Lost Pleiad*, published in 1845. But in *Eonchs of Ruby* (1851) and *Virginalia* (1853), there is evidence that he had, for a moment or two at least, considered Poe's judgment and searched through Tennyson.

John Olin Eidson includes in his list of Chivers' poems showing Tennyson's influence three from *Virginalia:* "Rosalie Lee," "Bessie Bell," and "Lily Adair." I cannot subscribe to this view. Mr. Eidson bases his belief on the similarity of the rhythm of these three poems (all are four-stress trochaic, the 2nd, 4th, etc., being catalectic) to that of "Locksley Hall" (eight-stress trochaic catalectic). Tennyson wrote his poem in couplets; Chivers' poems, according to Mr. Eidson, differ only in that the eight-stress couplets have been broken down into four-stress quatrains, rhyming *abab*, the catalectic beat occurring at the end of each *b* line.[124] Had Chivers suddenly come upon this cadence, had he used it first after the 1842 edition of Tennyson's poems, then such a process as Mr. Eidson suggests might well have taken place, since the "Locksley Hall" meter was popular in America and since Chivers was deeply interested in rhythmical effects.

But the catalectic foot was one of Chivers' favorite devices to produce a rocking, continuous rhythm, and one which he experi-

mented with in a number of early poems. For example, in Chivers'
1834 volume, *Conrad and Eudora,* appear three poems which
make use of the very same four-stress, trochaic *abab* quatrain
with alternating acatalectic and catalectic lines which Mr. Eidson
uses to indicate Tennysonian influence.[125]

I can agree that Chivers felt Tennyson's influence in terms of
meter in one other poem in *Virginalia,* namely "The Queen of
My Heart," a poem which uses Tennyson's "Locksley Hall" meter
exactly enough.[126]

More important than any of the four poems just discussed is
"Isadore," a poem which must play its part in the analysis of
Chivers' influence on Poe's meter in "The Raven." Mr. Eidson
draws a parallel between it and "Locksley Hall," noting that
"The first two and last two lines of every stanza of 'Isadore' fit
the 'Locksley Hall' cadence exactly . . . although the other lines
vary it. . . ."[127] The first two and last two lines of every stanza of
"Isadore" are the four-stress trochaic lines we have noted in the
1834 volume, the second of each pair being catalectic. In addition
to the evidence that Chivers had already used the line, and thus
does not need to share whatever influence his poem had on Poe
with Tennyson, we may note that the rhyme scheme of "Isadore,"
abaabab, produces an effect far different from the couplets of
Tennyson; the very stanza of "Isadore" which Mr. Eidson quotes
as proof indicates that Chivers was less interested in the catalectic
effect than in the final rhymes:

> While the world lay round me sleeping,
>   I, alone, for Isadore,
> Patient Vigils lonely keeping—
> Some one said to me while weeping,
>   "Why this grief forever more?"
> And I answered, "I am weeping
>   For my blessed ISADORE![128]

I could conclude that Chivers was not so obviously influenced
by Tennyson's popular meter as Mr. Eidson would suggest; Tennyson's success with catalectic trochaic meter may have caught
Chivers' attention, but he must have recognized it as something
he himself had tried before.

Furthermore, Chivers' comments on Tennyson may lead us to
an understanding of why so little of the Tennysonian influence

is found in Chivers' themes. Chivers found fault with Poe's poetry because it did not contain elemental Truth, and the same objection kept him at a distance from Tennyson, who did not "sing Truth." Tennyson's early poems, particularly such as "The Lotus Eaters," might well have delighted Chivers, as they did Poe, had Tennyson gone further in his revision of "The Lotus Eaters" than he did. Chivers might admire the atmospheric conditions which Tennyson could produce, but, as poet-prophet, he could never think him worthy of the first rank. Chivers at one point identifies "the Divine Idea" with "Passion" as distinct from "sentiment"; he goes on to criticize both Poe and Tennyson: "Like Tennyson—which is Tennyson's greatest fault—he was totally destitute of that *primum mobil* [*sic*] of the soul of the true Poet— namely passion."[129] Later generations have agreed with Chivers, if in somewhat calmer terms and if for different reasons. Chivers could begin a poem in terms much like Tennyson's,

> In the rosy Bowers of AIDEN
> With her ruby-lips love-laden,
> Dwelt the mild, the modest Maiden.[130]

but in the next line he has used this setting to pay a tribute to Poe: "Whom POLITIAN called LENORE," the next line, begins Chivers' evocation of Poe's struggle against the world's evil. Occasionally he does produce description which is close to the Tennysonian romance,

> Down in the acromatic streams
> Meeting the luminiferous beams
> With which the air forever teems,
> The golden mail of minnows gleams.[131]

but the whole poem is devoted to praise of God as He appears in the beauty of the hour.

Tennyson's well-known names, Lilian, Oriana, and Eleanore, as Mr. Eidson points out,[132] are close to Chivers' Rosalie Lee, Lily Adair, Isabel, and so on, all from *Virginalia,* and to Cecilia, Isadore, and Eulalie, from *Eonchs of Ruby,* the two volumes which show whatever influence Tennyson did have on Chivers; but whether such similarity indicates any deep influence is doubtful.[133] He delighted in them as end-rhymes, just as Poe did, and there is no doubt but that he may be charged with plagiarizing when he uses words which, as Professor Damon notes, have Poe's "brand" on them,[134] but, no matter whether Chivers uses names familiar to readers of Tennyson, before or after 1842, Tennyson's "brand" was and is not on them.

It may be noted in conclusion that almost none of Chivers' poems attempt to create the mood music so effective in Tennyson's early work, and that while Tennyson was attempting to reform himself in his corrections in the 1842 volume to a poet concerned with serious themes, his themes, as corrected, do not find parallels in Chivers' work. Tennyson's lack of a "higher purpose" in terms of man's relations to God and the poet as God's prophet kept Chivers from admiring and following him as closely, say, as he did Shelley. The difference that exists between Tennyson and Shelley is perhaps the very difference which might allow Chivers to sympathize with the poet who bled upon the thorns of life, seeking the Ideal, while he called Tennyson "effeminate."

Chapter Three

ᏮᎡᏅ Poe and Chivers

An evaluation of the relationship which existed between Poe and Chivers contains only one unalterable fact: Poe, clearly the finer poet, will retain his higher stature no matter how definite or important Chivers' influence upon him may prove to be. However, the fact of Poe's superiority does not grant him, automatically, precedence whenever his work and Chivers' seem to be similar. That Poe's sources were various, and that at least once (in *The Conchologist's First Book*) he silently appropriated what was not his are admitted facts. Yet it is not inevitable that the result of such appropriation or influence will not surpass the original in effect. "In weighing a man's originality, the fundamental question is not whether he has borrowed, but what he has done with the material he has taken."[1]

The intimacy with which Chivers and Poe argued over Tennyson's position as a major poet suggests something of the nature of their friendship. Chivers' arguments are long and detailed, obviously the result of careful preparation; Poe's are rapid and conclusive, just as obviously the words of a man whose primary interest lies elsewhere. This symbol of their respective attitudes is borne out in their other correspondence.

It is possible to analyse Chivers' friendship with Poe, his correspondence with him, Chivers' charges of plagiarism, and the similarity among a number of their poems; but at the end point of such analysis, when synthesis is attempted, the complexity of the relationship will inevitably dictate an ambiguous answer. Time has removed the literary atmosphere in which both poets wrote; it has obscured a number of details of Chivers' life; and it has produced misinterpretations of the Chivers-Poe friendship, which, save for one hint from Poe, dropped at the close of his life, was warm and surprisingly intimate. It has only been for the last twenty-odd years that the true nature of Chivers' relationship with Poe has been suggested; one of the most important critical editions of Poe's work, that edited by James A. Harrison, the one which Poe scholars and readers turn to for text and bibliography, appeared far too early to have partaken of recent investigations, and the result is that the common view has always known Chivers as the mad Georgia poetaster who accused Poe of plagiarism, when clearly the influence ran the other way. It is necessary to remove such distortion, for not only does Chivers have something to tell us about Poe, he also deserves to be known by the light of his own particular genius.

Just how early that genius came into contact with Poe's writings cannot be stated exactly. Chivers himself suggests that he knew of the 1831 edition of Poe's poems, and he refers familiarly, offering comparative texts to reinforce his comment, to the early *Southern Literary Messenger* text of Poe's "To Helen" and to the first text of "To One in Paradise," noting that this poem appeared in 1834 in *Godey's Lady's Book*.[2] It is certain that Chivers would not neglect Poe's writings, for he devoured literary journals, and, in later years, kept a file of the more important magazines of the day.

In the March, 1835, number of the *Southern Literary Messenger* appeared a notice of poems sent by "T. H. C., M. D.," which concludes that his work contains a "great deal of feeling . . . but . . . not much poetry."[3] The criticism has been variously assigned; Professor Damon believes it is Poe's, but others have expressed doubts that he was writing criticism for the magazine that early.[4] That Poe *did* see Chivers' poems sometime between August, 1834, and September, 1835, is testified to by a letter of his to Chivers, apologizing for a harsh criticism: "What I said of your grammatical errors arose from some imperfect recollections of one or two poems sent to the first volume of the Southern Literary Messenger."[5] Poe's first literary criticism, says David K. Jackson, appeared in August of 1835; but Poe's letter suggests that if he did not write the notice he at least saw the poems (or others like them, we may presume) which provoked it.

There is no evidence of any direct connection between the two poets until 1840. But Chivers had been following Poe's career; Poe sent him a prospectus of the *Penn Magazine,* for which he was then seeking financial support, and Chivers replied in terms which indicate familiarity with Poe's criticism:

In the Paradise of Literature, I do not know one better calculated than yourself to prune the young scions of their exuberant thoughts. In some instances, let me remark, you seem to me to lay aside the pruning-knife for the tomahawk, and not only to lop off the redundant limbs, but absolutely to eradicate the entire tree.[6]

Chivers knew Poe's writing, clearly enough; exactly how Poe knew enough of Chivers to send him the prospectus is a matter for supposition. Chivers had published three volumes of poetry, but no review of any one of them has been found. The first volume, *The Path of Sorrow,* was printed in Tennessee; the second, *Conrad and Eudora,* printed in Philadelphia, was, as always, gotten up at his own expense; *Nacoochee,* printed in New York, apparently achieved wider circulation. Lowell had a copy of it and it is virtually certain that Poe saw one. Some twenty of Chivers' poems had appeared in magazines, including such as *The Knickerbocker* and the *New Yorker.* Chivers certainly had a formidable reputation in Washington, Georgia, but it is doubtful that he was widely known in New York. Conceivably he was on a list of subscribers to the *Southern Literary Messenger,* or that of some other magazine, which Poe might have used when sending out his prospectus. Such a listing quite possibly was one reason for the inclusion of Chivers' name; but when Poe saw whatever list it was, Chivers' name must have been familiar, for there is almost irrefutable proof that he based at least one of his own poems on a poem from *Nacoochee.*[7]

Chivers said he would be most happy to aid Poe in his projected magazine, going on in the letter to offer transcendental speculations on the divinity inherent in literary work, and finally asking pardon for his "meanderings of metaphysical thought"; he received no answer. But in December of 1841, in *Graham's,* Poe offered a note on Chivers in his "Autography" chapters.

Dr. Thomas Holley Chivers, of New York, is at the same time one of the best and one of the worst poets in America. His productions affect one as a wild dream—strange, incongruous, full of images of more than arabesque monstrosity and snatches of sweet, unsustained song. Even his worse nonsense (and some of it is horrible) has an indefinite charm of sentiment and melody. We can never be sure that there is any meaning in his words—neither is there any meaning in many of our finest musical airs, but the effect is very similar in both. His figures of speech are metaphors run mad, and his grammar is often none at all. Yet there are as fine individual passages to be found in the poems of Dr. Chivers as in those of any poet whatsoever.

His MS. resembles that of P. P. Cooke very nearly, and in poetical character the two gentlemen are closely akin. Mr. Cooke is, by much, the more *correct,* while Dr. Chivers is sometimes the more poetic. Mr. C. always sustains himself; Dr. C. never.[8]

Chivers' reaction may be imagined; he wrote twice to Poe, complaining, in the first, of the "Autography" squib; in the second, which Poe dates June 11, 1842, Chivers included texts of poems he wanted published. That he should dare to put more poems in the path of Poe's criticism indicates both his self-confidence and his desire to establish a correspondence. Some comment in this last letter may have jolted Poe loose from his silence, for he replied in July of 1842:

I fear you will have accused me of disrespect in not replying to either of your last three letters; but, if so, you will have wronged me. Among all my correspondents there is *not one* whose good opinion I am more anxious to retain than your own. . . .

Your last two letters I have now before me. In the first you spoke of my notice of yourself in the autograph article. The paper had scarcely gone to press before I saw and acknowledged to myself the injustice I had done you—an injustice which it is my full purpose to repair at the first opportunity. . . . You will not suppose me insincere in saying that I look upon some of your late pieces as the finest I have *ever read.* . . .

It is now my intention to resume the project of the *Penn Magazine* . . . . As I have no money myself, it will be absolutely necessary that I procure a partner who has some pecuniary means. I mention this to you, for it is not impossible that you yourself may have both the will and the ability to join me.[9]

Poe was apparently more concerned about the future of the *Penn Magazine* than in justifying his criticism. Chivers must have been delighted by his admission (as quoted previously) that his opinion had been based on poems he had seen in 1834-35; juvenilia it was and juvenilia Chivers was content to have it remain. He replied immediately, in a letter which indicates his financial status, and his early opinion of Poe, of himself, and of his poetry:

I am now on my way to the South. . . . My brother has written me a letter informing me that the division of my father's estate will take place on the first of August, and I must hasten to my plantation to receive my portion.

I receive, with grateful pleasure, your polite remarks in regard to the autograph article. I had always spoken so highly of your talents as a poet, and the best critic in this Country, that, when my friends saw it, believing you were what I represented you to be, they came almost to the conclusion that they were not only mistaken, but that I was a bad writer, and a fit subject for the Insane Hospital.

. . . I have had mighty dreams in my life. The embers of enthusiasm are still glowing with a quenchless heat in the centre of my heart. Music and poetry are my chief delights. . . . In regard to the "Penn Magazine," all I can say at present is, that I will do all I can to aid you in the procurement of subscribers for it. I would take great delight in becoming the associate of a man whom I am proud to recognize as my friend, and whose superior talents I can never cease to admire.

I do not know how long I shall remain at the South; but, long or short, I will do all I can to benefit you.[10]

Chivers closes the letter with a long prayer for Poe's success and health; but he had to write twice more before he drew an answer from Poe. Certainly the possibilities of Chivers' expected inheritance must have pleased him, for his next letter thanks Chivers for obtaining four subscribers, and says "[if you] can command about $1000 and say that you will join me, I will write you fully as respects the details of the plan. . . . I am sure of our community of thought and feeling, and that we would accomplish *much*."[11] Chivers wrote three times in answer, noting, finally, in a letter dated June 15, 1844,[12] that the estate was at last to be divided during the approaching July; Poe replied on July 10, still certain they would be successful should Chivers join him, and apologizing for his almost two-year silence. In this letter he paused to do what Chivers wished for so much; he chatted with Chivers on literary and philosophical matters. He had written twice in 1842, and once in 1844; in each of these letters there is some short bit of literary discussion, usually over poems which Chivers had sent to him for comment and criticism; Chivers wrote once in 1840, once in 1841, five times in 1842, and once in 1843 and in 1844; in all but one of these letters (four of which are not extant), Chivers indulged in observation on the literary scene, speculation upon the theory and nature of poetry, and exultation about his position as poet-prophet. The difference in interest is obvious from this far perspective, and almost surely was evident to Chivers himself. Poe needed financial support, and Chivers, who had the means, seemed curiously reluctant to commit himself, despite Poe's appetizing offer of a partnership. Had Poe extended himself a little further and expressed more than the incidental interest in Chivers' poetry his letters contain, Poe's future and Chivers' position in American literature might well have been different.

In 1845 Chivers was in New York, where he made himself known to Poe; within a week of their first meeting (sometime before July), Chivers met Poe, drunk, on Nassau Street. Walking on together, they met Lewis Gaylord Clark, whose controversy with Poe was then of long standing, and who had recently criticized the *Broadway Journal* in a particularly nasty tone. Poe attacked Clark verbally for his criticism of an anonymous article in the *Broadway Journal* (which Poe had written), and the resulting scene, as recounted by Chivers, adds another incident to our knowledge of Poe's crowded career.[13] The terms of the introduction which preceded the argument are of course Chivers'; Poe introduced Chivers, saying,

["] Here is my friend Dr. C.—from the South.["] "What!" exclaimed Clark, giving me his hand—"Dr. C., the author of so many beautiful Poems?" "Yes, by G—d" said Poe—"Not only the author of some of the beautifullest Poems ever written any where, but my friend, too by G—d"[14]

He continues his sketch of Poe by a quite realistic view of Poe's homelife, and a series of "Conversations" which indicate that at last he had managed to find Poe in a mood to discuss literary matters. There is no mention of the *Penn Magazine*.

The ratio of their correspondence continued after Chivers left New York, Chivers writing three to Poe's one. There are indications that Chivers understood their friendship now to be on quite intimate terms, as he asks Poe to conduct business matters for him, and indulges in even longer dissertations on contemporary poetry. Poe, in desperate need of money, continued to ask for Chivers' help; he had evidently asked for $50, for soon after their New York meeting he writes, "What you say about the $50, too, puzzles me. You write—'Well I suppose you must have it'—but it does not come. . . . For Heaven's sake [send it]——as soon as you get this—for almost everything (as concerns the paper) depends upon it."[15] Chivers replied quickly that his regard for Poe does not depend upon the paper and its success; his friendship is personal, "abiding, disinterested, heartborn." He had received, upon his return to Georgia from New York, enough money to fulfill his promise to Poe, but had given it to a friend whose wife was expecting a child. "I am sorry that I cannot accommodate you at present, as it would give me great pleasure to do so. I will send it to you as soon as possible."[16] The letter is full of ecstatic comment over his happiness with his wife, and about the review Poe had written of his *The Lost Pleiad*. Poe replied in November, in a letter which contains a mixture of certainty over his partial success with the *Broadway Journal* and anxiety that he will not be able to get the final $140 he needs to pay for the printing. He again asks Chivers' aid, pausing to answer a question of pronunciation Chivers had asked, and concludes: "Write soon—soon—& help me if you can. I send you my Poems. / God bless you— / E.A.P. / We *all* send our warmest love to yourself, your wife & family."[17]

Poe's warmth drew from Chivers six letters, all sent to 195 East Broadway, where Poe had been staying. But during the interval he had moved to Fordham, and it was only by a fortunate chance that the letters were forwarded; Poe received all of them on the same day, and wrote to Chivers at once:

I had long given you up (thinking that, after the fashion of numerous other *friends,* you had made up your mind to desert me at the first breath of what seemed to be trouble) when this morning I received no less than 6 letters from you. . . . My dreadful poverty has given [my enemies] every advantage. In fact, my dear friend, I have been driven to the very gates of death and a despair more dreadful than death, and I had not even *one* friend, out of my family, with whom to advise. What would I not have given for the kind pressure of your hand!

Your professions of friendship I reciprocate from the inmost depths of my heart. Except yourself I have never met the man for whom I felt that intimate *sympathy* (of intellect as well as soul) which is the sole basis of friendship. Believe me that never, for one moment, have I doubted the sincerity of your *wish* to assist me. There is not one word you say that I do not *see* coming up from the depths of your heart.[18]

The arrival of the batch of letters meant a great deal to the despairing Poe, and his reply is in the warmest possible terms; the result was that Chivers soon asked him to come and live his life out in the South. "If you will come to the South to live, I will take care of you as long as you live—although, if ever there was a perfect mystery on earth you are one—and one of the most *mysterious.* However, come to the South and live with me, and we will talk all these matters over at our leisure." What Chivers refers to here is not certain; we know Poe wrote to Chivers before January 30, 1847, a month before Chivers' invitation (a letter not extant),[19] which may have contained matter puzzling to Chivers. But he was serious when he asked Poe to come South; he adds a postscript: "P.S.—I do not intend this for a letter, but write to let you know that New York is not the place to live in happiness. . . . Come to the South."[20]

But Poe did not come, nor did he answer. Chivers sent another letter in April, a jumbled, nervous inquiry: "What is the matter? Where are you? . . . I long to hear from you. What shall I say to induce you to answer my letter?" The inducement he decided upon indicates his eagerness to continue the friendship: "I have made an ocean of friends since I saw you last. Write me immediately upon the reception of this. How would you like to come to the South and establish a paper here? Write to me."[21]

Poe wrote, over a year later, a short note, informing Chivers, who was in New York, that he has just returned from Lowell and has not, therefore, been able to see him. He offers specific instructions to Chivers on how to get out to Fordham, saying, "I am *very* anxious to see you—as I propose going on to Richmond on Monday. Can you not come out to Fordham and spend tomorrow and Sunday with me?"[22] Chivers noted at the top of the manuscript that this was "the last letter that I ever received from him." What went on during that weekend, if indeed Chivers found his way to Fordham, is unknown. Poe mentioned Chivers only once again, and then to write Mrs. Clemm, "I got a sneaking letter to-day from Chivers."[23] Evidently Chivers tried to continue the correspondence; in all probability he continued also to avoid Poe's requests for financial assistance. The "mystery" which Poe had come to represent to Chivers may have grown deeper; at any rate there is no indication that Poe ever saw Chivers again.

This account of their correspondence has necessarily omitted many literary references, most of them in Chivers' letters, but it does suggest an interpretation of their friendship which is not entirely complimentary to Poe. Professor Woodberry concludes, "Poe, I think, played with Chivers to make something out of him; but there was nothing to be made of him but a friend. . . ."[24]

It is easy to evaluate Chivers' part in the relationship. He had established a correspondence with the famous Poe, a man whose poetry he admired greatly, whose work he had followed almost from the beginning, and who might understand the "mighty dreams" which he delighted in. If only Poe would respond in similar terms! His final letter to Poe suggests that he knew his speculations were not holding Poe's interest; he was willing to help start a paper in the South to keep Poe near him. I believe his offer to support Poe was genuine, motivated partly by his own desire to continue the association, and partly by his reaction to Poe's continuing appeals. It is singular to note that Poe's most enthusiastic response centers about the years in which Chivers was expecting his share of his father's estate. Ironically and tragically, Chivers' desire for literary companionship and stimulation and Poe's desperate need for financial assistance were frustrated by Chivers' basic stinginess. He repeatedly dodged Poe's pleas for help. It hardly seems surprising that Poe failed to accept or even reply when Chivers finally extended an offer of real aid, and asked Poe to come and live with him. Poe had heard Chivers' promises before, and his previous disappointments prevented him from understanding the sincerity of Chivers' offer.

Not once in any of their letters is there a hint of the plagiarism which after Poe's death became the central issue in discussions of their relationship. It will be seen, I think, that both poets were aware of their similarity in technique and theme; if anything, such similarity drew Chivers closer to Poe. He knew Poe well enough to see his personal faults, to remonstrate with him about his drinking, yet never to doubt his genius. Not even in the hottest days of the *Waverly Magazine* feud (in 1853), when he accused Poe of plagiarism, did he cease to insist upon his ability and genius.

Any study of those poems of Chivers which resemble Poe's, or which may have influenced him or been derived from his poetry, must be based upon just such a study of their correspondence as has been made above. Knowing that they communicated, in particularly friendly terms, for some eight years, it must be obvious that they knew one another's poetry; Chivers, in particular, made a habit of quoting stanzas or sending whole poems to Poe. Of course it was easy enough for Chivers to get Poe's work; his early interest in it has already been testified to. It is with a background of such knowledge that the complexity of influence must be understood. Given the similarity of mind, which Poe referred to as a sympathy of intellect and of soul, it is difficult to see how cross influence could have been avoided. Chivers' high-flying charges

146 ·

of plagiarism are certainly exaggerated; the critical silence which greeted his own poetry changed whatever legitimate claims he might have had into an obsession. But equally unfortunate are the counter-charges against Chivers, in whose light, alone, he was known until 1930.

There is seldom evidence of malicious intent or simple copy work obvious in plagiarism cases; the motivations for plagiarism or charges of plagiarism are manifold and deeply bound up with psychological and sometimes subconscious motivation. Chivers' attacks on Poe are of a particularly definable character, since they followed the supposed plagiarism by some six to eight years; such delay indicates that the explanation of them goes beyond Chivers' basic belief that Poe derived something of his success with "The Raven" from his work.

Poe's death occurred the year before the publication of *Eonchs of Ruby* (1850); the last volume Chivers had published during Poe's lifetime had been *The Lost Pleiad* (1845), essentially the resting place for his grief. There is not much there of the later experiment with sound and rhythm. During the five year silence Chivers was publishing in magazines, and in particular was pouring out his opinions and prejudices in a series of letters to the *Georgia Citizen,* letters which are under datelines of New York, New Haven, Middletown, and Boston. Chivers was traveling the literary circuit; in New Haven he lived just down the street from Yale, and in Boston several poems were accepted by established magazines. He was by no means silent, but the majority of his published expression was in prose.

It is my belief that during this time of comparative poetic silence Chivers increased his experiments with those forms of expression which gave him the reputation of a strangely mad imitator of Poe: the atmosphere of "Avalon," "Rosalie Lee," "The Poet of Love," or "Apollo" seemed typically Poesque. Together they mark a development in style that indicates a careful and deliberate study in the effect of sound for its own sake, beauty to evoke beauty with the belief that its creation is a deliberate emotional experience worthy of expression.[25] They go far beyond anything that Poe attempted; by the very distance they transcend something like "The Bells" they are at once effective and chaotic.

The development of this style was a gradual thing; meanwhile Chivers would act as literary commentator for his friends back in

Georgia. Poe was a source of inspiration, surely; when Griswold published his attack on the dead poet Chivers began researches and correspondence to create a rebuttal. The disturbance which the Griswold article stirred up no doubt inspired Chivers to voice his own private information about Poe and his genius. Among his praises of Poe was the startling statement that "The Raven" had been inspired by two of Chivers' poems.

No extant letter indicates Chivers voiced this belief during Poe's lifetime. Chivers believed he had been close enough to Poe to write a biography of him; they had exchanged criticisms of each other's poetry: now Chivers was left alone to tell the world what he knew of the famous poet over whom such a controversy was raging. The critic of the *Literary Union* offered praise, in April, 1850, of Poe's originality in "measure and style"; Chivers replied that this was all very well, but Poe was not as unique as many might believe. In fact, "The Raven" had been drawn from his, Chivers', poetry.

That Poe himself never claimed anything more than originality in the combination of ingredients is of course true; and Chivers, in this first comment on the uniqueness of Poe's verse, did not insist that he had. He was objecting only to comment by someone who did not, in his belief, know the full facts of the case. The facts were as he, Chivers, would now prove.[26]

From such a comparatively obscure beginning arose the whole controversy over influence and plagiarism. Before this date no one had ever said publicly that Chivers resembled Poe or that Poe's poetry resembled Chivers'. And Chivers' present comment went only to the short reaches of Georgia. One year later he pointed out parallel passages in two prose articles, and devoted a short paragraph to a reiteration of the fact that "the style" of "The Raven" was derived from "To Allegra Florence in Heaven."[27] Again there was no comment from the literary world.

It was not until two years after this that Chivers launched his infamous series of accusations in the *Waverly Magazine;* again he wrote in reply to a critic who praised Poe's creation of a new measure and style.[28] During the two year interval he had praised Poe and begun to collect information for his *Life of Poe.*

Such, briefly, is the history of the beginning of the Chivers-Poe controversy. It indicates that Chivers never at any time denied Poe's genius, but always insisted that his own poetry had stood as inspiration for Poe. He voiced this belief only when someone praised Poe as "original." His first comparatively reasoned statement apparently passed unnoticed, as did the second brief paragraph; twice Chivers had voiced his belief and no one had contradicted him. Is it strange then that when he came to write of the influence a third time he spoke in convinced terms? His letters to Simms and to Duganne,[29] saying that he believed everyone already knew the facts of Poe's sources, indicate that he thought his earlier criticisms of Poe had been read and accepted.

I believe the convinced terms which he uses in his articles on Poe help explain the background that the charges of plagiarism proceeded through. At Poe's death Chivers felt he knew him well; as one who knew him he stated in public what appeared as truth to him. He does not say at that time that such borrowings are particularly heinous; he praised Poe for this method of combining the various elements which had gone into the poem. He was one of these elements.

What, after all, could be more natural than for two poets of similar poetic bent to exchange ideas and beliefs, themes and methods. Chivers, at least, would quickly unburden himself on all literary matters. Probably "The Raven" struck him as an able and successful piece of poetic manipulation; there was no thought of plagiarism. It took three years of thinking, three years of having his biography of Poe (which does not mention plagiarism or influence) turned down by publisher after publisher, and letters from literary leaders like Simms to convince Chivers of the seriousness of Poe's debt.

What, exactly, is plagiarism? Does it occur when a poet uses another's theme? Only when such a theme is earmarked, is so fully identified with its original user that the public will associate him with it. Does the use of another's imagery or diction incur the charge? The same answer holds. Is it plagiarism if a second author uses another's work more successfully and effectively than its creator? Not at all. And what of the intent of the plagiarist? Only when he carefully and dinstinctly sets out to utilize that which is another's without changing it to make it his own is he open to the charge of plagiarism.

Under all of these criteria Chivers' accusations in 1853 that Poe was a plagiarist must be flatly denied. Even given the fact that Poe was influenced by "To Allegra Florence in Heaven" and "Lament on the Death of My Mother" he cannot be accused of misuse; for he most obviously made them his own. It is important to accept this distinction, for it is the distinction that Chivers himself implies in his first comment on "The Raven." His later writings on the subject are the products of frustration, not of sensible belief. At no time did anyone of literary importance except Poe offer Chivers companionship; we have seen his desperate seeking after Poe's good feeling, and the latter's momentary responses to such desires. Then, when Chivers spoke, as he believed, as an authority on his friend, he was first greeted by silence which he interpreted as agreement, then by violent and satiric disagreement. Poe was one of the very few who understood him, Chivers felt; he had himself noted the "sympathy" existing between them. When by implication this friendship and resulting knowledge was denied, Chivers' reactions were bound to be extreme. Perhaps he was self-convinced; perhaps he was the victim of his own loneliness. Whatever the reason, his tones are psychopathic, and by the violence of his own charge Chivers almost destroyed any claim he might have had.

The immediate reaction to Chivers' charges is to suspect the accuser himself of being the criminal; Chivers, it is reasoned, was reacting to a sense of his own guilt. Frustrated by comparative neglect, he spent the five years between *The Lost Pleiad* and *Eonchs of Ruby* working and reworking his rhythms and rhymes, constantly under the influence of the widely-known Poe. When the latter died he felt safe to put the products of this influence in print. His charges are simply a device to throw the critic off the scent.

Were the problem that simple, there would be no point in disputing it; Chivers could be conveniently relegated to a sub-paragraph proving Poe's wide influence. It is because various factual data refute such a conclusion that an alternate interpretation must be found. I have attempted to indicate an explanation of Chivers' charges of plagiarism; it remains to be proven that such influence as Chivers first insisted upon does exist.

The primary contention that Chivers put forth in a series of articles in the *Waverly Magazine, Dodge's Literary Museum,* and the *Georgia Citizen,* from 1850 to 1853, was that Poe's "Raven" had been derived from two of his poems, "To Allegra Florence in Heaven" and "Lament on the Death of My Mother." The January

27, 1845, publication of Poe's poem echoed loudly in the literary journals, and it is even possible that Poe sent Chivers an advance copy of *The Raven and Other Poems* before its publication in November.[30] Nowhere in their extant correspondence is the poem mentioned. Chivers did not speak of it until after the death of Poe, when he included his charges in the prose articles he had been writing for the *Georgia Citizen* (July 12, 1850):

Immediately after my Poem "TO ALLEGRA FLORENCE IN HEAV-EN," was written, I wrote Mr. Poe a letter in which I copied the following verse, requesting him to let me know how he liked it:

> "Holy angels now are bending
> To receive thy soul ascending
> Up to Heaven to joys unending,
>   And to bliss which is divine;
> While thy pale cold form is fading
> Under Death's dark wings now shading
> Thee with gloom which is pervading
>   This poor broken heart of mine!"   [ll. 49-56]

Chivers dated this poem *"Dec. 12th, 1842"* when he published it in *The Lost Pleiad* (pp. 15-16). That it was written before March of 1843 is shown by a highly critical review of it in the "Editor's Department" of the March-April number of the *Orion,* a literary magazine published in Athens, Georgia, which quotes the first stanza and several other excerpts.[31] There is a record of a letter Chivers sent to Poe in the early summer of 1843, which may be the one he refers to.[32] It has been suggested further that when Poe praised a poem which he called the "Heavenly Vision" in his July 10, 1844, letter to Chivers he may have been referring to "To Allegra Florence in Heaven," although other evidence does not bear this out.[33]

These various indications that Poe probably knew "To Allegra Florence in Heaven" are not important unless the similarity between it and "The Raven" can be indicated, however. Chivers suggests that his poem is really hexameter, not tetrameter, and quotes the final stanza, writing two lines as one:

> And as God doth lift thy spirit up to Heaven
>   there to inherit
> Those rewards which it doth merit, such as
>   none have reaped before:

Thy dear father will, to-morrow, lay thy body,
    with deep sorrow,
In the grave, which is so narrow—there to rest
    forever more!

Such a pattern, with the resulting caesuras, is exactly like that of the first four lines of stanzas two and six of "The Raven"; in the other sixteen stanzas Poe does not use internal rhyme in the second line. Taken in its original tetrameter form, Chivers' rhyme-scheme, *aaabcccb,* is exactly like that of the actual rhyming pattern of the two Poe stanzas; and it is this combination of internal and end rhyme which makes the poem effective. Professor Harrison's reading of "The Raven's" rhyme scheme agrees with my understanding of it. He says, "Its metrical form is at first glance trochaic octameter, but in reality it seems to be a four-time tetrameter verse."[34] Chivers would seem to have made a point.

The meter, which is trochaic, the fourth and eighth lines being catalectic, is also exactly the same as that in the first four of Poe's lines; moreover, it was a cadence which Chivers had used often enough in the past, apparently admiring the pause thus obtained.[35]

Poe's refrain Chivers felt had been taken from his "Lament on the Death of My Mother." The poem, one of a number written to his mother soon after her death in 1838, has a refrain of "No, never more!" To this refrain Chivers added a note, saying, "I think that Madame De Stael has said somewhere—perhaps in her Corinne—that the most musical words in the English language are 'no more'."[36] It is possible that Poe saw the poem; it is obvious that Chivers, like Poe, was impressed by the "musical" quality of the refrain. Chivers did not mention the fact that one of his earlier poems, "The Dying Year,"[37] utilized the same phrase.

Both of the poems Chivers cites are elegies, as is "The Raven"; Chivers believed that he had been the first to use trochaic rhythm to express an elegiac theme.[38] If Poe did actually see Chivers' "Lament on the Death of My Mother," he may also have obtained the structure of "The Raven" from it; like Poe's poem, it is a series of negative statements, although Chivers does not use dialogue. It was there that Chivers found Poe's true genius: "That he possessed a most consummate power to appropriate and transmute, is proven by the chrysomelphonian Dialogue, which he uses in 'THE RAVEN,' compared with the Poem from which it was taken."[39]

It is important to notice that both of the poems which Chivers offers as Poe's sources were published in *The Lost Pleiad,* a volume which Poe reviewed in quite glowing terms. He notes the single theme, death, and finds truth in Chivers' expression of it: continuing, he says,

Is it not, indeed, a miracle that today a poet shall compose sixty or seventy poems, in which there shall be discoverable *no* taint—absolutely none—of either Byron, or Shelley, or Wordsworth, or Coleridge, or Tennyson? In a word, the volume before us is the work of that *rara avis,* an educated, passionate, yet unaffectedly simple-minded and single-minded man, writing from his own vigorous impulses—from the necessity of giving utterance to poetic passion—and thus writing *not* to mankind, but solely to himself. The whole volume has, in fact, the air of a rapt soliloquy.[40]

Before commenting on this, it might be well to insert what Poe wrote to Chivers just after it was published:

The "Morning News" of this city had, also, a handsome notice [of *The Lost Pleiad*], digested from mine in the B. J. Colton's Magazine will also have a favorable one. You may depend upon it that I will take good care of you [*sic*] interest & fame, but let me do it in my own way.[41]

The letter concludes, "Virginia and Mrs. Clemm send their warmest love to you & your wife & children. We all feel as if we knew your family. / God bless you, my friend."

What is to be made of the suggestion inherent in these two comments, one for public and one for private reception? Poe must have recognized the meter of "To Allegra Florence in Heaven" and the refrain of "Lament on the Death of My Mother" (he was at this time getting *The Raven and Other Poems* ready for the press). If these poems with their similarity to his own work had been unknown to him before, would he have *stressed* Chivers' originality? He was always extremely touchy on the subject of plagiarism, and it is doubtful that even his hope for financial aid from Chivers could have moved him to this extreme. If he had known Chivers' work and considered his own use of it as plagiarising, on the other hand, the emphasis on originality which he placed on Chivers' work must be interpreted as a kind of inverse attempt to forestall any comment on whatever similarity might exist between Chivers' poems and "The Raven"; such an interpretation seems too twisted and artificial to be valid. But if he had used Chivers' work in a thoroughly normal manner, as an element which went into the complex of "The Raven," and if Chivers himself understood such usage as the result of their similarity of poetic intention and theory, then Poe's delight in *The Lost Pleiad* and his continuing warmth toward the lesser poet are quite genuine. I do not believe any other interpretation can be placed on these statements of Poe's without intimating either a surprising lack of critical insight or a warped and malicious intention. Poe, I believe, knew of Chivers' poems before their publication in *The Lost Pleiad;* if he did not utilize what Chivers had attempted then he recognized a kindred spirit and was glad to welcome poetry which followed theory similar to his own.

The factual evidence of early publication and availability makes a substantial case for Chivers; Poe's praise of the poems indicates that there was never in his mind any thought that he might have infringed on either ethical or aesthetic boundaries. Chivers' later charges are distorted; there is strong evidence that they were enlarged from just such friendly interplay of influence as has been described. Had Chivers never made such charges, it would be simple today to suggest him as a probable influence among the intermingled sources of "The Raven." Attempting to weigh these charges correctly, there are two possible conclusions available: (1) That among the many influences on "The Raven" are Chivers' meter, rhyme, and refrain; or, (2) That only through extraordinary coincidence and because of the similarity of their temperaments and beliefs, Chivers and Poe made independent use of these elements. I believe the first conclusion to be the correct one.

In his *Life of Poe* Chivers quotes a poem entitled "The Departed," which he says is Poe's although not included in any of his works. The poem has not been generally accepted as Poe's, but Chivers offers an explanation for his belief:

One day while I was in the office Mr. Poe said to me, ["] Have you seen the last Number of the *Broadway Journal?* It is a good one—every article in it having been written by myself, except one Poem." From his looks as well as manner at the time, I was particularly impressed with the belief that the Poem was his own. After looking over the *Journal* and after having read the Poem, I was then more particularly impressed than before with the belief that Mr. Poe was the author of it—the reason why he did not acknowledge it, at the time, being that it was written . . . after the manner of my Poem *To Allegra Florence in Heaven*—

Nothing else would have made him disown a Poem of as much Beauty—
Its Poeishness, at the same time, betraying its origin.[42]

The poem is in the same form and meter as "To Allegra Florence
in Heaven," as Chivers noted; its theme, one common to both Poe
and Chivers, is the grief of a lover for his loved one, now dead.
If the poem is Poe's, then it would seem to be conclusive evidence
that he not only utilized Chivers' work but, if we grant the
accuracy of Chivers' quotation, indicated as much to Chivers, and
did so, I believe, in a pleasant, if deceiving manner. Killis Campbell believes that the poem is Chivers', and that he introduced and
quoted it in his *Life of Poe* "in a spirit of pique, or of jealousy
of Poe. . . ."[43] He quotes lines from "The Departed" which are
similar to one in "The Vigil in Aiden" as proof of Chivers'
authorship, concluding that it was a subtle attempt by Chivers to
prove the influence of his work on Poe.

As far as substance goes, the poem might be from either pen;
the form is Chivers'. But if the poem is his, its inclusion in the
Life of Poe marks a radical departure from the tone and intention
of that work. In the entire volume there is no hint of anything
but praise for Poe's poetry in terms of what Poe was trying to
accomplish, despite the fact that Chivers objected to Poe's poetic
theory. Professor Campbell agrees that Chivers was devoid of
guile; I cannot believe that he would include a poem of his own
in the biography, assigning it to Poe, in hopes that a future critic
or a reader of the biography would seize upon it as evidence of
Poe's indebtedness to Chivers.

Chivers, I am certain, believed the poem had been written by
Poe; the very tone of his introduction suggests the naturalness of
his belief. Furthermore, the manuscript of the *Life of Poe* indicates that the text of the poem was not taken from Chivers'
voluminous notes and files, but "Copied Verbatim et Literatim"
from the *Broadway Journal*.[44] Surely he would have kept a text
of the poem had he written it, particularly since he believed it
contained so much "Beauty." And to suggest that Chivers, remembering the incident of their meeting in Poe's office, destroyed his
own copy of the poem, and had it recopied from the *Broadway
Journal* stretches probability.

Poe may not have written the poem; Chivers surely did not. Poe
may even have believed it to be Chivers', recognizing its similarity

in form and subject to "To Allegra Florence in Heaven" and to "The Raven," and silently included it in a number of the *Journal* he believed a "good one." Such a conclusion would indicate that the poem was not written by either man, but by some other author who had been impressed by "The Raven," published only six months earlier or by "To Allegra Florence in Heaven."

Chivers was not the kind to be devious when he believed himself plagiarized; in the fervor of his charges in the *Waverly Magazine* he quotes a stanza from the poem, which he says is Poe's, and insists that it was taken from "To Allegra Florence in Heaven."[45] We may discount the tone of this statement, but its substance is the same as Chivers' belief as expressed in his *Life of Poe*, where his tone is more rational yet equally convinced. He was sure the poem was Poe's. He may have been mistaken, but if Poe was not the author, then that unknown artist had taken the trouble to analyze the true metrical effects of "The Raven" or knew "To Allegra Florence in Heaven."

Those poems which Chivers believed contributed to "The Raven" appeared in *The Lost Pleiad*. The publication of *Eonchs of Ruby* in 1851 brought comment, both private and public, on his similarity to Poe. Simms wrote to him, after having received a presentation copy, "I have received & read your last volume, with pleasure & regret. Pleasure because you have a rare faculty at versification. Regret because you do not do it justice—because you show too greatly how much Poe is in your mind. . . . Give him up as a model and as a guide."[46] Chivers replied in strong terms: "There is not a Poem in that book modeled, as you suppose, upon anything that Poe ever wrote." His sense of outrage is apparent when he says, "But all these things are *mine*. I am the Southern man who taught Mr. Poe all these things."[47]

The reviews of the volume were mixed. Most of them manage to quote two or three unfortunate passages, but these are often set off against stanzas which are favorably appraised:

Here is a little volume, the transcendental character of which its very name discovers. Its author undoubtedly possesses poetical taste and talent, evinced by passages of rare power and beauty, gleaming out from the rubbish of unintelligible nonsense peculiar to writers of his class. Shelley or Mrs. Browning are not more ingeniously and laboriously obscure, than he is. At times, too, he rivals them in touching pathos and beautiful sentiment. . . .[48]

The Message-Bird, whose review was copied in several other magazines, had much the same thing to say:

[Most of his work is of] a very scholastic if not pedantic character . . . promising little for the writer as a man of real genius. . . . [Yet] Chivers gives evidence in this little volume of the possession of high poetic power, placing him a thousand cubits above two thirds of the jingling bards who comprise . . . our American Parnassus. That he has many faults is too apparent—faults of imitation, and of reduplication of ideas and expression . . . much of the matter in this volume . . . seems but the reflex of Poe, and others of the intense school. . . .[49]

Comment of this sort would hardly sit well with Chivers, whose belief in his own originality never wavered. He wrote the day after the review appeared to Augustine Duganne, the editor: "There is not a single Poem in that whole Volume imitative of either Wordsworth, Tennyson, or Poe. . . . Poe stole every thing that is worth any thing from me. This I thought you *knew* perfectly well."[50]

Those poems which drew such comment resemble Poe's in atmosphere and tone; it is worthwhile noting that no reviewer accused Chivers of plagiarism. And despite Chivers' objections, a number of his poems do resemble Poe's.

"Isadore" is perhaps the most controversial. Professor Damon has drawn the parallel which exists between it and "The Raven"; here Politian (a name from Poe's *Scenes from Politian,* published in 1835-36) weeps for his lost Isadore, suffers the tortures of a Voice which questions why he sorrows, since she has been borne up to Heaven while he will live in Hell forever, and finally drives the questioner "Back to Hell, thou ghostly Horror!" The theme is not unusual in Chivers (the very poem he felt Poe took his refrain from "Lament on the Death of My Mother," is essentially the same), but "Isadore" has virtually every element of sound effect and rhythm Poe used in "The Raven." One element in the poem, Isadore pleading to her love not to remarry, is a familiar theme in Chivers' poetry.[51]

The trochaic tetrameter is one Chivers had used long before, as has been noted above, but the rhyme, *abaabab,* with the *ore* rhyme of the second, fifth, and seventh lines repeated throughout, is new:

> "Back to Hell, thou ghostly Horror!"
> Thus I cried, dear Isadore!
> Phantom of remorseless Sorrow!
> Death might from thee pallor borrow—
> Borrow leanness ever more!
> Back to Hell again!—tomorrow
> I will go to Isadore!"[52]

The likeness is unmistakable; the only question is one of date. Professor Damon cites an article by Warfield Creath Richardson, in *The Boston Evening Transcript,* April 24, 1897, in which it is stated that "Isadore" was published as early as 1841. Would that the place of publication had been given![53] Unfortunately, the only absolutely verifiable evidence of the poem's existence before its publication in *Eonchs of Ruby* is in a letter Chivers wrote to Poe on February 21, 1847, sympathizing with him over Virginia's illness. There, as Professor Damon notes, he quotes three lines from "Isadore":

> Come, come to the Pure Land lying
> Far up in the sky undying—
> Where is rest forever more.   [11. 129-131]

Chivers quotes the poem "without author or title, as something with which Poe would be perfectly familiar."[54] Clearly, Virginia's deathbed was not a place to quote a poem which had been stolen from one of Poe's; but it might very well raise a flood of memory and association if it had stood as inspiration for Poe's most famous poem. But this is speculation, reasonable speculation, I think, but unbuttressed by documentary proof. Chivers' poem is an effective one, and the theme, by just as much as it differs from that of "The Raven," seems typical of Chivers. Poe's successful use of dramatic situation lifts "The Raven" above Chivers' generalized statement of tortured grief.

Definite proof can be offered that Chivers did exert influence upon Poe's "The Conqueror Worm"; Chivers' "The Death of Time," published six years before Poe's poem in *Nacoochee,* offers the metaphor of a play, with God as dramatist, and Christ as leading man, as the setting for the end of the world. It is full of typical Chiversian thunderings on the Judgment Day, but the framework of metaphor is the same as that Poe used. Perhaps, as Professor Damon implies,[55] the success of Poe's substitution of

158 ·

the Worm for Christ, and the resulting irony, marks the difference between the poetry of the two men. Such bitterness, and such a climax, would never have occurred to Chivers.

It might also be claimed that Chivers experimented with the effect of repeated sound, as Poe did in "The Bells" (1849), in his "The Mother's Lament on the Death of Her Child," dated August 10, 1841, and published in *The Lost Pleiad* (1845):

> The funeral bell keeps tolling, keeps tolling,
>   Keeps tolling for the dead;
> Whose azure sound goes rolling, goes rolling,
>   Like water, o'er my head![56]

The influence is almost surely in the other direction in Chivers' "Morcia Funebre," published four years after "The Bells." It is a "Requiem on the Death of Henry Clay":

> Toll, toll, toll!
> Let your great Thor-hammer strike upon the bell,
>   Crushing from out his iron heart the dole—
> To sable all the world with his funeral knell!
>   For the passing into glory of his soul—
> For the Requiem of the soaring into glory of his soul!
>   Then toll, toll, toll!
>   Till the billow of your moan
> From your iron heart that inwardly doth groan, groan, groan,
>   Shall, like raging seas, roll on, on, on,
> To the Goal, to the Goal—
> To the glorious golden Goal—
> Where the mighty Man is gone—
>   To the Kingdom of the Soul—
> From this Valley of Dark Shadows to the Kingdom of
>   the soul![57]

Such is the cross influence at work.

Professor Damon has outlined probable sources of Poe's "Ulalume" in Chivers' "Nacoochee," published nine years before Poe's work.[58] It is clear from the above comments on "The Conqueror Worm" that Poe knew the volume in which it was published; it is also clear that Chivers thought it one of Poe's better poems:

["Ulalume"] possesses a Greek classical Olympian sombreness not only artistically wonderful, but mellifluously [*sic*] enchanting. There is an Ambrosial Epicurianism [*sic*] of Logic about it, which tastes of the Gardens of Hesperides. Ullalume [*sic*] signifies the *Guiding Star of*

Love—or the *Luminous Guiding Star of Ireland.* A Star was called by this name in the days of Fingal, as it was the heavenly beacon to those who sailed by night from the Hebrides, or Caledonia, to the coast of Ulster.[59]

His interpretation of *Ulalume* is interesting, and if such a reading is rejected by a philologist, it certainly could stand as a subtitle to his own or to Poe's poem.

So far the majority of the evidence offered has indicated that Poe knew and made use of Chivers' poetry; in every case he adapted the material to his own genius, and the action is not to be condemned on either ethical or aesthetic grounds. It has been charged,[60] on the other hand, that Chivers unethically took the name *Israfel* and the explanatory note following it from Poe's poem of that title in his 1831 volume. Poe's note there reads, "And the angel Israfel, who has the sweetest voice of all God's creatures: *Koran.*" Later Poe inserted the phrase "whose heart-strings are a lute" into the note; such an addition was necessary to explain further the source of the theme of his poem. Chivers uses the name as Poe spells it nine times in his poetry; twice he utilized Poe's interpolated phrase as an image;[61] he added an explanatory note four times.[62] The note reads, "The angel Israfel, who has the most melodious voice of all God's creatures." The source is given either as "Sale," "Sale's *Koran,*" or "SALES' KORAN." Interestingly enough, Chivers' reading of the note is correct, and is from Sale's *Preliminary Discourse* (iv, 71); Poe's *sweetest* is his own invention. At no point does Poe refer to Sale or to *most melodious.* Both poets found their original reference in Moore's *Lalla Rookh,* note 293, which reads, "The angel Israfil, who has the most melodious voice of all God's creatures.—*Sale.*" Moore had used Sale and the *Koran* extensively in his work, referring to them variously as *"Sale," "Koran," "Sale's Koran,"* or *"Sale* on the Koran," which probably explains the confusion of Chivers' source references.

Chivers followed Poe's spelling of the name; in *The Lost Pleiad* and in *Eonchs of Ruby* he used Moore's footnote, and in *Virginalia* he twice used Poe's "heartstrings" phrase as an image within the poem, not as a note. Chivers' first reference to Israfel came in 1839;[63] he used the *Lalla Rookh* note for thirteen years before adapting Poe's image.

Such data indicate that Chivers, who had derived several images

and concepts from Moore, had been struck by the idea of the singing angel and had no knowledge of Poe's use of Moore's note until
the late 1840's, before he published *Virginalia*. The facts do not
confirm the belief that Chivers plagiarized from Poe; what he did
do, in *Virginalia*, was to utilize Poe's improvement, his "heart-
strings" phrase, as a simile.

He knew Poe's "Israfel," and admired it deeply. It is

. . . not only the most ethereal—least passionate—, but comes up *more*
to *his own ideal* of the art— (which he contended consisted in being
wholly *passionless*) than any that he ever wrote. In many senses, it is
truly a remarkable production—being not only an Ariel in its physiology, but in its psychology an Aeolian Harp.[64]

Such praise was sincere; it was written to provide testimony to
Poe's genius in Chivers' biography of him. Chivers' implication
that Poe's lack of "passion" was the most characteristic element in
his work seems valid; his meaning has been echoed by more modern critics, who note the essentially contrived nature of Poe's verse.
Chivers, of course, believed *his* inspiration was genuine, not artificial; later he insisted still further:

Mr. Poe, being a man of no passion, and knowing that every body, who
knew any thing at all about him, was perfectly well acquainted with
this fact, and would find fault with him, as a Poet, because he was want-
ing in this element, set himself to work to prove that "True passion is
prosaic—homely."[65]

It seems to me that this difference in belief—the one demanding
control and subjugation, the other delighting in ecstasy—marks
the difference between Poe's "Israfel" and Chivers' "The Song of
Seralim," which appear, at first glance, quite similar.

Poe's "Israfel" was published first in 1831; it was republished
in 1836, 1841, 1843, and 1845; and in 1842 Chivers wrote "God
Dwells in Light" and included it as lines 13-36 of "The Song of
Seralim" when the latter was published in 1843;[66] an "extract"
from "The Song of Seralim" appeared in 1847, and was included
in *Virginalia*.[67]

The rather complex publishing history of "The Song of Seralim"
shows both its popularity and Chivers' efforts to revise it. The final
text in *Virginalia* is a dialogue among Raphael, Gabriel, Michael,
Seralim, and a Chorus of Angels. Raphael begins,

> The Stars are pausing in their orbs tonight,
> And silence is the concert which they hymn. . . . [ll. 1-2]

In Poe's "Israfel" the lightning "Pauses in heaven" [1. 15]. Chivers' Chorus sings,

> From thy celestial lyre,
> O! SERALIM!
> Scatter through Heaven the radiant note of fire!
> And from thy soul-uplifting tongue,
> In concert with each golden wire,
> Pour forth the living tide of song—
> The sweetest, holiest hymn
> That ever Angel sung!   [ll. 13-20]

Israfel's music (in the poem's final text) is from "The trembling living wire / Of those unusual strings." [ll. 21-22].

In these lines only does Chivers' imagery resemble Poe's. Yet the first quotation above is not from Poe at all, but from Young's *Night Thoughts* (IX, 1258-1259), an image which Chivers used twice elsewhere.[68] The second quotation from Chivers' poem helps to show the complexity of the cross influence between Poe and Chivers.

The first texts of "Israfel" show progressive improvements in the imagery depicting Israfel's song. The original version (*Poems,* 1831),

> That Israfeli's fire
> Is owing to that lyre
> With those unusual strings.

is hardly effective, but Poe made no changes in the poem's publication in the *Southern Literary Messenger* for August, 1836. In *Graham's Magazine,* October, 1841, the image was improved to read:

> That trembling living lyre
> With those unusual strings.

Before the next publication Chivers printed "The Song of Seralim" (January, 1843), with its image of "each golden wire." Two months later Poe's image had been modified to

> The trembling living wire
> Of those unusual strings.

This evolution of Poe's image is a credit to his taste as well as a study of his method of composition. Chivers' poem must have come into his hands, and he saw the improvement which could be effected by changing *lyre* to *wire*.

Thus the apparent debt Chivers owed to Poe is reversed; "The Song of Seralim" is hardly a "direct imitation"[69] of "Israfel." Furthermore, the purpose of the two poems differs. Chivers' poem is an evocation of Heaven itself as a state of music; Poe's is a carefully constructed reference to the beauty of the angel's song, but its whole point lies in the two final stanzas, in which Poe bemoans the lack of such song here on earth and speculates that were he in Israfel's position, and Israfel in his, he might sing "a bolder note" [1. 50]. Poe is conscious of himself; Chivers is transported out of himself and whatever identification there may be between him and Seralim is kept wholly implicit. Such, I believe, is one of the major differences between Poe and Chivers.

Both "Israfel" and "Seralim" had their inspiration in Moore's note, and while Chivers had seen and admired "Israfel," Poe in turn saw and utilized "Seralim." There can be no thought of plagiarism. It is rather an example of close interaction of inspiration and stimulus.[70]

Chivers did not always succeed in translating his materials into his own terms; the result may safely be called imitation. "To One in Paradise" (*EofR*, p. 150) has much the same theme as Poe's poem of that name, although there exists a manuscript of Chivers' poem in the Chivers Collection entitled "To the Beautiful Dead," dated *"Dec 25th* 1841." Chivers indicates that he knew the earliest text of Poe's poem as it was published in "The Visionary" in *Godey's Lady's Book,*[71] and that appearance was probably the source of his inspiration.

In addition to this obvious imitation, Chivers made the mistake of utilizing certain words which were clearly Poe's. *Auber, Weir,* and *Politian* immediately bring Poe to mind. Chivers uses them, as Poe does, for end rhymes, and the resulting pattern of rhyme often comes very close to the effects Poe achieved.[72] However, Chivers was genuinely interested in the effect of the rhymes; he combines them with true place names, such as *Coosa* and *Tallapoosa,* two rivers which meet in Alabama, in "The Lusiad," and *Cuscovilla,* a Seminole village in Florida, in "Lord Uther's Lament for Ella."

"The Lusiad" has been set down as a "graceless parody of Poe's 'The Haunted Palace' ";[73] the only similarity lies in the meter, which is generally trochaic. Certainly the theme and emphasis are not like Poe's, Chivers' poem being a rhythmic elegy on a young girl whom he taught to blow on an "eonch" shell. Poe said his poem was "to imply a mind haunted by phantoms—a disordered brain. . . ."[74]

The accusations which have surrounded Chivers must be carefully sorted; there are a few, however, which can be dismissed succinctly. Chivers' "Nacoochee" (N, pp. 5-26) was not inspired by Poe's "Al Aaraaf," nor was his "Lost Pleiad" (LP, pp. 5-12) or his "Song of Le Verrier" (EofR, p. 145). Chivers' "Catholic Hymn to the Virgin" (EofR, pp. 142-145) does not echo Poe's "Catholic Hymn." Both Chivers and Poe wrote poems to "Eulalie"; Chivers' (EofR, pp. 160-163) has no hint of Poe in it. He does not steal Poe's idea of a dying woman transferring her soul to her unborn child, used in "Morella," for his tragedy The Sons of Usna (Philadelphia, 1858).[75]

"The Vigil in Aiden" at first seems outrageously imitative of Poe. Published in 1850, it has a varying refrain of "Never—never more," and concerns itself with the love of Politian for his Lenore.

> Then, beside the silent river,
> Where he waited still forever,
> By her lonely grave that ever
>   Seemed to Heaven the only door—
> A white Swan, all heavenly-gifted,
> Like to living snow uplifted,
> On her saintly pinions drifted,
>   Came her dying song to pour!
> Like the crescent moon sedately,
> On some cloudless night, all stately,
> Or, as on her couch lay lately,
>   The incarnate Moon Lenore—
> Breathing out her soul in silence
> For the Heaven-uplifted Highlands
> Of the floating argent Islands
>   Sailing now her soul before—
> Floating now this argent Naid,
> As in Heaven would float some Pleiad,
> In the hyaline embayed,
>   Anchored near him on the shore.

> Then he cried out broken-hearted—
> Ever true to the departed—
> In this desert-world deserted—
>   "Are we not to meet, dear Maiden
>   In the Rosy Bowers of Aiden,
>   As we did in Days of Yore?"
> And the voice of that sweet Maiden,
> From the Jasper Reeds, of Aiden,
> With her lily-lips love-laden,
>   Answered, "Yes! forever more!"
> And the old-time Towers of Aiden
>   Echoed "Yes! forever more!"[76]

Politian can only be Poe himself; Lenore is Virginia Clemm. The poem interprets, in symbolic terms, the final months of Poe's life. It is only his love for Lenore which keeps Politian from the tempting "Lethe" of Lucifer, who appears to lure him from his constancy. Chivers identifies the poem specifically in a letter to Simms:

I wrote you in my last that *The Vigil in Aiden* was founded upon Poe himself. But why do you think it is an *"imitation"* of *The Raven?* Because it contains the word *Lenore?* But is not Lenore common property? Mrs. Osgood, as well as the German Poet Korner, made use of it. Is it because I make use of the word *Nevermore?* Is it because it is written in the same rhythm? But all these things are *mine.* I am the Southern man who taught Mr. Poe all these things.[77]

Aesthetically and ethically Chivers is within his rights in using the name *Lenore* in an elegy on Poe; but when such diction as this is found in a poem not directly associated with Poe, then Chivers has erred.[78] *Lenore* is not "common property." That Chivers spoke the truth when he told Simms that the Poesque touches in "The Vigil in Aiden" were there because it was an elegy to Poe is indicated by his revision of "The Fall of Usher," inspired originally by Poe's tale, but published four years before Poe's death. When Chivers reworked the poem for inclusion in *Virginalia* (1853) he added lines referring directly to Ulalume in an effort to conjure up the image of the grief-stricken poet, a technique similar to that used in "The Vigil in Aiden."

Any conclusions which may result from this study of Poe and Chivers must, I think, establish the similarity of mind, interest, and method between the two poets. The multiple instances of borrowing, of inspiration from common sources or from each other further suggest that neither poet had a clear and separate influence upon the other; the evolution of Poe's "Israfel" cannot be interpreted any other way, for example, than as evidence of cross influence. Their correspondence, while originating largely from Chivers' end, was comparatively long and full, although the object sought differed in each poet, and it would not have continued had either man been self-conscious about the other's influence upon him.

Chivers' charges of plagiarism must be understood for what they are, the frustrated orations of one who has been told that he suffered from being guided by a man whom he regarded as a friend and fellow-poet rather than master, and whose pride would never permit outward discipleship. The gradual change from the simple comment in 1845 that Poe had modeled a poem after one of his to the fanaticism of the *Waverly Magazine* attacks in 1853, however, was a product no less of his failure to find an audience than of his egotism, although his need for an audience may perhaps be interpreted as egotistical.

And it is in terms of audience, of the literary atmosphere of the time that their relationship may best be understood. Chivers recognized Poe as a genius, sought and tried to hold a friendship with him, and exercised a minor if revealing influence over his poetry. Only the first two elements of this sequence were important to Chivers until Poe had died and the temptation to share some of the dead poet's fame became too great. Then he spoke out, at first in comparatively calm terms, in the midst of the turmoil of charge and countercharge about Poe after his death. It is vital to remember that Chivers was preparing his defense of Poe's genius and ability and minimizing his personal idiosyncrasies in his *Life of Poe* at the same time that he was arguing about the sources of "The Raven" as Fiat Justitia in the *Waverly Magazine;* he did not wish to do anything except clear the air for an understanding of the genius he recognized in Poe in his biography, and, in the beginning, the comments on Poe's ability (widely recognized today) to adapt and assimilate material from his, Chivers', poems was in much the same vein. But he could not hold such objectivity for long, and the resulting accusations in 1853 succeeded in damaging his reputation so effectively and distorting his friendship with Poe so badly that for almost fifty years after his death he was forgotten.

The summary just concluded may help to define and explain that friendship in literary terms, which are the only valid criteria in such a case. The evidence here offered that Poe was influenced by his work in no way lessens the success of Poe's poetry, but it may help to mitigate the apparent absurdity of Chivers' charges of plagiarism. Yet what Poe did was not plagiarism; he was reacting honestly and effectively to the stimulus of an erratic, extreme, often chaotic emotional poetry, just as Chivers was inspired by his few glimpses of the contemporary literary world, as seen over Poe's shoulder, to become a minor but important figure in American literature.

The distinction between each poet's borrowing from the other must be made in terms of each poet's ability to assimilate the other's work. There is no doubt that Poe was eminently successful in this, as the difficulty involved in tracing Chivers' influence on him testifies. Likewise, there is no doubt that Chivers sometimes failed in his attempt to manipulate the inspiration Poe had given him. Neither poet thought that the other was breaking either an aesthetic or an ethical boundary in reacting to the other's influence.

Today we may certainly agree that no ethical code was broken, particularly when we recall the essential immaturity and amateurishness of much of the country's literary effort in the first half of the nineteenth century. Poets were everywhere, an astounding number trudging after Byron's flights and protecting themselves from failure by using his themes and phrasings, and an even larger number inspiring one another to such identical efforts that the contents of the popular gift books of poetry might be republished again and again as long as the title and binding were changed, for contents were never unique.

Perhaps, however, the aesthetic of the relationship existing between Chivers' poetry and Poe will cause objection. The finest genius receives multiple influences and digests them so well that no man can call the result anything but original and unique. Those of lesser rank, of smaller capacity, never fully assimilate such influence, and their productions reflect other men's light rather than transmit their own. Chivers belongs somewhere between these categories, for while he passed the influences exercised upon him through his own personality and talent, that personality and that talent were not deep enough to prevent reflection of others' work.

Poe inspired him, and without the stimulation he received from Poe and the literary world he represented Chivers would not have succeeded as well as he did. Poe, the man of greater ability, used whatever suited him in Chivers' poetry, while Chivers, the enthusiast and the extremist, could not always change Poe's influence from example to inspiration.

Chapter Four

❧ Subject Matter

It would be interesting to read an autobiography of Chivers' early life; his life before his fateful first marriage we know only through inference from a series of poems published throughout his writing career. He dealt with emotion in extreme terms always; so we must temper our knowledge gained from his autobiographical poems. But had Chivers ever written an autobiography, I feel it would not differ greatly in tone from the poems on his childhood; we would know more detail, and could do our tempering from a firmer basis, but perhaps it is the attitude with which he remembers his youth which is more important in any case.

His early days in the small Georgia town were for him a symbol of good which has passed and may never come again. Once he had crossed the awful line of his first marriage, and felt the ensuing emotional disturbance, "the velvet lawn— / The gravelled walk—the poplar avenue"[1] must have seemed an oasis. And since all the details we know of that home come to us from this side of that borderline, we may doubt that the lawns were much more than coarse field grass cut to a manageable height and that the gravelled walks were as tidy as his lines suggest. He planted a China tree and played with his mother and his sister Adaline in the neighboring oak groves, whose branches "sang the music of truth"[2] to him. He could never refer to the setting of his early home in any but a longing, wistful tone, and echoed Byron with "Precious youth! how soon ye vanish! / Leaving manhood's pleasures blind. . . ."[3] We know few details from his accounting, but from his vision of his home and its peace and beauty he could draw strength to face his world:

> My heart is as a mountain set on fire,
> Which melts into its centre all unseen—
> A shrine burnt down amid its own desire
> To live without enjoying what hath been!

A thing all labouring, but shall never tire,
That flags for moments to revive again—
Whose unconsuming core shall always burn
Till life's bright spark shall unto God return.
My heart is as a lyre of many strings,

. . . .

It is, as 'twere, a fount of many springs—
A thousand streams set over golden sands—[4]

But no matter how ideal his early life impressed him as being, and there is wide evidence that he remembered it in only superlative terms,[5] the spectre of his wife Frances, whom he speaks of in his poetry as Angeline, provided him with subject matter more important to his development as a poet.

We have today only Chivers' view of the failure of his first marriage; just as surely as he exaggerated the beauty of his childhood home did he exaggerate the pain and distress of the relationship between his first wife and himself. In "The Dream," one of the chief sources of autobiographical information, he presents the normal stages of a love affair between two very young people, their marriage, and then, tragically, the break-up of that marriage.[6] He speaks of the first days of that marriage in terms which leave little doubt as to the young couple's happiness, but soon "a fiend" (his wife's aunt) takes his wife from him, and even though she returns eventually with their daughter, he is not allowed to see the child. He speaks of becoming attached to another woman, and of his wife's refusal to grant him a divorce. The tale is continued in "The Lament of Youth," where he reassures his reader that in his youth he had been a quiet, sober boy, reared innocent of guile, and identifies the motive of the "fiend" as that of "envy" of their (or his) happiness. In the second Canto of the poem Chivers speaks as though he has returned home after a long absence (presumably at medical school), to discover that he still loves his wife, and she loves him, but that circumstances, circumstances which, unfortunately, are never explained, prevent her going away with him as he leaves a second time (presumably on his trip into the Midwest).

He eventually obtained his divorce; he even returned to Georgia in 1835. His first wife and their daughter, whom he refers to as Ada,[7] probably outlived him, as his will testifies, but whether the scandal of their break-up dispersed because she moved away or whether the town forgot its local gossip I do not know. In referring to his wife in the other poems from which this account is drawn, Chivers' tone varies from the warmly cordial to the bitter,[8] but whenever Chivers' mood is such that he remembers the ugliness of the affair, he is always certain that the fault is hers. She is a "passion vender"[9] and he has left home because her inconstancy has quelled all passion and all hope. His bitterness has increased by the time of publication of "The Voice of the Exile," in 1837:

> The last dark wave that lashed affection's shore,
> Is passing now upon my weary soul!
> The syren mistress of its tides shall be
> A lamp hung out beyond eternity![10]

Many of the poems Chivers devoted to this subject show him to be distressingly egotistical; many indicate that he must have been at certain times a frightful prig: but the question is not so much whether a consciousness of his own guilt in the matter produced such reactions or whether he suffered from wrong done him, as he constantly claimed; the question is whether his tragic experience forwarded or retarded his poetic career. In his first volume he bitterly thanks those who defamed him:

> There is a glorious magnitude of bliss,
> Which I shall never waste — my eyes shall see
> What they have never seen; and, for this loss,
> I am indebted for that legacy—I own
> The knowledge of mankind—the mighty cross
> Which rends the heart—disturbs the soul. . . .[11]

And throughout his poetic career he declared that his greatest inspiration came always from grief; sometimes his sorrow produced eloquent poetry; often his sentimentality embarrasses the reader.

The defiant tone which Chivers adopted to defend himself in these sorrows passes when he writes of his mother. She held a large place in the young man's memories of his childhood, and a series of poems dated from the West during the years immediately following his career at Transylvania University (1828-1830) all show Chivers in the role of solitary wanderer, longing for the love and peace which his mother symbolized.[12] In his loneliness he is driven to exclaim, "Would I could find thee in some precious wife!"[13] In both *The Path of Sorrow* and *Conrad and Eudora* Chivers expresses his sense of solitude, but finds consolation:

> That other world which my existence loveth
> That inner heaven which my young spirit moveth;
> That vision sphere which in me never sleepeth. . . .[14]

Already there are stirrings of the world to which Chivers was to turn for his most successful subject matter. In his early work he confined himself to narrowly autobiographical subject matter, and had he continued such confinement, his poetry would be of little thematic interest today.

Chivers occasionally wrote of himself without direct or primary reference to either family or environment, and, when the picture thus afforded is added to what we have already seen, the young poet appears as a sensitive man, perhaps given to morbid specula-tion (a characteristic of the age), occasionally prideful and egotis-tical, but most importantly finding himself and his subject matter in a world divorced from the material.

> How sordid are all things on earth this even!
> Where death takes birth as soon as life is born!
> How dark are all things on this dubious sod,
> When thou hast told me, earth is not my home!
> But one long life, where all men meet their God!
> Thou art man's heaven! thou art my home, blue sky!
> Thou art my heaven! thou know'st my heart must die.
> Thou art that gate through which we pass on high.[15]

He can write that "existence belongs to the past,"[16] and wonder, longingly, when he can escape time's pressure, as in "Apostrophe to Time" (*LP,* p. 15); he can be self-centered enough to write "But your grief were *whole ages* of pleasure, / Compared with *one* moment of mine!";[17] and he is not hesitant to show his homesick-ness, as he calls to the wind,

> Kind spirit! didst thou laugh on all my hills?
> And lure no tones from long loved visions past?
> Heard ye no voice speak near my silver rills?
> Felt ye no thrill, like this, so solemn cast?
>   Come home, come home!
> Oh! spirit! singst thou not through all these woods?
> And pay'st thee not, each tree, obsequious bows?
> Thou walk'st through earth—through all her solitudes,
> And still thou bringst me this—these solemn vows—
>   Come home, come home![18]

He confesses, symbolically perhaps, that when the world's forces become too much for him, he retreats to a woodland cave, there to praise God,[19] foreshadowing his later images of the same retreat in two longer poems, "Nacoochee" and *Atlanta*.

The consensus of these poems, most of them drawn from his earlier work, is that the world impressed Chivers with its malicious ways; his certainty of the weight of his cross drove him inward to a personal evocation of a personal Heaven, as we shall see. That his father was wealthy enough to allow him to wander about the Eastern Seaboard without the necessity of working for a living impressed him not at all in the face of his early marital tragedy, and, most particularly, when he later watched four of his seven children die.

He married Miss Harriette Hunt on November 21, 1837, in New York,[20] and only three of their children outlived their father.[21] The loss of four others confirmed the poet in his certainty that only sorrow awaited him on earth; the effect was great enough for him to contemplate suicide—"From Death's bony hand I now empty the Phial—"[22]—despite his obvious interest in his mission as a poet.

The death of Allegra Florence, his first child by his second wife, was a disaster the effect of which never really left him. She was his favorite child; he had seen her face in a vision years before her birth,[23] and she, among all his children, seemed the most angel-like. On the morning of her birth he wondered how such beauty could remain on earth;

> I feel, while gazing on thy beauteous face,
>   That so much of the Cherub has been given
> To keep thee mindful of that glorious Place—
>   That we shall scarcely keep thee back from Heaven.
>
> Thou art prophetic of what is to be—
>   A Heaven on earth, which tells of Heaven above—
> Wherein all that my soul has longed to see,
>   Is seen—revealed to me in heavenly love.[24]

Her death did inspire one atrocious stanza, in a poem which is by no means as false in its similes as the one example would imply:

> As an egg, when broken, never
> Can be mended, but must ever
> Be the same crushed egg forever—
> So shall this dark heart of mine!

· 173

> Which, though broken, is still breaking,
> And shall never more cease aching
> For the sleep which has no waking—
> For the sleep which now is thine![25]

The critic of *Orion* was the first to respond to this miscue:

Shade of Blair, what a figure of speech! An egg and a heart in the same category! With what intensity does the poet declare the important fact that a broken egg cannot be repaired![26]

That Chivers could write all three of the stanzas quoted above is indicative of the weakness of his powers of selection, but a poet is not to be condemned forever for one incredible stanza; the ease with which similar blunders could be culled from better and better-known poets is a mitigating one. Chivers could make poetry from his personal tragedies:

> Kindling the high-uplifted stars at even
>   With thy sweet song,
> The Angels, on the Sapphire Sills of Heaven,
>   In rapturous throng,
> Melted to milder meekness, with the Seven
> Bright Lamps of God to glory given,
> Leant down to hear thy voice roll up the leven,
>   Where thou art lying
>   Beside the beautiful undying
> In the valley of the pausing of the Moon,
> Oh! AVALON! my son! my son![27]

But the Gothicism of the times did Chivers no good. "The Lost Pleiad" is a long elegy on the death of his children, and in it it becomes painfully obvious that Chivers observed those deaths with a clinical as well as a poetic eye:

> And then, with more than mortal dread,
> I laid my hand upon her head!
> It was as clammy cold with sweat,
> As rose leaves in the frost-dew wet!
> I wiped away the death-cold dew—
> Her once soft pearly nails were blue!
> The cramp was in her hands and feet!
> Her breath, that once was *more* than sweet—
> Than Jessamines when first in bloom—
> Smelt like the cold earth of the tomb![28]

Unfortunately the quotation might be continued with equal effect. That Chivers was not unique in his preoccupation with death and the deathbed during the early nineteenth century is testified to by any number of popular novels; but such correspondence is an explanation rather than an excuse.

The only consolation which he could find in the face of such tragedy was his deep and certain belief that he would, in terms which seem trite to twentieth-century sophistication, meet his children in Heaven. Almost every one of the poems devoted to his dead children concludes with a prayer that such a time may come soon. And it is to that Heaven and Chivers' views of it that we may now turn.

The terms in which Chivers envisioned Heaven are strangely personal ones, strange though personal because they so often present familiar and traditional imagery utilized in a unique manner. That Heaven and its God existed Chivers never doubted; both his early Baptist training and his own visionary experiences aided in providing his troubled spirit with a place where complexities would become clear, sin be unknown, and hate impossible. Early in his life he witnessed the tragedy of his young sister's death and was tormented by his inability to visualize her soul's rise to Heaven:

> Oh, dying sister!
> How can I emblem that I never saw? how
> Can a brother's words depict that which he
> Only saw reflected from the mirror
> Of your infant soul?[29]

The frustration he felt at that time changed gradually in later years as he compromised with the non-pictorial strength of his emotional belief. He could not paint what he felt in terms which others would understand. What he could do was invest his poetry with the same strength of emotion his belief incurred within his own heart and image that emotion in terms at once undefined yet suggestive, often involving Biblical metaphor and traditional symbol.

It was easy for him to populate Heaven with the figures of his children; more than once the reader is startled by an angel whose features strongly resemble those of one of his dying children.[30] And after reading several of his poems on this subject, the reader

· 175

becomes increasingly aware that the terms Chivers uses to describe Heaven are always much the same.

The most frequent reference is to Heaven as a state of music, "Vibratory . . . blissful music . . . melodious impressions."[31] There is no evidence that Chivers was ever a musician, but he was certainly sensitive to large, sweeping musical effects, and later he undertook poetic experiments in the nature of sound and on how it might be suggestive of sense.

> Swift as the rolling spheres
> Diffuse their circular orbit-tones on high—
> Spreading till they embrace th' Eternal Years
> With their dilating, wave-like melody—
> Winnowing the calm, clear, interstellar air—
> Does thy sweet, spiritual music spread up there.[32]

Whenever Chivers undertook to represent angels or cherubim, he described them as singers, whose melodious voices enchant their God and all the spirits. In "The Song of Seralim," Raphael, Gabriel, and Michael introduce Seralim; then, in chorus, they sing,

> From thy celestial lyre,
> O! SERALIM!
> Scatter through Heaven the radiant notes of fire!
> And from thy soul-uplifting tongue,
> In concert with each golden wire,
> Pour forth the living tide of song—
> The sweetest, holiest hymn
> That ever Angel sung!

SERALIM SINGS

> Praise God, ye Angels of the Heavens above!
> Praise Him, ye Seraphs who can never die!
> And you, Archangels! whose delight is love,
> Thunder your anthems through eternity!
>
> Let the uncounted Realms of endless Space
> Join in their orbits to unite in praise—
> (Whose light is the reflection of His face—)
> Loving aloud the ANCIENT ONE OF DAYS!
>
> Lift up your voices, Children of the Earth!
> Praise God, ye Spirits of the countless spheres!
> And you, ye HABITANTS OF HEAVEN! pour forth
> The tide of song through Heaven's eternal years!

> Fill up the canopy of Heaven above
> With song's immortal, everlasting sea;
> And drown the Stars in one wide sea of love
> Poured forth in praises of the Deity.[33]

This "Celestial Melologue" suggests several elements common to much of Chivers' poetry of this type. The reference to such well-known hymnal phrases as "ancient [one] of days" can be duplicated frequently enough; but sometimes Chivers made the reference his own. Such is the following, which began, probably, as Elijah's chariot:

> Up through the hyaline ether-sea,
> Star-diademed, in chariot of pure pain,
> Through th' empyreal star-fires radiantly,
> Triumphant over Death in Heaven to reign
> Thy soul is gone, seeking its BLEST ABODE,
> Where break the songs of stars against the feet of God.[34]

"Seralim" is also typical in its suggestion of vast forces moving under the hand of an undefinable Creator. If Chivers was interested in astronomy, it was clearly in emotional terms only; the visible heavens served to suggest, like Blake's tiger, the magnitude existing before them.

> Circling the Cyclic-chorus of the spheres,
> Sphering the Epicycle of his song—
> He sings his anthems, through th' eternal years,
> Outside the orb-paths of th' Empyreal throng.
>
> Floating in chariot of celestial fire,
> Sphered Heavenward through th' Empyreal Ether-Sea,
> He rays his sphere-tones out unto the choir
> Of God until they fill Eternity.
>
> Tempestuous whirlwinds of deep melody
> Dash from his orb-prow on his spheric road—
> Rolling in mountain-billows on Heaven's sea
> Against the white shore of the feet of God.
>
> Shouting Excelsior to the starry choir
> Flooded with rapture, now he Heavenward rolls,
> Glinting those golden tones of lightning-fire
> Proceeding swiftly from the Angels' souls.[35]

Chivers felt close to such vast movements; in terms of them he could try to express the strong identification he felt with his God. He could not speak in calm tones when Heaven was his subject, and his poetry indicates both purposeful indefiniteness and apocalyptical vision. The Creation, Judgment Day, the ascent of a soul to Heaven were events which Chivers could experience emotionally. It is hardly careful theology or orthodox Christianity, but such dissensions would bother Chivers not at all.

In *Search After Truth,* a theosophical pamphlet in which Chivers uses the Socratic method to explain or prove the relation of God to man, the immortality of the soul, and the creation of the universe, Chivers' prose is careful and calm until he begins to speak of Heaven:

When God said, *"Let there be light; and there was light,"* the whole hierarchy of the Cycles and Epicycles of the glorified spirits in Heaven rose up in blazing majesty before the throne, and with one sudden gush of blissful rapture, flooded the ever-spreading Fields above with the thunder-deluge of their joyful jubilations. . . .[36]

Such an evocation was possible for Chivers not only because he could deduce Heaven's presence, analytically, as he does in this pamphlet, but also because he had himself experienced psychic visions. That the soul had the power to ascend to Heaven and know truth he never doubted;[37] furthermore it was possible to find such an Eden as he imagined Heaven to be here on earth. By expressing his own divinity, man can "live the future life while in this world—that is, he ascends to Heaven before he dies. . . ."[38]

Nothing could be more natural than for Chivers to have attempted to find some sort of possible recompense for the trouble he felt about him so often. He never doubted that he had proceeded through it innocently, and his early visionary experience suggested to him that for some there was a Terrestrial Eden in which all beauty might be found. Madness? No. Not as mad, perhaps, as the attempts of more "practical" philosopher-poets to establish Utopias. But Chivers was never practical in matters of emotion and feeling. And he did not, at any time, attempt to define a geographical or physical format for such an Eden; it is closer to the truth to say that such an Eden was a psychological one, a subconscious one, if you will, in which he quite probably existed as he wrote of it.

Atlanta: The True Blessed Island of Poesy, A Paul Epic—In Three Lustra, published in 1853, was his definitive attempt to evoke his Terrestrial Eden. Its title suggests Chivers' belief in the poet as God's prophet; its framework was taken from Chivers' earlier attempt "Nacoochee" (particularly in such details as the removed island, the canoe voyage to it, and in the theme of the search for eternal love or beauty). His Preface, which contains important statements on his poetic theory, only once implies the poem's contents.

. . . what was the Garden of Eden but an Opera of beauty written by the hand of God, in syllables of flowers, for the delight of the Angels?[39]

It is written "as an experiment upon the minds of the *Chosen Few,* wrought out . . . to introduce . . . a partial fulfillment of the demands required of the souls of all true worshippers of the Divine Beauty. . . ."[40] Such a statement, to Chivers, was more than the usual appeal to the ego of his reader; he really did believe that some few would understand the nature and the religious implication of the "demands," which he himself felt so strongly.

Atlanta is, structurally, little more than a verse romance. Ianthe and Julian, the young lovers, are separated when Lamorah, an Indian chief, kidnaps her and spirits her away to the Eden Isle. In the battle which precedes her kidnapping, Lamorah's son is killed; his action is one of revenge. Eventually, after Ianthe manages to send a desperate message to Julian, the latter disguises himself as Lamorah's dead son and persuades the old man to take him to Ianthe, after which Lamorah quietly disappears. Unless Chivers is given credit for symbolic intention, such a plot would be worthless; but when we remember Chivers' words in the Preface, it is clear that Ianthe represents true beauty or love, the higher consciousness. Julian must of course reunite himself with this consciousness. Professor Damon believes that Lamorah represents Julian's baser passions, what he would be without this higher self; eventually Julian succeeds in using them to achieve the unity he needs, here symbolized by the physical union of Julian and Ianthe.[41]

The action described above occurs in the first two "Lustra," or cantos. The third is devoted entirely to their nuptial feast, which is described in sensuous and evocative terms. It clearly stands as the climax of the poem in terms of structure, and just as certainly in terms of symbolism, through the descriptive passages. I do not believe that a symbolic reading of the poem is an exaggeration of Chivers' intention; he had announced that it was not for the general public; he had made use of earlier poems, particularly "Nacoochee," making them over to suit his more clearly defined purpose;[42] and all the finer poetry which he published in the 1850's, particularly in *Eonchs of Ruby*, deals, clearly enough, with just such subject matter as this, if in less symbolic terms. Furthermore, Chivers knew he couldn't write a verse romance; his old models, Byron and Moore, would have led him to an attempt before this had he envisioned success.[43]

Given the symbolic meaning I have just outlined, Chivers' description, always in sensuous terms, becomes even more effective. It is reminiscent of his poems describing Heaven, and the transformation of the natural detail to the exotic (and sometimes fanciful) is representative of the enlarging and purifying process through which Chivers passed his own experiences and emotion, as well as the facts or objects of the physical world, whenever the vision was upon him. Exalted himself, he might exalt all he touched.

> The golden grapes hung clustering in the sun,
> Oozing their luscious Nectar on the ground—
> Rare vintage ripe of rich deliciousness—
> Tempting the soul to eat continually.
> Large Orange-trees that blossom while they bear,
> Burthened with fruit of pure exquisiteness
> Like globes of vegetable gold on boughs
> Of lustrous emerald growing. . . .[44]

I have tried to emphasize, in this discussion of the form and content of *Atlanta*, that the poem stands as the natural and rather successful end to a long process. In his youth Chivers experienced what we must accept as a vision; he was convinced of its authenticity, and since we are not searching for absolutes here, his interpretation is the important one. The terms of the vision are suggestive of those he used later in his poetry.

. . . I had been sick, but was now convalescent—(the Elysium of this poor life—) and was lying in the middle of my bed in the middle of the room, reading the Psalms of David, when this vision appeared to me. I knew that God had couched my eyes to see it, for with my naked eyes I knew that I could not see a spirit; and, for fear that I was deceived, or, that it might be a *mere delusion*—I placed my hands over my eyes, but the glorious Vision still appeared to me as beautiful as before. Still doubting the truth of the Appearance—thinking, perhaps, that I *might* be deceived—I called my mother into the room, and crying out in the ecstasy of delight, I said, *"Mother! look up there upon the wall at the beautiful Angels singing and playing upon their harps!"* At which she looked up, intently, for some time, but could discern nothing. She then said, *"My dear! you are distracted! I can see nothing!"* *"Now,"* said I, *"they are gone!"* And they went away just as I have told you. When I turned my face toward the right side of the room, I saw a fountain of crystal water running down the wall, and breaking into a beautiful, musical, cooling and purifying cascade over the looking-glass. I told my mother of the Vision of the little crystal river of beautiful water, at which she smiled just as she had done at the Vision of the Angels. I then bade her go—(to satisfy her of the truth of the Vision)—and hold her hand under the glass. She did so; and I saw the living, crystal water splash down into the palm of her hand.[45]

He believed always that such experiences were possible for anyone whose eyes were "couched"; his Preface to *Atlanta* insists upon this distinction. Moreover, in addition to a telepathic experience he had while in the West, during an illness of his mother,[46] he was twice sure that his favorite daughter, Allegra Florence, appeared to him in a vision; I think the inspiration is genuine, as he describes her appearance with her brother:

> They were two infant Cherubim
> Who sang to me that Heavenly Hymn.
> One had the same cerulean eyes
> Of my first-born now in the skies;
> The other's eyes were dark, with light
> Therein like Hesperus to the night—
> Such as to my dear son were given,
> The Image of that One from Heaven;
> For my dear children had the eyes
> Of those bright Angels from the skies—
> The same as they appeared to me
> Eight years before their infancy.
> 'Twas in the flowery month of May,
> About the noontide hour of day,
> And on the same day in the year
> On which the Angels did appear,
> Revealing joys which were, to me,
> Prophetic of what was to be—

That tidings came to me what morn
ALLEGRA FLORENCE should be born;
And she was born—the very child
That came to me. . . .[47]

Here the appearance of Allegra Florence is described in simple diction, for he was explaining an experience, not reliving it or trying to evoke the emotions accompanying it. But *Atlanta* was something else; he was creating, not recounting, and the terms are as suggestive as the setting is exotic. Visionary experience began the establishment of a world in Chivers' mind which might be as sublime as he wished and as real as any physical object.

He sometimes used the vision as a purely literary device,[48] and once was torn by the feeling that the power to envision "the bright crystal waters," a direct reference to the terms used in describing his childhood vision, was now lost to him; his eyes were no longer "couched."[49] His distress at a temporary loss of his inner sight was genuine, for more and more as his productive years passed he depended upon the world it revealed for support and encouragement.

It was an era in which spiritualism, phrenology, and associated sciences were familiar and even respected; Chivers greeted the appearance of A. J. Davis' magazine *The Univercoelum, or Spiritual Philosopher* with great delight. And no matter how far from the contemporary mode his poems expressing such delight may now seem, he was inspired by his visions of eternity, in personal or in symbolic terms, to write much of his best poetry in praise of it. His terms were a combination of the familiar Biblical image and his own special diction; his tone is apocalyptical:

From the inflorescence of his own high soul,
The incense of his Eden-song doth rise,
Whose golden river of pure redolence doth roll
Down the dark vistas of all time in melodies—
Echoing the Island of the Sea
Of the vast immensity,
And the loud music of the Morns,
Blown through the Conchimarian Horns
Down the dark vistas of the reboantic Norns,
By the great Angel of Eternity,
Thundering, *Come to me! come to me!*[50]

THE NATION AND ITS DESTINY

It is clear that Chivers as a poet was a product of a particular area and a particular time, but seldom in his poetry does he give effective expression to that influence. The best part of his subject matter came from within his own mystic or semi-mystic inward experience, not from national or regional circumstance.

In one body of his poetry, however, he is concerned with the America of the decades before the Civil War. Some twenty-odd poems are devoted to exuberant praise of liberty and its stronghold, the United States. He was consciously, after all, a magazine poet, and voices such as Bryant's had been raised for some years in calls for the use of national subject matter and the national past. For Chivers this provided a suitable opportunity to declaim on the virtues of liberty and on its prime defender, Washington. Along with a series of poems on occasional subjects, these poems mark virtually the only point at which Chivers went very far outside his own personal experience for the subject matter of his poetry.

He was particularly conscious of the tradition that his country was the birthplace of liberty. Liberty itself carried with it suggestions of divine inspiration,[51] and Chivers wrote in praise of it wherever he found evidence of men defending it. Looking toward Europe, something which he seldom did, he found nations rising against that Old World evil, monarchy:

> So did these living columns of the indignant Free,
> Sweep onward to the Angel-voice of Liberty,
>   Over the desperate cataracts of Anarchy,
> Down to the opening Ocean of their Destiny—
>   Piling their rafts of slain along the vallies,
> Like fallen forests—prostrate monuments of slaughter—
>   To fatten Earth, or fill up Buzzards' bellies—
> For future Tyrants, now, shall know no quarter![52]

His image does not escape him here, and, if nothing else, the passage indicates the strength of the emotion with which he regarded the struggle of mankind to free itself from what he regarded as a basic evil.

Several of his poems concern themselves with specific examples of freedom's heroes leading their people. In an early poem, "The Siege of Vienna,"[53] Chivers writes in praise of Sobieski's relief of the Turkish siege on Vienna in 1683; Chivers could handle the subject best, apparently, when he was able to attach personality to the general concept. The poem is a monologue by Sobieski as he prepares for and fights the battle. Sobieski's motivation is not particularly that of a native patriot; rather, he speaks of the value and blessings of freedom in general, just as Chivers does. "The Blood-Stained Alder,"[54] published over twenty years later, shows much the same concern. Poland's struggle for freedom against Prussia was apparently of popular interest, for the poem was republished three times, even reaching the pages of the *Nantucket Inquirer*. From some source Chivers found the story of an alder tree which had been carried from Poland to the United States, there to grow strong itself, but, most importantly, to provide nourishment for the tree of liberty.[55] Chivers was very much aware of the polyglot nature of his country, but it is unusual indeed to find a poet celebrating, in 1853, the strengthening and life-giving qualities of immigration. One would have expected a Southern poet, writing for the magazines, to celebrate only native heroes. Chivers concludes the poem with a reminder to all Americans to study and honor the relics of their past as reminders of their own strength.

Continuing a belief which had its American origin in Puritan theological argument, Chivers saw the United States as the Promised Land. Here mankind was to have a new birth, a cleansing and a revivifying. Daring to name Christ as "The Radical," Chivers speaks for him:

> Thou dost despise the Ages that are past,
> Because their hearts are rotten at the core:
> For thou dost love that which was born to last,
> And *only* that which lasts forever more.[56]

It is clear that the United States will last; it is particularly clear that it is in no way rotten. Men have watched for the birth of this land over countless years, and the greatness of the vision forces Chivers to jumbled, exclamatory expression:

> Thus I sing to blest America, this land of many Nations,
> This bright Constellation of great States—the Exiles'
>   only bourne—
> This New Eden of Atlantides of Ancient expectations—
> Plato's loftiest Ideal realized—Columbia full of Corn—
> Here great *Liberty* was born.[57]

184 ·

In the inclusiveness of the concepts, which causes the stanza to fail, lies the interest of the stanza: Plato mixed with thoughts of the country as a haven and as a mother to all men.

This theme must have stayed with Chivers, for in the month following the publication of this stanza, he broke forth with a more typical and infinitely more effective evocation of the paradisical nature of America. "In the Autumn of the world, when the honey of the Summer still lay on the flowers of the years,"[58] Chivers finds himself transported to Heaven as he considers his subject. He offers several stanzas of impressionistic description of the Heaven he finds about him, and the poem rises to a climax which we, in our dislike of hero-worship and outwardly patriotic demonstration, may find difficult to accept:

> Then, like the unfolding of some antediluvian iron Scroll,
> With repercussive clang, like storm-winds when they rend
>   the bosom of the Deep,
> The Vail of Isis was rent in twain, revealing unto my
>   more than raptured soul
> The dark Aenigma of the grave, written in Dreams in the
>   House of Sleep.

This insight into the mysteries of death and heaven allows Chivers to be present at the climactic arrival of the man who more than any other symbolized to him the strength of freedom:

> Watching, my soul grew dumb with horror's wild
>   astonishment.
> Listening, entranced, before the presence of that
>   immortal One!
> Until, at length, strengthened by his sweet smile, my
>   soul gave vent
> To its new wonder shaping itself into the name of
>   WASHINGTON![59]

Washington is used again and again as the symbol of liberty and its coequal, truth. Upon the opening of his sepulcher for the removal of his body to the sarcophagus, Chivers was moved to write of his greatness of spirit in his search for truth.[60] Again, as he wrote in praise of "Liberty,"[61] he saw Washington's spirit leading the oppressed peoples of Europe to freedom.

Statesmen of America's past are not the only heroes to receive praise. "The Death of Jefferson"[62] expresses Chivers' admiration

· 185

for his spirit (Chivers would be a Jeffersonian of course), but he succumbed to popular contemporary belief in the following sonnet written upon the death of General William Henry Harrison. Chivers' motivation may have come from the essentially absurd but politically-effective evocation of the "log cabin" symbol, but his admiration dealt in larger terms:

> In the serene evening of his bye-gone days,
> The son of righteousness shed on his brow
> A holy light—more beautiful than now
> Appears high Heaven— too beautiful for praise!
> His goodness bankrupt leaves the mightiest tongue!
> For, as Heaven's arch, at night, with black is hung,
> With mourning is the Country of his fame!
> While, star-like, through the gloom, appears his name
> Making the darkness beautiful with rays
> That melt our sorrow, as the burning light
> Of Hesperus the darkness of the night—
> Defying all Earth's combined powers to raze
> One atom of his memory from mankind—
> As well may they attempt to fetter mind.[63]

Chivers' Whiggery is clear even if his genius is not. And one must not assume that his political expressions were concerned always with such impractical subjects; "Song of the American Freemen"[64] is an urging to all men to get out and vote!

But it remains to two long poems to show the reality of Chivers' concern with the essential, basic qualities of freedom. "The Mighty Dead" occupies twenty-one pages in *Eonchs of Ruby,* the volume which contains much of the most effective and typical of Chivers' verse.

As in "The Roll of Fame," Chivers begins with a series of stanzas describing Heaven, and his method of attaining the mystic view necessary to trace freedom's heroes:

> On every leaf that grows
> Beside the Living Waters, in each flower,
> A Song is written, which, while opening, shows
> An Angel's history, which, sung, gives power
> To those who hear to know the things to be,
> And see that which before they could not see.[65]

His belief that he could reach far enough to include the necessary perspective is not simply a literary device. It is a deep-seated belief

186 ·

in the visionary power of the poet. It has been noted that in virtually every one of Chivers' poems treating the theme of liberty or nationalism, Chivers attempted to equate the "free" and "freedom" with the "divine" and "divinity"; the structure of "The Mighty Dead" indicates that the theory is basic to his belief. Following the evocation of heaven, Chivers pauses to discuss the nature of the soul, and of death. Then, without further warning, the chief apostle of liberty appears, "Grasping the Parchment Scroll of Liberty, / Signed by the fearless Elders of the Free." Washington exists for Chivers not particularly as a revolutionary leader, but as symbol.

> The Mighty Ones of Old,
> Who saw the Fields of Immortality
> From earth—Oceans of panacoelian gold—
> Waving before God's breath—they died like thee—
> Died in their Manhood—with their Prophet-Eyes
> Fixed on the Future—ripe for Paradise.[66]

The prophet-quality of Washington is carried further as Chivers repeats his insistence that America is indeed the Promised Land, "The New Jerusalem of Liberty," "the Pride of Heaven! / Built of the columns of the ruined Past." Essential to this belief that America is the heaven-sent oasis for that hope which is ages old is the corollary that freedom itself has existed, in principle, from the beginnings of the world. The seers of the past have nourished this desire for liberty and it has come to flower in America.

> As on Oblivion
> God laid the Corner Stone of Nature, which
> The Fabric of this world was reared upon,
> With such immeasurable grandeur rich
> And wonderful in glory—so did they
> Their Altar, built for Liberty, that Day.
>
> .   .   .   .
>
> This monumental Fane,
> As did the uncreated world in God's—
> Lived archetypal in the souls of men;
> Till, springing upward from the dim abodes
> Of thought, it stood, like Nature on the Night
> Of Chaos, wonderful—star-spangled—bright!
> And this is Freedom's Home—
> Adown whose sculpture-columned aisles there rolls—

(Peopling, with living Thought, the years to come—)
Man's eloquence in thunders!—to all souls,
Like an inspired Rhapsodist, sublime,
Speaking Life's Cyclic Poem through all time.[67]

A further suggestion concerning Chivers' belief in his own duties as a poet is contained in the final stanza quoted; it is clear that Chivers is one of those who voice "Life's Cyclic Poem." When it is understood that liberty and divinity are prime essentials to that Poem, Chivers' attempts in these longer poems become more meaningful. He must continue the tradition of Doers and Sayers, in Emerson's words, by his praise and evocation of past heroes and eternal principles. In his selection of those heroes in "The Mighty Dead" we, in the perspective of a hundred years, may wonder at his sense of proportion. Milton and Shakespeare are suitable in our view, but it is of interest to note that Chivers' genius deserts him when he attempts to praise these two; he cannot achieve here the intensity which kindles throughout his continuing praises of Shelley, "The Israfel among the Sons of Song," or even the intimacy which marks his evocation of Byron. The latter two poets have been accorded respected places in the ranks of those who have sought liberty's ends, and the reader of Chivers has been prepared for their inclusion here by numerous shorter lyrics of praise. The nineteenth century would approve of the presence of Edward Young; Chivers raises him up because of his concern for "Life, Death, Immortality," eternal subject matter to the far-reaching mind of Chivers. The inclusion of Felicia Hemans is an indication of her contemporary popularity, although she has been virtually forgotten today; Chivers quotes from her poetry many times in his shorter pieces. Here the reader begins to understand that the listing of heroes in "The Mighty Dead" is dictated as much by Chivers' admiration of the effect each poet had upon him, as by standards set by history or contemporary opinion.

Certainly the inclusion of Andrew Jackson to stand alongside Washington, as well as the brief note on General Harrison, indicates this further. Perhaps it is this purposefully random quality about the work which helps make it one of Chivers' better long poems. Here he had a theme which meant much to him, and he was able to use a favorite six-line stanza to present separate images which the theme would hold together.

In June of 1856, the town fathers of Washington, Georgia, asked their resident poet to prepare a Fourth of July poem to be read at the local celebration. Chivers replied that the request did not give him time to prepare adequately; so the townspeople missed what would have been a fascinating performance. He did manage to write the poem, however, regretting that "much of [its] charm is lost . . . for the want of the voice of the Nuncio." [68] His *Birth-Day Song of Liberty* would have indeed been an oration, for its theme drew twenty-nine stanzas of twenty lines each from Chivers. The occasion demanded treatment of America's success in the Revolution, of her ideals of liberty. Chivers offers this, but his primary emphasis is less upon the details of that struggle than upon his belief that God had directed it, preparing America to be the home of the "Christ-Freedom." His belief is confirmed as he watches Europe's monarchies fall one by one, and he eulogizes the movement of freedom everywhere.

> Now the Olympian thunders no longer shall rattle
>   Their chains on the summit of Heaven's proud Hill;
> Nor the clarion of War call the Gods down to battle,
>   For the Angel of Peace walks in triumph here still.
> Thus the chain that once clanked round the limbs of the angel
>   On the Caucasus-Rock, by the Prophet is riven;
> For the lips of the Lord spoke that withering Evangel
>   Which smote down to Hell the Usurper from Heaven.
> Now the last solemn swing of the Death-bell goes tolling,
>   From the watchtowers of Freedom, across the deep sea,
> For the Tyrant's swift death, like an ocean-wave rolling
>   Through the Land of the Beautiful, the Land of the Free. [69]

Not a unique belief, and certainly appropriate to the occasion, Chivers' certainty of America's destiny was a genuine one. Writing always of the ideal in his poetry, he could reserve his hatred of abolitionists and his sectional feeling for his prose and evoke here the "Freeman's Thor-Hammer" with which all might build the strength of freedom everywhere.

Such was Chivers' concern with the theme of liberty, of freedom, always closely associated with the presence of divinity in its evokers and in its leaders. In "Ganymede," a poem which he identified as having been "Grounded on an actual occurrence," [70] he describes a mystical experience from his early youth, in which, inspired by the glory of his land, he rides to the mountain tops, "Like God's great Prophet," and in the moment of his ecstasy is inspired by two emotions: the love of Beauty in women and the adulations of America and her chief defender, Washington. This experience is emblematic of the themes which continued to inspire him. He writes often of America as God's New Jerusalem, and the primary characteristic of that Jerusalem is always liberty, just as he is always its prophet.

Keeping his Southern sentiments regarding slavery for expression in his prose, he spoke in large terms of the nature of liberty, of the magnificence and destiny of his country, and of the strength of her heroes. He writes in a declamatory style, one which requires strong emotional participation by the reader if the poem is to be successful. That style he reserved almost entirely for such subjects as we have been treating here, and it might well have been enhanced by Chivers' own reading of the poetry. If such a conclusion seems to require too much supposition, then it is at least safe to conclude that Chivers' poetic theory was in part moulded by his consciousness of America's oratorical tradition. When the theme was right, he could break forth with large emotional statements of what he regarded as Eternal Truth, voiced in the tones of the evangelist.

Since America's past seems to contain many events provocative of emotional reaction, it might be hoped that Chivers made use of the American background as natural, national subject matter. He had traveled in the American West, and several of his poems bear date lines of "Beyond the Mountains" and "Cherokee Nation." Unfortunately, he went no further than most of his contemporaries in his treatment of the American Indian or of the landscape about him, for no poem shows that he profited particularly from his visit in the West.

In "The 'Falling Garden' " dated "St. Louis 1833," Chivers summarizes much of what was being said by American poets and American critics about their land. Like Bryant in "The Prairies," Chivers stands before a natural scene which evokes certain speculations within him. He looks upon an Indian burial mound, wondering who these people were, how long they have been buried, what their history was, and so on. After his questioning Chivers decides, "America should be reckoned old, / To know thy race is run!"[71] Here the Indian serves as symbol of the age of the continent, and offers to the poet a subject matter which is sufficiently aged to permit competition with the romantic antiquities of Eng-

190 ·

land and Europe. The American poet felt he had no ruins and no castles, no history, in short, out of which he might write. Just as Cooper moulded Scott's form to include the American experience of the frontier, so Chivers here appears to be reaching into the available American past for subject matter which might provoke romantic and suggestive antiquity.

Had Chivers continued in such a vein, he might well have produced authentic American experience. But unfortunately he was not temperamentally equipped to treat of America's background in any but romantic, distant terms. "Malavolti,"[72] for example, records the hero's death at the Alamo, but there is no attempt on Chivers' part to make the fort's defense anything but a Byronic, narrative adventure-romance. Nor is there detail of the wilderness through which he must have traveled to reach St. Louis; his poems from his Western trip deal with his fond memories of the home left behind, but not with the land of the people around him.

The American Indian did provide him with certain materials, however, although Chivers always viewed him as an exotic. He was conscious, to be sure, of America's need for national expression, but he found himself unable to evolve the realistic scene, the authentic detail, which was necessary. As a result, Chivers' poems on the Indian do not contribute much to America's heritage.

One group of poems ostensibly makes use of the Indian as subject, but usually he is little more than a vehicle for a larger purpose. "Nacoochee," the title poem of the 1837 volume, is representative. Chivers began with a combination of several "Indian" legends, each involving a heroine who dies with her lover or to protect him.[73] The legends hardly seem particular or even native; they have the flavor of countless others which are more romantic than antiquarian. But the valley of Nacoochee was there, in White County in Georgia, and all records indicate its beauty. Chivers would not miss such subject matter, and the result of his knowledge of the myth and, presumably, his visit to the valley, is a poem only superficially concerned with the Indian. Nacoochee herself becomes a symbol of holy love existing, temporarily, upon Earth. At the climax of the poem she is carried to Heaven by the Angel of Death. Her lover, Ostenee, seeks her as the vehicle of ideal love; before the poem concludes Ostenee has become Chivers and Nacoochee Chivers' recurrent symbol of the ideal. He was to use this myth of the earthly paradise again in *Atlanta*.

But an earthly paradise is not the background America provided or even the habitat of the Indian. At the opening of the poem Ostenee's father is characterized thus:

> [the] old chief stood upon the sand,
> Like copper sculptured into majesty!
> For on his dusky brow there sate command,
> And on his lips sublime austerity!
> And on his cheeks there sate, convulsed, the sea
> Of that dark passion of his heart within,
> That changed upon his lips tempestuously,
> As if his soul were cradled into sin
> By those long waving years that made him ghostly thin![74]

This is hardly a view of the American Indian. It could as well be from pseudo-Italian melodrama, which, indeed, "Nacoochee" would be were it not for two things: Chivers' own technique of description and his symbolism, both of which are discussed elsewhere. The Cherokee legend has been submerged beneath Chivers' preoccupation with the earthly Eden.

The hint of the sinful character of the pagan Indian in the above description of Ostenee's father, is belied in another poem, "The Chickamauga Indian's Conversion,"[75] in which Chivers traces the story of an Indian sachem's son who, after his father is killed in battle, is taken away by his mother and raised to revenge his father's death upon the white man. But suddenly, "between his soul and heaven, / A cloud as white as snow, was driven,"[76] and he becomes a Christian. That the process of conversion is not fully explained is clear; perhaps this is so because Chivers' point was not the method but the fact of conversion. The Indian is susceptible to a sense of sin, and thus can be Christianized. Such a view was not unknown among American theologians, but that it should be offered by a Georgian, whose state had been freed of Indian troubles only in 1832, is interesting.[77]

Chivers was apparently aware also of the emotions of the Indians as they were dispossessed and forced further west. In "The Last Arrow"[78] Yanassa, the only remaining survivor before the attacking white men, pleads for destructive strength as he strings his last arrow. The couplets of the poem do not permit the swift rush of narrative that would be necessary to capitalize on such a situation, however, and the result is strangely static. It also sinks to one of Chivers' lowest points of anticlimax: Yanassa speaks, as he seats the arrow, "I plucked it from an eagle as he flew / Up to the sun— which no one else could do!"[79]

In such poems Chivers is attempting to create narrative poetry. His mottoes give notice of his intentions: Campbell's "Gertrude of Wyoming," Chateaubriand's "Atala," Byron's "Corsair." He is taken with the problem of creating an absorbing plot, and in his attempt to devise suitable trickery and climax, he reached much too far. The result is complete unreality, even of impression. The action overcomes common sense, and Chivers' verse suffers badly from neglect. Chivers eventually realized that he did not have the ability to write sustained narrative verse; in the Preface to *Atlanta* he says as much, and offers a quite logical alternative, a series of short set pieces, held together by common mood and tone.

In virtually no other group of his poems does he attempt this narrative form. He did not have the power to focus his vital imagination upon a complex and distant goal, and he knew it.

It might be said further that Chivers, while himself a product of America's aspirations and culture, could not speak of his own land in terms which identify it. His world was an inward one, and the movements and color of his outward experience were drawn into that inner, imaginative world where all things were ideal, where all things were greater than life size. Chivers was too busy experimenting with the details of this apocalyptical domain to find inspiration in the realities of his own land. To him, reality was not one of human movement or factual experience, but of the larger concepts of Liberty, Freedom, Divinity, and Destiny. Chivers had an inward eye, not an outward one.

THE PHYSICAL WORLD

It has been said that Chivers' finest poetry came not from the stimulation of local, physical phenomena or experience, but from his ability to rise from the earth to a world of emotional identification with vaster forces, larger vistas, and non-personal experience in which Chivers, the man, is subordinate to Chivers, the identifier.

Such a background may be exemplified further by consideration of the place that physical nature holds in his poetry. Those poets whose influence shows most clearly in his poetry are not widely known as pictorial artists; Keats alone is concerned with the use

· 193

of intimate detail to produce the larger effect, and Chivers did not absorb enough of Keats to understand sensory lines such as "The hare limp'd trembling through the frozen grass." Physical detail is very scarce in Chivers' poetry, and when it is found, it consists largely of such romanticized items as fawns, purple mountains, and misty glades. His use of the backdrop of nature may help in defining his aims and capabilities.

Most of his nature poems bear dates of composition from the early 1830's, many of them written from "The West." The result is that a tone of sweet remembrance not infrequently mists the vistas he describes, where

> . . . emerald groves o'erlook thy shadowy aisles,
> Where verdant twilight lends sweet day repose.[80]

Under such terms we can hardly expect suggestive or provocative detail; about the only time he admits closer views to his poetry is in "To a China Tree" (*N*, pp. 51-53), where he attempts to re-create the setting of his childhood home. He does not often avail himself of the country surrounding his Georgia home, and, typically, "Tuccoa," a description of a particularly striking falls in Stephens County, Georgia, is built about a metaphysical metaphor comparing the stream to a "wandering vein of youthful blood"[81] in the bosom of a young virgin; such terms are hardly Wordsworthian. In his later poetry he does utilize several Indian river names (*Coosa, Tallapoosa*) but his interest in them derives from their fitness as exotic feminine rhymes rather than from their pictorial quality. The same suggestive romanticism is present in a famous stanza from "Rosalie Lee":

> Many mellow Cydonian Suckets,
>   Sweet apples, anthosmial, divine,
> From the Ruby-rimmed Berylline buckets,
>   Star-gemmed, lily-shaped, hyaline—
> Like that sweet golden goblet found growing
>   On the wild emerald Cucumber-tree—
> Rich, brilliant, like Chrysoprase blowing—
>   I then brought to my Rosalie Lee—
>   To my lamb-like Rosalie Lee—
>   To my Dove-like Rosalie Lee—
> To my beautiful, dutiful Rosalie Lee.[82]

Chivers was correct in his reference to a cucumber-tree, and that use, when added to the following detail of Georgian grapes, provides virtually the only pictorial image Chivers secured from his own wanderings through the South.

The description that follows is in many ways typical of Chiversian description at its best; there are enough details to provide visual aid to the reader, and the suggestive aura which surrounds the whole is useful in its context. In another way it is climactic, for the isle described is the Eden Isle, the terrestrial Eden, which in Chivers' mind necessarily evoked the most provocative detail of natural beauty.

> A flock of wild Swans, from the Jasper reeds,
> With side-long wings, rose up, darkening the sun,
> Whose clamorous shouts, redoubled by the Hills,
> Filled the wide Heavens with jubilations loud;
> And after circling on their snowy wings,
> Glinting the glory of the golden sun—
> Chequering the Lake with moving shadows—down
> They all descended, with Seraphic sail,
> On moveless wings, upon the lake again,
> Like living pearl, of Angels out of Heaven,
> Far out of reach of farthest shot of man,
> Floating among the reeds in jocund joy.
> Upon the sand, close by the water's edge,
> Where smote their little boat upon the shore,
> Clusters of luscious grapes were scattered round
> In prodigal profusion on the ground,
> And ebon Muscadines of lustrous black,
> Like drops of polished night, weighed down their vines,
> So, that, the cool lips of the crystal wave,
> Swayed by the presence of the noontide breeze,
> Lapped them with liquid kisses from the shore,
> Till they went dangling far away from land,
> Like little ebon barques upon the Lake.[83]

Such description cannot be classified as pictorial in the way some of Wordsworth's longer poems are, but the flavor of the early Keats is evident. I believe that Chivers made very little use of his eye as he composed, however, for the details above are not there as much for their pictorial quality as for their suggestiveness. Taken together they create an atmosphere which is necessary for the success of the poem.[84]

It is as though Chivers had translated the physical details of the world about him to a land where all is at once vague and yet vivid. He expects the reader to react with his senses, not his eyes, to such as the following:

> ... from the labyrinthine aisles of flowers,
> Upon the suckle-scented gales, shall flow
> The rich balsamic odours of the spring,
> And from the bare arms of the boughs, shall rain
> The luscious clusters, till their tones shall be
> As soft as the first audible steps of one
> Beloved, at the last meeting, heard at night.[85]

Odors represented as tones is typical of his description. Believing heaven to be a state of music, he could speak of odors, or colors, as though they radiated out from a given source in much the same way that a sound leaves its point of origin. Such radiation is necessarily not precise or defined, and little of Chivers' description is either. Vividness he could suggest through color, but again the description is impressionistic rather than detailed:

> Velvet moss of emerald lustre
> Laced the Rocks, dear Isabel!
> Where the Golden Grapes did cluster—
> Fare-thee-well!
> While the dazling emerald-glowing
> Of the leaves upon each tree,
> Verdant twilight there bestowing—
> Soothed the soul—farewell to thee![86]

It is a distant and exotic land Chivers has been describing; when he worked with details close at hand he was less successful, and seldom attempted such description unless it afforded him a stepping-off place, as it were, for philosophic or personal expression. "The Wilderness" finds him watching mountain streams cascade into a pleasant valley, where from "thyme enameled hills," he "Saw lordly oaks gigantic, / Throw twilight o'er the rills." The day passes, and soon the silence of the night "opened worlds before me, / Which had no time for sin."[87] He has used the natural scene, described in romantic terms, as inspiration for personal fears and griefs. There is no delight in the scene for its own sake. In yet another poem he builds a woodland setting for some fifty lines, glorying in its beauty, the true purpose of the description becomes evident when he suddenly asks if such earthly beauty must not postulate an even greater heavenly beauty awaiting him after death.[88]

His tone is normally quiet and calm in such descriptions, turning to the more exclamatory when he draws his parallel or asks his philosophic question. Occasionally, however, he does not pause to build up the tone, but begins at once in a declamatory style. For example, many of Chivers' poems which utilize nature or this earth only incidentally, in terms of a larger purpose, resemble "God," an early effort which also indicates something of his moderate pantheism:

> Thou speakest Thy language through this universe!
> Thy voices, through this world, are borne on winds!
> With sunbeams Thou dost write creation's verse!
> Thy songs are writ in stars—Thy stars on minds!
> And on the sea, and on the shore, at morn and even!
> Thy music, rolling spheres! Thy voices, songs in heaven!
> Thou art, oh God!—Thou makest this world thy rest!
> Thy words are thunders!—breath, each morning's breeze!
> Thy smiles are suns!—Thou art from east to west!
> Thou movest down rivers! Thou dost roll through seas!
> Thy name's Eternity! Thyself man's soul!
> Thy house all space!—Thine everlasting whole![89]

Nature, the earth, became to Chivers a visible sign of God's presence and love; from it, man might learn the truth of himself. As early as 1834 he writes of "the book of nature"[90] and of its demand for close study. Chivers never applied himself fully to the transcendental task of recognizing God in nature, usually being content to use the spring time of the year, in a most orthodox fashion, as symbol of the eventual resurrection of man. He addresses Spring quietly:

> Thou art an emblem of Man's resurrection
> From the cold embrace of the silent tomb;
> When his bright soul, with all the flower's perfection,
> Shall meet his body in immortal bloom.[91]

Such thinking is typical of Chivers in that it illustrates his method of using a particular scene or experience as something from which he can move, philosophically or emotionally, toward a further elaboration. When this movement is philosophic, his success is perhaps limited; when it is emotional, he manages the transition more smoothly. Stirred by the sight of the Mississippi, he does not detail the scene, counting on the reader's common understanding of the river's strength and power, but instead uses a metaphor suggestive of its fertile nature as he calls to the river:

> Oh! speak from the North where thy travels begun,
> And tell me the first with thyself to unite,
> Who walked down the valleys like lovers at night,
> Till thou, with thy freedom majestic and deep,
> Bestrode like an emperor walking in sleep.[92]

As the poem progresses, the Mississippi becomes the symbol of America's strength and power, again by extension of the original scene.

It is not often that Chivers can keep the first person out of his descriptions. Once, at least, he manages to suggest his own participation in the scene without becoming obtrusive; he is moved by his first sight of the ocean.

> Madness is thy chief delight,
> Sometimes transports intervene—
> Oftener we explore thy might,
> Oftener are thy beauties seen!
>
> Breakers! cease thy ceaseless roar—
> Foaming cease,—oh! frantic deep!
> Battle thou with winds no more,
> Calmly chide thy waves to sleep!
>
> Crystal-glittering ocean, cease!
> Struggling with thy tossing breast,—
> Yearning long for silence—peace!
> Ocean! let me, let me rest!
>
> Evening wanes!—declining sun
> Lingers languid, clothing thee!
> Shedding glory, pregnant one,
> Over all!—immortal sea![93]

Chivers certainly was conscious of the landscape about him, but when he transmitted that landscape in poetry it automatically took on tones and details which remind the reader of the later generation of English romantic poets rather than the earlier; Wordsworth, in particular, seems absent from such a description as is found in "Invocation to Spring," one of Chivers' more successful attempts at romantic atmosphere:

> The green blades of the grass
> Lean over on the margin of the brook,
>   And on themselves, beneath, in its clear glass,
> Shadowed at noontide, ever tireless look;
> While their green banks above, whereon they grow,
> Seem resting on their images below.
>   The golden humming-bird,
> At intervals, among the blossoms flits,
>   Chirping, as soft its lulling wings are heard—
> Swift-darting, glinting back the sun in fits—
> Humming caresses to each flower it meets,
> While rifling it of all its odorous sweets.[94]

The same is true of the following:

> Down in the acromatic streams,
> Meeting the luminiferous beams
> With which the air forever teems
> The golden mail of minnows gleams.[95]

But Wordsworth does appear in Chivers' poetry, although not in such a way as to indicate that Chivers profited greatly from his study of him.

"Agnus" is a bathetic story of a young lamb who strangles to death while pulling Chivers' sister Adaline about in a tiny wagon he had constructed. It is full of Wordsworthian descriptions of nature, and seems to be modeled rather carefully after that poet's "Lucy Gray"; Chivers calls it "A Pastoral," and it is apparently in a sense of domesticity that he uses the word. The manuscript of the poem indicates that Chivers was not pleased with it, for the revisions are numerous and contradictory. Chivers could not loose his genius when restricted by Wordsworth's simple diction and sometimes prosaic subject matter.[96] And although the title page of *The Lost Pleiad* and of *Eonchs of Ruby* has a motto from Wordsworth, there is no evidence of his influence there or on any other volume beyond the rather vague acceptance of nature as teacher and sometimes as symbol.

Occasionally Chivers achieved a light, gentle touch with a tone of happy remembrance dominating a romantically distant scene. In "Georgia Waters" native details help achieve an intimate atmosphere.

On thy waters, thy sweet valley waters,
   Oh! Georgia! how happy were we!
When thy daughters, thy sweet-smiling daughters,
   Once gathered sweet-william for me.
Oh! thy wildwood, thy dark shady wildwood
   Had many bright visions for me;
For my childhood, my bright rosy childhood
   Was cradled, dear Georgia! in thee.
On thy mountains, thy green purple mountains,
   The seasons are waiting on thee;
And thy fountains, thy clear crystal fountains,
   Are making sweet music for me.
Oh! thy waters, thy sweet valley waters,
   Are dearer than any to me;
For thy daughters, thy sweet smiling daughters,
   Oh! Georgia! give beauty to thee.[97]

The sources of Chivers' inspiration may well have begun in the beauty of the physical world, for his Eden Isle is clearly a physical paradise, but he took that inspiration within himself, heightened and exaggerated the detail, covering it with an atmospheric suggestiveness reminiscent of the early Keats, and produced poetry that is neither pictorial nor exact in its imagery. He would explain this transformation of the natural world to one of the imagination as revealing the *true* nature of its beauty, not the superficial, so that it might be "seen in all its crystalline entireness."[98] Poetry which revealed such beauty was the opposite of indefinite. "There are some Poems," he said, "whose imagery leaves upon the brain an indistinct impression, precisely because they possess no other merits than those of nebulosity which are recognized 'through a glass darkly.' But what has this to do with pure Beauty?"[99] It may well be that his own suggestive imagery conjured up in Chivers' mind something other than the indistinctness apparent at first glance. In any case, to achieve "pure Beauty" was part of his aim, and he utilized the natural world as a starting point from which he might abstract that Beauty.

CONVENTIONAL LYRICISM AND DIDACTICISM

By this time it has become obvious that Chivers' value to the student of American literature lies largely in those areas in which he attempted to extend the boundaries of the subject matter, diction, and form of his poetry. His continual search for Beauty, in its manifold forms, led him to an inward world in which he might create the ideal, perfect world which he dreamed of. This desire to perfect found expression in a variety of ways in the poetry of Romanticism, both in America and England. Chivers' own conception of it depended upon certain theological beliefs, as we have seen.

But Chivers was not only an experimenter who achieved success often enough to secure a place for himself in our literature; he was also a typical product of the society in nineteenth century America and of that society's habits of expression and publication. It has been noted that there was a particular form of public Renaissance in the middle years of the 1800's, a form which demanded and got public participation to an extent which has not been evident since. One of the primary methods of expression which that public utilized was the literary journal, the magazine of good reading, devoted either to a particular sectarian cause, or simply to the purveying of literature which might both entertain and elevate its audience. Editors established their own list of "correspondents" who might be depended upon to send poetic efforts regularly; the bottom of the odd column of many a magazine was rounded out by an occasional lyric, sonnet, or elegy. These correspondents varied from the more established poets, who might expect to receive a nominal sum for their efforts,[100] to the anonymous and sub-literary authors who sought their living in other fields but who recognized the production of poetry as a sign of culture, a token of social position, and, occasionally, as the vehicle for personal expression. Their names are difficult to trace today, and their productions have little intrinsic value. To a cultural historian, however, the mass of their verses offers evidence of the temper of mind of those years, of the public interests, and of America's growing interest in her own nascent powers of expression.

Occasionally a poet rises from these ranks to offer further evidence that the creative spirit was indeed abroad in the land, and one of this number was Chivers. It is necessary to emphasize that the magazine market for which Chivers wrote demanded comparatively little in the way of individual expression or unique format. That he went beyond the familiar lyric or the quickly forgotten occasional poem is testimony to the creative impulse within him, for the magazines did not demand it, and in no way was he dependent upon his writing for financial support. He was a poet, and for all the uneven criticism or more frequently silence which greeted his verse, for all the lack of selectivity of both editor and public, he must express himself.

But to say that he removed himself completely from the realm of the magazine column-filler type of poem would be incorrect. He had enough money to publish his own work in book form, and depended upon that outlet from 1832 to 1858; but within the boundaries of this period Chivers sent poem after poem to the literary journals, to his local paper, the *Georgia Citizen,* to established magazines, the *Knickerbocker, Graham's Magazine,* the *Ladies' National Magazine,* or to such as *The Univercoelum, or Spiritual Philosopher,* A. J. Davis' magazine devoted to spiritualism. And he was most anxious that his efforts be published. Poetry was not incidental to Chivers.

It would be comforting to be able to say that he accommodated himself to the desires and standards of his magazine audience, to insist that his less effective efforts were the product of a conscious restricting of his power. Such is not the case. Although Chivers was able to choose his best work for book publication, he was not a good critic of his own work. An enthusiast, he would defend a poor poem almost as readily as a successful one. His themes in this work vary with his mood, but he was certainly aware of the public demand for sentimental love lyrics and occasional pieces.

Those poems which concern themselves with themes of love and beauty, beauty in the orthodox sense, are among the least successful he ever wrote. The "Songs of the Heart" section of his second volume, *Conrad and Eudora,* a collection whose main importance to Chivers lay in the title verse tragedy, testifies to the fact that he did not separate the public's demands from his own desires; the majority of these poems are standard, orthodox pseudo-lyricism, touched only occasionally by the genius he was to show later. Following as they do his early, extremely personal verse in *The Path of Sorrow,* they indicate that Chivers had become conscious of himself as a poet, and probably turned to the contemporary journals for inspiration and pattern, not objecting in the slightest to the essentially temporal nature of the poems he found there. They testify further that Chivers was very much a part of the public Renaissance of the nineteenth century, for, were they inserted carelessly in a typical gift book of poetry (a form of collection which reached its peak about 1850, when the average year saw the publication of sixty such volumes)[101] it would be difficult to find any individual touch to identify them as Chivers'. The influence of Felicia Hemans, an extremely popular English poetess whose work was widely known in America, can be found everywhere, in his sentimental themes, his love lyrics, his romantic descriptions of nature, full of "sylvan vales" and soft-eyed fawns, but no testimony can be offered that it was her work in particular that led Chivers on, for almost any journal of the day contained the same sort of poetry.[102]

Many of these poems concern themselves with descriptions of the beauty of a woman:

> Sweet ladye! my fair dove! I give thee praise,
> And love thee, gentlest!
>
> .   .   .   .
>
> Thy snow white lids, beneath each darksome lash
> Protect thine eyes, which are my fancy's heaven!
> Through which thy soul doth now sedately flash,
> Like fitful lightnings on some April even.[103]

Such verse as this does not indicate the later and less conventional Chivers. While suitable for incidental reading, it will not attract the reader more than once. Most of these poems are vaguely personal, in that the narrative structure involves the speaker. They deal with his love for various women, all of whom are spoken to but never speak, or with Chivers' mother. Commonplace situations provide the necessary and usually artificial stimulus; the worship of a woman's physical beauty, his sorrow at parting, petitions for the love of a stranger passed in the street, even one castigating a woman's inconstancy—all are here.

First lines suggest the nature of this poetry: "Hear me, my love! thou art my soul," "Sweet ladye! time may change my outward form," "If the meeting be short, let the parting be tender," or "Thine eyes are bright, sweet lady love";[104] these poems are uniform in their orthodox romantic content and style, a romanticism which becomes soft and even sticky after a time. They are not Chivers at his best; they are Chivers trying to find himself as a poet, and practising with the contemporary forms and themes. Only infrequently does the later Chivers imagery come through:

Thou hast heard plaudits borne on morning's breeze,
When spring's jocundity went high as heaven;
And nature slumbered in her own alarm!
Thou hast now pinioned thought and wedded heaven!
Made God thy banquet, and got drunk on love!
Thou hast been sitting in some twilight bower,
When all thine energies were radiant suns;
And heard some vaulted rock respond thy voice.[105]

It was not often in his early magazine-style that Chivers tried to evoke the imagination. Usually his verse concerns itself with his personality as it reacts to given situations, and that reaction seldom provided a song for its own sake. "Medora of Ultramontane" is one of the few songs in his early work that provides imagery which hints of his later extensions beyond fact.

Come, hie o'er the mountains where deep rivers flow,
Come, hie where the red roses every day blow;
Come, go, where the wild valley maidens have eyes
As dark as the night, and as blue as the skies!
Come, go where their rose-leafy lips are so fine,
That angels would call them all cherubs divine;
Where songs, rapt in echoes, throw bliss over pain,—
Come, hear sweet Medora sing ultramontane.

Come, hie where their soft rosy blushes make love,
Come down on thy soul, like some charm from above!
Where virgin reproofs fall as soft from each tongue,
As down from a swan, that is tender and young—
Come, hie where the wild valley maidens are free,
As birds overcast with their love song and glee;
Whose soft silver notes cureth love sick and pain—
Come, hear sweet Medora sing ultramontane.[106]

The verse is in places rough, several of the images are trite, and one seems forced, but the final stanza line does suggest that later ability which Chivers had to a surprising degree, an ability which provided him with many and often startling images. Many of the poems of *Conrad and Eudora* are dated from the first years of the decade, and may have been disinterred to fill out the volume. Our interest in the collection is dictated by the fact that it contains so many of his less successful poems, poems which I have chosen to call magazine-filler verse.

It was through his early practice with such love lyrics as those which have been described that Chivers prepared himself for future success. "Rosalie Lee," one of the most typical and successful of these later lyrics, depends for its effect upon the evocation of apparently standard romantic detail, but arranged so as to produce an other-worldly atmosphere, an atmosphere which draws much of its effect from rhythm. The Beauty he describes here is not only that of a woman. She becomes part of another world.

> On the banks of the yellow lilies,
>   Where the cool wave wanders by,
> All bedamasked with Daffodillies,
>   And the bee-beset Crowtie;
> More mild than the Paphian Luna
>   To her nude Nymphs on the Sea,
> There dwelt, with her milk-white Una,
>   My beautiful Rosalie Lee—
>   My high-born Rosalie Lee—
>   My child-like Rosalie Lee—
> My beautiful, dutiful Rosalie Lee.
>
> More coy than the wild Goldfinches,
>   When they hunt for the Butterfly,
> Which the dew of the morning quenches,
>   In the psychical month of July;
> Like an opaline Dove's neck chiming
>   Cherubic beauty for me,
> Were her ovaline arms in their rhyming,
>   Of my beautiful Rosalie Lee—
>   Of my lamb-like Rosalie Lee—
>   Of my Heaven-born Rosalie Lee—
> Of my beautiful, dutiful Rosalie Lee.
>
> .   .   .   .
>
> Through the Valley of Avalon lonely,
>   By the light of the argentine Moon,
> From the presence that lived for her only
>   On the banks of the Rivers of Rune;
> Through the Star-Islands studding the Ether,
>   With the Angels that took her from me—
> (Though my soul in its sorrow went with her—)
>   Soared my beautiful Rosalie Lee—
>   Soared my Christ-like Rosalie Lee—
>   Soared my God-loved Rosalie Lee—
> Soared my beautiful, dutiful Rosalie Lee.[107]

There are extremes in such a poem; Chivers fully intended them, believing that by use of a constant and almost hypnotic rhythm and exotic diction he could utilize descriptive, romantic details to evoke the ideal of undefined and essentially impersonal beauty he admired.

"Eulalie" is more conventional in its form, but, like so many of his poems, offers images that are strangely effective:

As when the summer South
    A rose-bud doth dispart,
The lips of her sweet mouth
    Seem opened by her heart.
.   .   .   .

Mild as some breeze at noon—
    Soft as the pale cold light
Rained from the full-orbed moon
    Upon the down of night
.   .   .   .

Sweeter than voice of swan
    Upon some Summer sea,
Piling to Heaven, at dawn,
    His clarion melody.

For when she sings at night,
    The stars appear to me
To burn more Heavenly bright
    In her sweet symphony.

Soft words from off the caves
    Of her sweet lips now fall,
Like dew drops from the leaves
    Of roses—rhythmical.[108]

It is obvious that the woman whom Chivers describes never changes; it is the same image each time. He was stimulated to place her in a variety of situations, normally as subject for his more unusual rhythms and similes. Because of the constancy of the image presented, and of the repetition of certain details, his love lyrics seem all of a kind; the only distinguishing feature is the structure and rhythm of each poem.

One particular concept grew in Chivers' mind as he wrote such lyrics as we have examined, and that was that the beauty of a woman's song symbolized Heaven; believing that Heaven was a state of music, his worship was inspired by song. His repeated use of the concept of Israfel, "who has the most melodious voice of all God's creatures," to symbolize this state testifies to his belief:

> My swift-winged soul is driven
> Upon thy song to heaven![109]

Other than his ecstatic reactions to song, only a scattering of poems celebrating the physical beauty of woman need be noted to complete this study of Chivers' use of love and beauty as theme. Occasionally he was more sensuous than might be expected,[110] and at least once he achieved a unified picture:

> As graceful as the Babylonian willow
> Bending, at noontide, over some clear stream
> In Palestine, in beauty did she seem
> Upon the cygnet-down of her soft pillow;
> And now her breast heaved like some gentle billow
> Swayed by the presence of the full round moon—
> Voluptuous as the summer South at noon—
> Her cheeks as rosy as the radiant dawn,
> When heaven is cloudless! When she breathed, the air
> Around was perfume! Timid as the fawn,
> And meeker than the dove, her soft words were
> Like gentle music heard at night, when all
> Around is still—until the sound of care
> Was soothed, as noontime by some waterfall.[111]

Chivers is not at his best in this work. Limited by a preconceived subject, one which had definite conventional and romantic boundaries, he was unable to mould such material to his own delight in beauty; it is interesting to note that despite his assertion that poetry must speak of the truly beautiful and that God is Love, few of his poems on physical beauty or earthly love are successful. The earth was not the place for his genius, a fact which becomes immediately obvious when his instructive verse is examined. Chivers could create a mood or move the imagination, but he could not draw a picture or guide his reader.

Except in those poems which indicate his experiment with diction and rhythm, Chivers' essentially theological delight in Beauty apparently did not extend its inspirational powers to the physical beauty of women, nor to the orthodox concepts of romanticized love. Limited by his inexperience in the *Conrad and*

Eudora lyrics, and by defined and conventional romantic boundaries even when he attempted such themes in his later work, this poetry serves to link Chivers to the magazine poets of his age rather than raise him above them. Physical beauty or earthly love did not inspire his genius; the earth did not inspire his genius.

His connection with these magazine poets becomes even clearer through study of his instructive verse. As has been suggested, Chivers failed to understand how argument might be conveyed in verse, and he was seldom able to bring his wild flights back to earth by attaching a moral at the conclusion of the poem. His poetry is personal rather than directive; while most of the scenes and experiences he writes of he believes to be universal in appeal and in detail, he would persuade implicitly, by the recreation of his own delight in the experience rather than by explanation and argument.

Yet because he believed himself to be a prophet, a seer, he would attempt instruction occasionally. There were examples enough about him, reaching a climax in the immense success of Longfellow's "benign didacticism" in the 1850's.[112] Many of Chivers' instructive poems propose vaguely sentimental Christian and humanitarian concepts. "Religion" provides a typical and unfortunate example, with such tortured homilies as "For where thou art, there can we find relief, / As, when relief is sought, there thou art found!"[113] Such didacticism is not Chivers' forte, possibly because his own religious belief was so entirely emotional in its expression.[114] He coaxes the reader to forego earthly pleasures in hope for others more divine, and consoles man with the thought that God will aid his puny might in time of trouble,[115] but he seldom does so with success.

Instructive verse of this sort appears throughout Chivers' publishing career, seldom impressing with its facility or its reasoning. A poem published in *Virginalia*, "Words to the Unwise," is successful only within the extremely limited effects he desired; his directive poetry is never large in scope, never undertaking to explain any but the simplest rules or truths:

> Ye have no echoes in your souls
>   Of Heaven's celestial music-tones;
> Such Angel-language never rolls
>   Out of your hearts, ye simple ones!

· · · · · · ·

The experience of Earth's early youth—
    The foregone Ages—all combine
To teach thee that undying Truth
    Which made even Christ on earth Divine.

If thou wouldst live in endless youth—
    Like Angels through Eternity—
Be thou the unembodied Truth,
    And thou shalt never, never die.

Fathom the depths of thine own soul,
    And then wilt others understand;
Who knows himself, will have the whole
    Of human Knowledge at command.[116]

There is little evidence in Chivers' poetry that he was concerned with ethical or social concepts. Whatever instruction he might offer would be in theological terms. Occasionally, by curbing his own emotional response to religion, Chivers could succeed in producing a controlled theological statement:

Lord! like the desert fount that flowed
Fast by the feet of Hagar bowed,
Thirsting amid the desert wild
She wandered with her outcast child—
Oh! pour upon me thy soft beams,
And circle me with heavenly streams.

  .   .   .   .

If, from the chaos of old Night,
The stars were whispered into flight!
If, when another word was given,
The sun stood on the hills of Heaven!
And if these things were made for me,
Lord! tell me what to do for thee!

  .   .   .   .

If night doth prophesy to night
The language of the morning light;
And if the morning doth appear
To whisper to the evening near;
And if these things pour forth to thee,
Lord! what should not be said by me!

Are not the songsters of the grove
Vocal with thy redeeming love?

Are not the burning stars of even
The members of thy church in heaven?
And if they are but lamps to me,
Lord! teach me how to worship thee.[117]

Chivers never came closer to orthodox homilies. Much of his value for us today lies in the fact that his temperament led him away from the moralizing characteristic of so much of the magazine poetry of the 1800's. Neither conventional images of earthly love and beauty nor didactic conclusions interested Chivers for long unless he could translate them into his own particular idiom of Divine Beauty and Truth, and when he achieves this translation he removes himself from the concerns of the majority of magazine "correspondents" and becomes a poet of true worth.

Chapter Five

✑ Technique

Perhaps the measure of Chivers' success with the themes most typical of his poetry may be in part determined by an examination of his theory of poetry, and his understanding of the duties and desires of the poet. Not an analytical critic or a particularly acute surveyor of the contemporary literary scene, he wrote few objective reviews, most of his expression on literary theory occurring in the Prefaces to *Nacoochee, Memoralia,* and *Atlanta.* Very often such discussion becomes a defense of his own poetry.

Chivers did not greatly modify his poetic beliefs as expressed early in *The Path of Sorrow;* his later theories are, in large part, developments of his determination in 1832 to write from the world of his imagination,[1] and his certainty that the true poet was divinely inspired.[2] As he wrote and experimented further, he came to change the terms of these theories; but they remain, in principle.

One of his earliest decisions was no doubt brought about by his own distress and grief over his first marriage. He will sing, he says, only of grief; there is reason to believe that his early tragedy focused his desire to write poetry. He had been happy, and indeed in early youth had composed a number of incidental verses, but after a period of mourning, grief "tuned up [his] heart strings to music again."[3] Chivers' belief that sorrow could draw the poetry from him was never changed; *The Lost Pleiad* (1845) is a volume which testifies to the seemingly endless variety he could achieve upon the single theme of death and sorrow, and while such melancholia was quite in keeping with Romantic tendencies, it is obvious that he felt more than a theoretical motivation.

But even the most depressed of poets needs must find relief from such woe, and Chivers' most important interpretation of his calling arose from the necessity to find another outlet, another world in which he could create all that this one, he believed, had failed to supply him with. The mystical world of the terrestrial Eden and the emotional evocations of Heaven which are such an important part of his poetry provided the necessary outlet. His understanding of that world came from within himself; so there was no need to square it with the reality he saw about him. He speaks often enough of the horrors of this world, of loss, death, and loneliness, but never does he evoke Hell; his glance moved only upward (if inward), a move which he once developed a metaphor to describe:

As the penitent Pilgrim, on his way to Mount Zion, reclines, at the noontide hour of the day, from the burning heat of the tropical sun, in the cool refreshing shadow of the Rock of Rimmon, so does my wearied soul hide itself away into an ecstasy underneath the odoriferous dove-wings of the Divine Queen of Heaven.[4]

It is not difficult to understand the motivation for such a hiding away; the world would not receive his poetry in the manner he believed it deserved; his happiness with his second wife hardly compensated for the death of four of his children; and as a Southern Transcendentalist, he found himself out of place in both North and South.

The result of his inward-turning is such a poem as "The Poet of Love," in which he attempts to explain his source of inspiration and to exhibit its effects at the same time:

> The Poet of Love receives divine ovation;
>   Not only from Angels' hands while here on earth,
> But all the Ages echo back with salutation
>   The trumpet of the Skies in praises of his worth;
>   And all the islands of the Sea
>   Of the vast immensity
>   Echo the music of the Morns
>   Blown through the Corybantine Horns
>   Down the dark vistas of the reboantic Norns,
>   By the great Angel of Eternity,
>   Thundering, *Come to me! come to me!*
>
> From the inflorescence of his own high soul
>   The incense of his Eden-song doth rise,
> Whose golden river of pure redolence doth roll
>   Down the dark vistas of all time in melodies—

> Echoing the Islands of the Sea
> Of the vast immensity,
> And the loud music of the Morns
> Blown through the Conchimarian Horns
> Down the dark vistas of the reboantic Norns,
> By the great Angel of Eternity,
> Thundering, *Come to me! come to me!*
>
> With the white lightnings of his still small voice,
> Deep as the thunders of the azure Silence—
> He makes dumb the oracular Cymbals with their noise,
> Till BEAUTY flourish Amaranthine on the Islands
> Of the loud tumultuous Sea
> Of the vast immensity,
> Echoing the music of the Morns
> Blown through the Chrysomelian Horns
> Down the dark vistas of the reboantic Norns
> By the great Angel of Eternty,
> Thundering, COME TO ME! COME TO ME![5]

The excesses of the poem are perhaps annoying; yet it is successful, I believe, in the effect Chivers desired to create, for not only does it explain an important theme, but also it attempts to recreate the emotional state of the poet as he experienced that theme.

Furthermore, it exhibits almost all of the theories Chivers developed in prose regarding his theory of poetry. Chivers drew a distinction between the poem as such and experience as such which modern critics have found valid, and he would answer the critic who objected to the excesses of such a poem as this by saying, "There is nothing in the world that is not equivalent in brightness to the poetical manifestations of it. People too often mistake the *relations* of things for the *things* themselves."[6] That is, the experience he creates here was, to him, the experiencer, just as frantic and bright as the poem in which he tries to explain it. Many of Chivers' poems are of the same sort; seldom have we found him as interested in the "brightness" of "things," although their brightness is insisted upon, as in the actual experience of his appreciation of that brightness. A nice distinction, perhaps, but a necessary one, and one which helps to explain Chivers' statement that all true poetry is dramatic, for at first glance his poetry appears to be singularly undramatic. What he means is that the true poet describes not the scene before him, but his experience in reacting to it. Because of his participation in the scene it becomes dramatic, animated, although the drama is usually implicit.

"The Poet of Love," by its very title, suggests further explanations. God, he believed, was Love. The true poet partakes of that Love and attempts to express it. In what may it be found? In the poet himself. What inspires it? His answer helps explain his poetry:

> . . . Poetry is the soul of his nature, whereby, from communing with the beauties of this earth, he is capable of giving birth to other beings brighter than himself; and of lifting up his spirit to the presence of those things which he shall enjoy in another state; and which he manifests to *this* [world] through the instrumentality of certain words and sentences melodiously concatenated; and such as correspond with the definite and wise configurations of the mouth in the communication of thought through language.[7]

I very much doubt that any poet writing in the South in 1837, except perhaps Poe, had developed his own aesthetic so completely; Chivers' beliefs may not be suitable for the twentieth century, or, for that matter, popular in the early nineteenth, but they were definite and defined. We have grown away from any theory of poetry which depends upon inspiration of such a seemingly nebulous character; Chivers was close to it, and he depended upon it to write poetry. He said, in the Preface to *Birth-Day Song of Liberty,*

> Inspired by that self-rewarding enthusiasm which always fills the heart with rapture—being the first-born Cherub of the soul's rapport with the infinite splendor of God—I composed the following Paean of Glory. . . .[8]

Sometimes his sense of this identification may have been self-induced. That is not as important as the fact that it *was* induced. Poetry was not a matter of incidental composition to Chivers; it was tied very closely to his deep belief in an after life which would compensate for the toils and turmoil of this one. So when he soars upward in his description of Heaven, he is tasting joys which, to him, were just as much reality as the earthly vistas about him.

But those earthly vistas were, as he notes, important to evoke the needed inspiration. And since the following development of his theory comes close to that expressed by Poe in *The Philosophy of Composition* (1846), it is necessary to point out that Chivers had established, to his own satisfaction, the basis of his later expression in the Preface to *Nacoochee* (1837): by communing with "beauties" he will be empowered to produce further beauty which will in turn produce a "lifting up [of] his spirit." I do not suggest that Poe derived his belief that poetry's province was that of beauty which produced "pleasurable elevation, of the soul" from Chivers, but that such similarity as exists here is further evidence of a more inclusive similarity of judgment and taste. Poe's language apparently impressed him, however, for Chivers depended more and more upon the word *beauty* to express his desires after Poe's statement was published.

Poe believed poetry should concern itself with beauty, not with passion or with truth; Chivers disagreed,[9] insisting that passion was an integral part of any poem and that Poe's poetry suffered from its absence. And Chivers' interpretation of beauty differed in an important point from Poe's; it was *divine* beauty that Chivers sought, in connection with his belief that poetry was a vehicle by which the soul might rise to God.[10] Chivers attempted to set up an interesting distinction between earthly beauty and the divine, a distinction which probably resulted from his personal failure to find heavenly beauty in the physical world:

No Nation, with the exception of the Hebrews, ever enjoyed so serene a vision of the Divine Glory as did the Greeks. Their religion was Beauty. It was out of the manifold analysis of Nature that they created their world-renowned Synthesis of Beauty, called *The Venus de Medicis* [sic]. For, as there was nothing in Nature perfect enough to represent the Divine Beauty, they had to resort to Art, which is the Synthesis of the highest sensation united to the loftiest thought. Thus, by glorifying sensation, which is finite, into thought, which is infinite, thereby creating an Image, they gave birth to the Apollo. . . .

Now, the more palpably this thought is made manifest in the IMAGE, through Art, the more lucid will be the *Revelation of the Divine Idea.*[11]

Having established the fact that he was reaching toward a purpose which was as much ethical as aesthetic, Chivers goes on to define the difference between Art and Thought, which taken together produce Divine Beauty. Every poem contains two beauties, the outward, that of form, the vehicle, and the inward, that of passion, of Nature; when they are correctly combined a "pure"

· 215

poem results, one which will "enchant the souls of men." Passion, to Chivers, represented both thought and action, both the consciousness that contact with God could be established and the act of identification itself. A transcendental belief, surely, the transcendental nature of which is even clearer when Chivers speaks of the poet as having "the perfectly couched eyes of an illuminated Seer," to whom "all things appear beautiful that are *really* so."[12]

As seer, or prophet, it is the poet's job to become the mediator "of the revelation of the influx of the Divine Life of God into the soul"[13] of man; he is the voice of God and the echo of Nature.[14]

In statements such as these, Chivers tried to define why he wrote as he did; occasionally he went on to speak of how the true poem might achieve the desired ends. He agreed with Poe that no true poem was anything but a lyric. Although he did not set as definite a limit on the length of a poem as Poe did, he based his objections to epic poetry on much the same belief as that which Poe had, that the soul wearies after a time and cannot absorb the beauties before it. A poem must be complete in itself, and the only way a long poem might be written was through the method Chivers used in *Atlanta,* by creating a narrative or symbolic framework against which separate images may be placed. These images, Chivers believed, must constantly be varied; the "true mystery" of angelic pleasure is the continual reception of varying delights.

One device which is helpful in producing this necessary variation is the refrain, which is not simply an ornament to a poem, but part of that poem's "essence": he describes its importance in typically Chiversian terms.

It is to a Poem precisely what Ovid says of the outward golden tire of the many-spoked wheels of the Chariot of Apollo, that makes a continual, ever-recurring Auroral chime at every revolution of the wheels, proportionate to their velocity, which is never lost, or dies away into an echo, but forever returns upon itself, like the menstrual changes of the Moon, but only to be made the same sweet Moon—the same sweet Auroral chime.[15]

Again a reference to "The Poet of Love" will indicate Chivers' meaning; the refrain returns the poem and the reader's attention to the central theme once more, or, as in a poem like "Rosalie

Lee" (*V*, pp. 31-32), it provides a melodious and slightly varying structure about which the theme is developed. Chivers experimented with the refrain, varying its place in the stanza (beginning, middle, or end), shifting its content slightly each time (as Poe did in "The Raven"), or using it to establish the desired rhythm.

Rhythm was particularly important, and although Chivers' statement of its importance was undoubtedly derived from Poe, he was experimenting with it before Poe defined a poem as "the rhythmical creation of beauty."[16] Interested in music, and familiar with the Negro songs of the South, which he praises highly, Chivers would naturally utilize strong rhythm to produce the essentially hypnotic effect of some of his evocations of Heaven.

And although he never fully stated his implicit belief that the poet's province entitled him to coin whatever words were necessary to express his emotions, it is clear that when he says that no poem can be wholly successful unless the poet has "the highest knowledge of the true Art of musical language,"[17] he means just that. Much of the unique effect some of his poems have is derived from his interest in sound as such, which often demanded that he invent onomatopoetic words.

Chivers insisted that the Age does not make the poet, but that the poet establishes the essential character of the Age.[18] Insofar as he adhered to the standards and theories which have been elaborated here, Chivers spoke the truth about himself. Although certain elements of his belief can be traced to New England Transcendentalism, and the wording of others to Poe, the poetry which resulted from the application of his theories is virtually unique in any anthology of nineteenth century American verse. Concerned with establishing his identification with what Emerson called the over-soul and with what he called Heavenly Beauty or Divine Beauty, he was very much of the nineteenth century, however, in the essentially theological base he chose to give his poetry. Furthermore, that poetry of his which does not concern itself with Divine Beauty, as a considerable amount does not, is typical of the magazine expression of his Age. No better proof than his intermittent application of his poetic beliefs, as well as the nature of those beliefs themselves, could be offered in testimony to the fact that Chivers was both a product of the nineteenth century and his own master.

FORM AND STRUCTURE

The development of Chivers' technical ability throughout his publishing career is a gradual one, moving from the use of standard *abab* quatrains, which were so simple and so popular, to a manipulation of stanza form and meter to achieve unique poetic effects. Chivers was a conscious artist, deeply concerned over the appropriate form his expression might take.

His very first volume, *The Path of Sorrow*, indicates that the young medical student had been paying as much attention to form and structure as to the woes he wished to express. Although depending largely on single and double quatrains for the majority of his poems, he experimented, at this beginning point in his career, with such diverse forms as Spenserians and blank verse, even pausing to invent a nine line stanza, *ababcdcdd*, which he hoped might round out the formal double quatrain to something more organic. Throughout his career he experimented with the basic eight line stanza, varying the pattern to such extremes as *aaaabbbb* and *abaabbaa*, and while many of these efforts are not successful, the fact of his experimenting, occurring as it does so early and continuing so long, helps to present another perspective on his nature. He was not simply a theorizer, but an artisan, attempting to mold his forms to particular ends. His second and third volumes indicate an early and sustained interest in the use of the refrain, an interest quite in accordance with his poetic theory, and the third, *Nacoochee*, contains "Malavolti," a poem which, as Professor Damon points out, may well have been inspired by Coleridge, whose "Christabel" utilizes varying forms to suit the several moods;[19] in "Malavolti" Chivers includes stanzas of *abab* rhymes, *aaaabbbb* rhymes, couplets, and an *abbacca* form.

The Lost Pleiad (1845) marks Chivers' first use of the sonnet, and his attempts to evolve a new pattern of rhyme for this form are as numerous as they are unsuccessful. All told, Chivers tried eighteen different variations, the majority involving changes in the Shakespearian sonnet, although he also tried to manipulate the octave and sestet of the Petrarchan form. However, he lacked the precise control necessary to achieve variation within the strict form of the sonnet, and most of his efforts indicate he understood the sonnet to be simply a fourteen line lyric. "The Grave,"[20] for example, rhymes, in iambic pentameter, *ababacacacacac,* and although it is an effective lyric, it hardly illustrates the subtleties of a sonnet.

His last three books, *Eonchs of Ruby, Virginalia,* and *Atlanta,*[21] are more interesting in terms of diction and sound than of form, although his early interest in the refrain here becomes almost an obsession. Usually he used his refrain to carry certain repeating hypnotic or melodic effects through the poem; so its use must have sprung directly out of his interest in sound and rhythm rather than from any artificial influence or example.

Chivers' forms are seldom completely orthodox. If he utilizes a simple double quatrain, he is likely to make it unique by alternating trimeter, tetrameter, and pentameter lines. His stanzas vary from tercets to an eleven line stanza. Blank verse appealed to him in his early work, although he used it only twice after 1837. It will be worth while to examine the effect of some of his less orthodox attempts.

Chivers' new stanza, *ababcdcdd,* a variation from the Spenserian, is usually marred by the obviousness of the experimentation. "The Prophet's Dream," for example, concludes many of its stanzas with the final line beginning with an all-too-obvious *And,* the result of which is not all that Chivers was hoping for. He speaks of the coming of Christ:

> His hand shall help creation's alien race;
> His wings shall hover o'er the contrite child!
> The mighty men of earth shall see his face,
> But no man shall presume to say, He smil'd.
> He shall be sanctified by heaven's dew,
> And he shall be a stone—a steadfast rock!
> And he that doth his path, in love, pursue,
> Shall shine again, exempt from hell's foul shock;
> And He shall be a pillar on Jehovah's rock.[22]

Perhaps Chivers realized that he had not fully integrated the final line with the rest of the stanza, for in "Apollo," many years later, he used the same scheme but changed the repeating final rhyme into a varying refrain.

> Like some deep, impetuous river from the fountains everlasting,
>> Down the serpentine soft valley of the vistas of all Time,
> Over cataracts of adamant uplifted into mountains,
>> Soared his soul to God in thunder on the wings of thought sublime.

With the rising golden glory of the sun in ministrations,
   Making oceans metropolitan of splendor for the dawn—
Piling pyramid on pyramid of music for the nations—
   Sings the Angel who sits shining everlasting in the sun,
   For the stars, which are the echoes of the shining of the sun.[23]

The repeating final phrase of the seventh line does help to control the long varying lines. Chivers' efforts to thus end-stop the double quatrain are effective only when he so arranged his content that the added line does not appear tacked on.

The blank verse which Chivers used in the three long autobiographical poems of *The Path of Sorrow* is of a particularly unique kind. Chivers knew Byron, but that poet's adept manipulation of the line apparently did not have as much effect upon him as his own wish to achieve a coherence through some sort of a carry-over from line to line. Realizing perhaps that steady, regularly accented pentameter lines might not achieve the flow he desired, Chivers tried to create something more organic by dividing his lines after the fourth or fifth beat in the line, and placing the resulting extra syllables at the beginning of the next line. The effect does not always succeed, partly because he often utilized this method artificially and without reference to the content of the line:

>   My
> Soul is drunk with thy omnipotence. There
> Seems to be, within my very life, a
> Longing after immortality, in love.
> There is an ideal something in my soul,
> Which swells my bosom lord nigh bursting! What
> Is it?—from the very morning when I
> Woke a child of sorrow, I have espoused
> The cause of nature; and I love the world——
> Not that I feel adhesiveness for man——
> For sinful man! but, there is a glory
> In its contemplation, which pervades my
> Very being. There is a fixedness,
> Undaring purpose in my heart, which time,
> With all her multitude of ills, shall not
> Eradicate. The basis of my heart——
> The center of my being—shall remain
> As firm and steadfast as the wreckless rock
> Of Heaven! it shall endure, though hell, with all
> Her panoplied and plumed array, consign
> Me to their grief.[24]

Chivers' method creates a caesural pause before the fourth or fifth beat of the line. It seems probable that by this pattern he hoped to achieve something like Milton's blank verse paragraphs. The subtleties of Milton's technique escaped him, and his enjambment does not always create the organic effect he desired; while his attempt shows his lack of experience as a poet, it also shows his interest in technique itself. But in his poems written in this enjambed blank verse, he is trying to duplicate the emotional effects of an experience (not the experience itself), and the surge of each line into the next is occasionally successful in its context, even though the tendency toward regularity of enjambment is in itself static.

Not all of Chivers' blank verse attempts such carry-over. "The Soaring Swan," whose subject is a symbol of Chivers' own desires, keeps its accents:

> Thou art soaring around the throne of light,
> Bathed in the tingling radiance of the sun
> Whose bright effulgence, gilding thine abyss
> Of burnished glory, scales the heights of heaven!
> For on the velvet vesture of the hills,
> Throned in the fulgence of the hills,
> In desert embrace—bosomed by the groves—
> And where the liquid flowings of the waves
> Woo the enamoured banks—thy home shall be.[25]

But blank verse could not serve him long, for his spirit would rise as does his swan, and the broken lines of "The Death of Adaline" or the long paragraphs of "The Lament of Youth"[26] soon give way to more complex patterns, forms in which Chivers might establish a rhythm and break it where he wished.

One of Chivers' answers to this problem, the necessity of finding a strict form which might be endlessly varied, led him to utilize more and more the refrain, before, within, or at the end of each stanza, with the hope of thereby achieving a varying continuity, change plus exact cadence. In the Preface to *Virginalia*, he compared the refrain to the recurring chime at each revolution of the wheels of "the Chariot of Apollo"; but, he notes, the wheels' sound (i.e., the refrain's effect) is "proportionate," in terms of the metaphor, to the "velocity" of the chariot's wheels, or, to the desired motion of the poem. Since this desired variation is close to Poe's theory as stated in *The Philosophy of Composition*, it is interesting that Chivers experimented with such refrains as early as 1834.

Chivers developed his use of the refrain gradually, from the simple one line final refrain in his 1834 volume to a complex seven line refrain containing elements of both theme and mood in 1856; generally, the advance in complexity was steady. *The Path of Sorrow* (1832) makes no use of the refrain at all, while *Virginalia* (1853) contains only a few poems which avoid it. Such a steady progress toward the organic type of refrain which he desired shows constant attention to the problem, and makes it doubtful that any particular outside influence determined his interest.

The orthodox use of refrain as a continuing set-piece appears throughout Chivers poetry; often it is there simply to provide atmosphere for the body of the poem. "To a China Tree," describing the idyllic surroundings of his early childhood, ends each stanza with "And shot with my cross-bow—my mulberry cross-bow—/ The robins that perched on the boughs near the gate."[27] Not an effective refrain, surely, but the type is familiar. He achieved a variation on the same type in one of the "Songs" of *Nacoochee:*

> Blessed of heaven! thy home shall be
> In the bright green isle of my love for thee,
> When thy form shall rest on my spirit bright
> Like the silver moon on the starry night;
> When thy voice shall float on my soul awake,
> Like the gentle swan on the azure lake—
> Blessed of heaven! thy home shall be
> In the bright green isle of my love for thee.[28]

Gradually Chivers' attempt to create an organic refrain evolved from simple parlor verse like the above. "Choral Song of the Temperance Legions" is an experiment that failed.[29] Here he repeated, in each stanza, the first, seventh and eight, and fourteenth lines of an odd fourteen line stanza, which attempts, as do a number of his poems, to present a shouted chant. The refrain lines presumably welded each bulky stanza to the next.

"The Angel's Whisper"[30] is one of the more complex of his poems which attempt to integrate the refrain within the stanza. Following an *ababbab* scheme, Chivers used the fourth, fifth, and seventh lines as a constant refrain, and made the sixth line a repetition of the third. The result is a poem which depends for its effect almost entirely upon the varying content of the third line, which, by its repetition as the sixth line, a line contained within the refrain, determines the meaning of the refrain, allowing it to develop and change with each stanza.

Much of the same ballad-like quality is found in a series of poems which make use of the repeated rhyme in the refrain without attempting to insert it within the body of the stanza. "Lily Adair" and "Rosalie Lee" are familiar to Chivers readers, and their background extends as far back as 1836, to a poem entitled "Ellen Aeyre," where the basic stanza form and refrain may be found. Again the simple double quatrain, *ababcdcd*, is the basis, but a *ddd* refrain is added to utilize the final pair of rhymes, the final *d* of the refrain doubling the length of the line.

> Like the Lamb's wife, seen in vision,
>   Coming down from heaven above,
> Making earth like Fields Elysian,
>   Golden city of God's love—
> Pure as jasper—clear as crystal—
>   Decked with twelve gates richly rare—
> Statued with twelve angels vestal—
>   Was the form of Ellen Aeyre—
>   Of my saint-like Ellen Aeyre—
>   Gentle girl so debonair—
> Whitest, brightest of all cities, saintly
>   angel, Ellen Aeyre.[31]

When Chivers came to write "Lily Adair" he had only to shorten the third line of the refrain:

> Where the Oreads played in the Highlands,
>   And the Water-Nymphs bathed in the streams,
> In the tall Jasper Reeds of the Islands—
>   She wandered in life's early dreams.
> For the Wood-Nymphs then brought from the Wildwood
>   The turtle doves Venus kept there,
> Which the Dryades tamed, in his childhood,
>   For Cupid, to Lily Adair—
>   To my Dove-like Lily Adair—
>   To my lamb-like Lily Adair—
> To my beautiful, dutiful Lily Adair.[32]

The same format for the refrain is found again in "Rosalie Lee," with the same varied prepositions and descriptive phrases in the final three lines. Each refrain of these poems contains different descriptions of the heroine, each changing the reader's understanding of her a slight amount. The lulling, melodic effect of such refrains was part of what Chivers was seeking; it helped to weave an aura of vague ethereal beauty about his subject, which was the only way he could effectively describe female beauty.

Eonchs of Ruby and *Virginalia* in particular show how much Chivers depended upon this strict *ababcdcd* structure to provide a pattern from which he might deviate. "The Place Where I Was Born" (*V*, pp. 80-81), for example, presents this form, but subtracts the last three lines and makes them the basis of a *dcddd* refrain. "The Moon of Mobile" (*V*, pp. 37-38) follows the double quatrain with a refrain of *efefff;* again Chivers seeks the hypnotic effect. "Avalon," a poem typical of Chivers and one of his best, utilizes the repeating refrain for atmospheric effects:

> Thy soul did soar up to the Gates of God,
>> Oh, Lark-like Child!
> And poured Heaven's Bowers of Bliss, by Angels trod,
>> Poured Wood-notes wild!
> In emulation of that Bird, which stood,
> In solemn silence, listening to thy flood
> Of golden Melody deluge the wood
>> Where thou art lying
>> Beside the beautiful undying
> In the Valley of the Pausing of the Moon,
> Oh! Avalon! my son! my son![33]

Such an atmospheric refrain was necessary, Chivers believed, not as an ornament, or as embroidery, but to complete the theme; statement was never as effective as suggestion.

The refrain might be made a part of the whole in other ways, too. Any repetition of thematic lines would draw the various stanzas together and create a unified effect. Perhaps I take liberties with strict meaning when I call the following repeating and organic lines a refrain, yet I think that Chivers would have cited this poem as one which achieved the continuity plus variation which he desired, and so I have included it here. "The Dying Beauty" repeats the introductory statement in the first line eight times, and it is followed on each occasion by an extended simile; the whole poem, by virtue of these varying images within the static structure, creates a veiled and romantic picture of the death of a woman:

> She died in beauty, like the morn that rose
> In golden glory on the brow of night,
> And passed off gently like the evening's close,
> When day's last steps upon the heavens are bright.
> She died in beauty, like the trampled flower
> That yields its fragrance to the passer's feet,
> For all her life was as an April shower,
> That kept the tear-drops of her parting sweet.
> And like the rainbows of the sunny skies,
> The dew-drop fillet of the brow of even—
> That blends its colours as the evening dies—
> Her beauty melted in the light of heaven.
>
> She died in softness, like the last sad tone
> That lingers gently on the midnight ear,
> When beauty wanders from her bower alone,
> And no one answers, but the voice is near.
> She died in beauty, like the lonesome dove
> That seeks her fledglings in the desert air,
> And hastes away from out the flowery grove
> To seek the little ones that nestled there.
> And like the humming-bird that seeks the bower,
> But wings her swiftly from the place away,
> And bears the dew-drop from the fading flower—
> Her spirit wandered to the isle of day.[34]

Several of the similes are effective; others are not, but whatever general success the poem has stems from the rigidity tempered by variation which the repeated line provides. Conscious, perhaps, that he had achieved something of his aim, Chivers used this formula in two other poems. "To My Mother in Heaven," published in the following year,[35] begins each stanza with "I see thee not!" and then enumerates, by stanza, the facets of his sense of loss. "Uranothen," published in *Virginalia,* is a revision of "The Heavenly Vision," which depends upon a repeating final line in each stanza, "She came from Heaven to tell me she was blest," to coordinate an essentially loose poem. In its revised form Chivers made the repetition less obvious, relegating it to the end position in the final line:

> The hyaline wavelets of her voice of love
>   Rose on the boundless ether-sea's calm breast;
> Amid the interstarry realms above,
>   To God in Heaven, telling me she was blest.[36]

There are endless examples of Chivers' structural devices, but most of them stem from the two categories developed here. He was constantly interested in involved stanza forms; "Threnody," written at the death of his son Tommy, indicates that he could be absorbed in the intricacies of form even in the midst of grief. In an attempt to slow down the movement of the opening of each stanza, he repeats the end-rhyme of the first stanza line as the first word in stanza lines two and three. The result is trickier than it is successful.

> How I miss him in the summer,
> Summer of the Golden Grain—
> Summer. . . .[37]

What Chivers could achieve by use of the basic *abab* quatrain in his attempt to create certain hypnotic, semi-rhythmic effects was paralleled by his use of this form to produce a species of declamatory poetry which cannot easily be duplicated in the nineteenth century until Whitman turned it into a philosophy and an ideal. Like Whitman, he begins his stylistic ventures by adhering to orthodox forms; like him, too, he threw them away when certain inspirations were before him. Unlike the Camden seer, he did not utilize his declamations to present any but the most orthodox sentiments.

The development of Chivers' style was of course gradual, and we have just seen to what ends he put his experiments in the use of the refrain. There are suggestions of his declamatory style in his first tragedy, *Conrad and Eudora*, in 1834, although they are overwhelmed almost always by metaphysical imagery or Shakespearian rhetoric. Perhaps the earliest inspiration for his use of the style was from Byron, for a poem like "Anastasius"[38] follows his formula for the narrative verse tragedy while it shows signs of declamation, unsuccessful as they are, which are absent from the other poetry of Chivers' first three volumes. Whenever an artificially imposed dramatic situation is present in his early poetry, as it rarely is, most of the poems being lyrical, Chivers attempts a rhetoric totally unlike the intimate style of his love songs or personal elegies. There is, however, a parallel between his development of the evocative, hypnotic effect which is exemplified in his later use of the refrain and the declamatory poetry under study here. In both styles he is likely to give way to exclamation and shouting which often obscure form, although the strictness superimposed by the varying refrain demands and gets attention where the blank verse or paeon-filled declamatory verse flows on from line to line without more than superficial notice of structure.

A series of what may be called patriotic poems best illustrates the development of this experiment. Chivers' quickly-incited fervor over any contest between liberty and tyranny was in some ways bound up with his desire to evoke or create the beauty of a Terrestrial Eden, for the Eden Isle is not far distant from the New Jerusalem which he saw embodied in nineteenth century America. And when Chivers chooses Heaven or its earthly counterpart as subject, he seldom tries to limit his effects. The emotion within him can best be expressed by exultation.

Yet it may not be said that Chivers lost sight of the less ethereal details of his world; we find the clearest beginning of his declamatory style in the "Choral Song of the Temperance Legions."[39] The poem is a series of trimeter quatrains arranged in the form of a chant, wherein the Legions shout their strength and purity to be answered by various Echoes—of the Sun, Moon, Constellations, or Angels. Its failure and its experimental nature are testified to by the fact he could revise it to "The Cry of Hungary"[40] by changing little more than its title and omitting the identification of the Echoes; their lines become a widely varying refrain. The evocation, this time of freedom, is equally vague. Such vagueness would not necessarily harm a declamatory poem, but as yet Chivers had not found the meter to create the necessary carry-over from line to line which would unify the poem despite its looseness.[41]

It was in 1854 that Chivers found and elaborated the form necessary to make his declamation effective. "To Allegra Florence in Heaven" had been written in lines which, although tetrameter in appearance, were actually broken octameters.[42] In "Where Liberty Was Born"[43] Chivers developed this meter in his favorite *abab* quatrain and kept the second and fourth lines catalectic. Like his earlier experiments in declamatory verse, the poem is marred by its extremes of imagery and diction, but the longer line goes far toward the effect of oration which Chivers was seeking.

"The Roll of Fame" is his most successful attempt in this direction, and its long, pulsing lines almost discard the stanza form and meter to achieve a rolling cadence now reminiscent of Whitman's carefully unmetered lines:

In the Autumn of the world, when the honey of the Summer still
    lay on the flowers of the years,
I stood on the evergreen banks of the beautiful River of Time,
And there I heard the loud thunders, rolled off from the prows of
    the crystalline Spheres,
Break calmly against the white shore of my panting soul in utter-
    ance sublime.

  .   .   .   .

Then the tranced Silence, wakened from her peaceful slumber
    In the Oasian Ocean of Saharah, hearing her mournful voice
Breaking against the Hills of Nubia, listening without number,—
    Fled to the Pacific Islands in those Seas whose billows make no
    noise.
But still it was far sweeter the Muezzin's mournful crying
    Uttered at daybreak from the Dome of the beautiful Omar,
Looking from the top of Zion up to the Mountain that is undying—
    Like the first great golden Iliad bursting from the soul of Homer.

  .   .   .   .

Then, like the unfolding of some antediluvian iron Scroll,
    With repercussive clang, like storm-winds when they rend the
    bosom of the Deep,
The Vail of Isis was rent in Twain, revealing unto my more than
    raptured soul
    The dark Aenigma of the grave, written in Dreams in the House
    of Sleep.

  .   .   .   .

Then I heard iron words, spoken as if by clanking chains
    Rattling in bottomless vaults rusted by tears wept by the utter-
    less Tomb—
Followed by rumbling thunders—after which there fell down hail-
    ing rains,
    As if hail fell instead of rain—freezing my lips to dumbness
    doubly dumb![44]

The control afforded by meter is here discarded in favor of a series
of chanted lines which, although the rhyme is kept, flow on without pause. The whole poem, thirty-four stanzas long, lacks any
really vital organization, but moves from stanza to stanza within
a very general framework of an emotional vision, in which Chivers
sees the Heavenly kingdom spread before him. The effect of these
short stanzas with their rolling lines, unhampered by any strict

progression, is of a series of impressionistic and sometimes symbolic images flashed before the reader. Like the majority of Whitman's long catalogues of images, they demand that the reader supply most of the pictorial detail, and depend for their effect upon the continuing cadence lines, lines which sometimes include as many as fourteen accents.

This is the furthest approach Chivers made toward the effects Whitman was to make notorious and then famous less than a year later. Published only four years before Chivers' death, a poem like "The Roll of Fame" indicates the extent of his interest in form as controlled only by cadence and sound. The 1850's saw the fullest development of Chivers' powers as a poet, and the poems of these years help to show the distance he has travelled since 1832. Never content with existing forms or methods, Chivers sought to expand the power and scope of poetry, and his attempt ought to entitle him to a position at least part way removed from the limited horizons of the mid-nineteenth century "public Renaissance" and nearer the broader and deeper limits of the true American Renaissance of *Leaves of Grass*.

SOUND AND RHYTHM

A considerable part of the effect of Chivers' most characteristic poems stems from their often unique diction. His habits of language indicate that descriptive or suggestive words that appealed to him found a repository either in his memory or in some sort of a card file. Images and phrases become familiar to the reader of Chivers, and sometimes their change and development may be followed throughout his volumes.

The Path of Sorrow (1832) marks the beginning of his experiments with various types of diction. The product of a young, inexperienced poet, that it should contain coinage of his own is surprising at first glance, but when we recall that he tried many varieties of meter and stanza form in the same volume, *obsecration, unburlesqued, gnomen,* or *domil* further the belief that *The Path of Sorrow* was a thoroughly unusual first book. Attempting to find a vehicle for the untutored poetry he had within him, Chivers misuses and coins words whenever it serves his purpose to do so. The prophet, Chivers says, moves

far
Beyond sycophants of terrene strife,—
While scintillations from his mighty star,
Shall pilot him to that eternal life,
Where oblectations shine, devoid of grief.[45]

Such diction is self-conscious and not entirely typical of the style he later developed. It does show, however, something more than early self-consciousness. Its essentially pedantic nature indicates that he was trying to mold what he thought of as esoteric diction to fit his own needs. An *orrery of tears,* an *ultramontaine sphere,* the *domil sun* are neither provocative nor suggestive unless they appear natural in their respective stanzas, and the poems of *The Path of Sorrow* are notable for their combination of standard poetic diction with such unique phrases as these. Delighted with unusual diction, Chivers had not yet found that it was possible to create poetry dependent almost entirely upon sound. The volume contains few color adjectives, and the greater part of the adjective usage is quite conventional in nature.

The urge to experiment in diction is not so much present in *Conrad and Eudora,* for the short lyrics in the book are, as has been suggested before, standard love songs whose content offered little or no incentive. The title drama indicates he knew his Shakespeare, although he cannot succeed in coordinating seventeenth century soliloquy with nineteenth century diction. And while a *run-mad heart* seems his own, Eudora says, echoing the Bible with some incoherence, "He, once the 'apple of mine eye,' cast off!/ If it offend thee, pluck it out!"[46] The violent rhetoric of the play is not good oration, but occasionally he succeeds:

> This fountain, which is stirred to bitter wrath,
> Which that insatiate wretch so rudely stung,
> And wounded with the arrows of his lust!—
> Shall turn an August to his life, and thirst
> For every drop that palpitates his heart![47]

Chivers revised and improved the play later as *Leoni; or, the Orphan of Venice.*[48] Here the rhetoric is improved, and lines which were loose and vague in *Conrad and Eudora* appear in a more effective, concise style. The Shakespearian diction is still present, but Chivers has managed to develop his own images:

> . . . never shall my soul find rest,
> Until the purple mirror of his blood
> Reflect the deep damnation of his deeds. . . .[49]

The fault of nineteenth century colloquialism is still present, how-ever, and exclamations of "By Jove!" appear violently out of place.[50]

But the rhetoric which occupied Chivers in his plays does not often appear in his lyric poetry, except in the patriotic chants dis-cussed earlier. He was busy developing what may be called his later style, which takes many of the unusual words of his earlier poetry and places them in a context which fits their nature. Compounds are very frequent, and *smile-beams, sapphire-paven,* or *zephyr-dimpled lake* become typical of the atmosphere he is trying to create. *Nacoochee* (1837) shows that it did not take Chivers long to realize the inadequacy of his earlier diction, or, rather, that that diction would not fulfill the purposes which were now uppermost in his mind. To paraphrase his own language, he would speak in *shell-tones,* moving in *pearl-tinct azure* (the sky) over the *crystal-line deep sea* to the *island-clouds* of Heaven. The title poem of the volume and "The Soaring Swan" contain the clearest examples of this later preoccupation; the other poems follow the essentially orthodox style of the lyrics in *Conrad and Eudora.* Some time in the years just preceding *Nacoochee,* he saw the collected poetry of Coleridge as it appeared in the Galignani edition republished in Philadelphia. The sight of "Kubla Khan" and "The Ancient Mari-ner" must have excited Chivers as much as Keats or Shelley did, for here was confirmation that he was right in believing that the boundaries of poetic diction might be extended. But surely he saw too the hypnotic effect Coleridge's romantic images created in "Kubla Khan"; and "Alph, the sacred river" as well as "Mount Abora" may well have drawn his attention to the fact that a wholly unreal image could be created by the judicious use of exotic dic-tion. It did not matter whether or not Mount Abora could be traced on a map; taken in its context it suggested just the remote romanticism that Chivers came to delight in.

Although Chivers learned more than exotic place names from Coleridge, his imagination was capable of producing such exoti-cisms as *Chalceldony, Boscobella, Oossanalla,* and *Meru,* and their use follows the date at which it is presumed he first saw Coleridge.

"The Soaring Swan" (1837) suggests that he was either immediately inspired by Coleridge or had been experimenting on his own:

> For there shall flow
> From out the circlings of thy floating form,
> Bathed in the flickering dalliance of the gems
> Of thy sun-cinctured dimples, like the pearl
> Of ocean set in beryl by the deep—
> A shell-toned music. . . .[51]

Such a picture is not realistic, nor is it detailed in the sense of being exact; it might better be called provocative, in that it attempts to set the reader's imagination to work with the poet's, suggesting colors and hues which may be filled in as the reader chooses.

Eonchs of Ruby and *Virginalia* mark Chivers' primary effort in the use of imagery that depends wholly upon suggestive diction, and the second volume indicates his increasing interest in the effect and theory of pure sound. Stanzas of "Rosalie Lee" have already been quoted to indicate Chivers' delight in certain passages from Keats, notable for this same suggestiveness. *Eonchs of Ruby* contains diction which still startles:

> In the mild month of October,
> As we did go
> Through the fields of Cooly Rauber,
> No one can know,
> But the great Archangel Auber,
> What songs did flow. . . .[52]

That Chivers is interested in the suggestive connotation of a phrase like *Cooly Rauber* rather than its denotation is indicated by the fact that the cooly rauber is a vegetable, a cross between a cabbage and a turnip. The same poem describes the "thousand oceans spooming" (1. 82). Or he could describe a natural scene in these terms:

> The cloud-sustaining, many-folded Hills—
> The soft, retiring mystery of the Vallies—
> The open frankness of the verdant Fields—
> The winding labyrinths of the emerald Alleys—
> The bending Heavens, with all the Stars in
> cyclic sallies—[53]

Lily Adair resides

> Where the Oreads played in the Highlands,
> And the Water-Nymphs bathed in the streams,
> In the tall Jasper Reeds of the Islands—[54]

Examples like these can be culled from a large number of the poems in these volumes, and they indicate a general trend. Chivers was less concerned with the denotation of his words than with the possible connotations dictated by the context of the poem; frequently he goes beyond the dictionary, to a land where the moon becomes a *melologue* (a word coined by Thomas Moore) and makes the *icy azure/Argently clear*. That is, Chivers could coin or distort language until it supplied him with the suggestiveness, the fantasy, he often desired. His imagination was not pictorial, nor was it, actually, dependent upon color so much as upon the connotations of the colors of precious stones; gem-mad, if you will, in the stanza from "Rosalie Lee" which he based on a scene from "The Eve of St. Agnes," he is interested in apples seen as "Ruby-rimmed Beryline buckets," and cucumbers as "emerald," "like Chrysopraz."[55] His descriptions of Heaven depend largely upon the twenty-first chapter of the Revelation of St. John, where the City of God is described in terms of precious stones.

Exotic place names, figures from Greek mythology, Biblical names, precious stones—all contribute toward the diction of Chivers' later style. Most frequently he utilizes the more unusual words as end-rhymes, realizing the emphasis thus obtained. There was an interesting connection in Chivers' mind between color and sound. He added a note to the phrase "Soft as the liquid tones of Heaven," saying that he was "Alluding to the harmony between a soft sound and a blue color."[56] Twentieth century psychologists, and even home decorators would agree, perhaps, and it seems probable, that Chivers' growing interest in color and its suggestive powers led him to experiment with the nature of pure sound in poetry. The mind that can record color in terms of sound clearly was sensitive to mutations in sound itself. Interest in suggestions of sound through alliteration and assonance led Chivers to write poems in which sound dominates, the thematic sense of the poem being of little importance. Coleridge certainly helped to lead him to such experimentation, and some of his lines are worthy of the English poet. Earlier he had written that the vultures "cleave their curve in the charnal air,"[57] a line which immediately suggests Gerard Manley Hopkins, and that his love's eyes were "Like the Lioness', lazy, their hazel hue."[58] He once tried to put this interest into concrete terms: the Angelus is described as

> A wave-like, azure sound,
>   Upon the pavement of new-fallen snow,
>   Pure as an Angel's garment on the ground—
>   Trembling the atmosphere with its soft flow—
>   Comes swiftly, with its Heaven-dilating swell,
>   From the Noon-ringing of yon far-off Bell.[59]

An *azure* sound suggests the nature of Chivers' ear, but here he depends, successfully, at least partially upon the picture suggested. "The Poet of Love," on the other hand, dispenses with such pictorial detail and relies upon the sweep of his language:

> With the white lightnings of his still small voice,
>   Deep as the thunders of the azure Silence—
> He makes dumb the oracular Cymbals with their noise,
>   Till BEAUTY flourish Amaranthine on the Islands
>   Of all the loud tumultuous Sea
>   Of the vast immensity,
>   Echoing the music of the Morns,
>   Blown through the Chrysomelian Horns
>   Down the dark vistas of the reboantic Norns
>   By the great Angel of Eternity,
>   Thundering, *Come to me! come to me!*[60]

"Apollo" achieves much the same effect:

> Like the lightning piled on lightning, ever rising, never
>   reaching,
>   In one monument of glory towards the golden gates
>   of God—
> Voicing out themselves in thunder upon thunder in their
>   preaching,
>   Piled this Cyeclop [*sic*] up his Epic where the Angels
>   never trod.
> Like the fountains everlasting that forever more are flowing
>   From the throne within the centre of the City built
>   on high,
> With their genial irrigation life forever more bestowing—
>   Flows his lucid, liquid river through the gardens of
>   the sky,
>   For the stars forever blooming in the gardens of the sky.[61]

The images of such poetry are not to be taken out of context, nor are they to be asked to produce their effects unless surrounded by others of the same nature. In these poems Chivers depends upon the multiplicity of his imagery, which in its suggestiveness often goes beyond intellectual comprehension, to produce an effect that is wholly of the senses. The reader is asked to forego his stable position and transport himself to Chivers' world, a world where "Chrysomelian Horns" and the "gardens of the sky" are wholly in place. The subject matter of poetry of this sort matters less than the emotional hypnosis the vast images and the exotic diction produce. It is not quite Xanadu, but it is not far from it.

Coleridge's world is most clearly evoked in a strange poem of Chivers' entitled "The Little Boy Blue," a title as deceptive as any ever offered. The poem tells the story of the poet's wanderings across the earth, led on always by the song of the little boy blue. It becomes clear only after some little time that this figure symbolizes Chivers' poetic inspiration, and the places they visit are suggestive of the wild heights of Chivers' imagination. It matters not at all what the exact sense of the stanza may be; the thirty-seven quatrains that make up the poem establish a cadence which, while it is completely different from the whirling lines of the poems quoted above, carries the reader through the exotic lands of Chivers' inner world.

> The little boy blue
>   Was the boy that was born
> In the forest of Dru,
>   On the mountains of Morn.
>
> Where the tongue of the sea
>   Piles the dirges on Lorn
> There he warbled for me
>   Mellow lays on his horn.
>
> Where the dregs of his moan
>   Shingle-sanded the shore,
> There he built all alone
>   Lays that live evermore.
>
> .   .   .   .   .   .
>
> By the cool crystal rills,
>   That meandered Lahawn,
> All along the green hills,
>   There he wandered at dawn—

From the forests of Dru,
 On the Mountains of Morn,
Blowing songs ever new
 Through the throat of his horn.

From the island of Arran,
 To the Vale of Lahore,
Where the fields are all barren—
 There he walked evermore.

On the green banks of On,
 By the City of No,
There he taught the wild swan
 Her white bugle to blow.

First, he sang of the land,
 Then he sang of the sea,
Then he wrote on the sand
 What I write now for thee.[62]

And it does not seem imperative that the reader recognize symbolic meaning in such stanzas; their primary effect, obviously, is to establish the atmosphere of another world.

Although "The Little Boy Blue" depends for many of its effects upon strange end-rhymes, the true nature of Chivers' interest in sound itself becomes clearer from an examination of his "Chinese Serenade." The poem is divided into six irregular stanzas, the first three introduced by lines which attempt to approximate the sound of a Chinese stringed instrument:

Tien-Tsze
Tu Du
Skies Blue—
All clear—
Fourth year,
Third Moon,
High Noon
At night....[63]

Strange music indeed for the stable pages of a reputable literary magazine! The subtly cadenced music of the Chinese appealed to Chivers, and his attempt to reproduce it is successful as far as it goes. The main body of the first three stanzas does not continue the music, however, as it tells the story of the love and the "King of Son-Tay." The final stanzas of the poem are an attempt to convey the sound of a gong:

Bo-au-awng, ba-ang, bing!
Bee-ee-eeing, ba-ang, bong!
So-au-awng, sa-ang, sing!
See-ee-eeing, sa-ang, song!
Bing, bang, bong![64]

Here he has gone beyond poetry to a type of phonetic reproduction which is less effective than the tonal music of the first lines. Chivers' ear was not always acute, but melody and certain rhythms attracted him, and his attempts to create poetry which might approximate what he heard are a fascinating undercurrent in American literature. The songs of birds attracted him, and he tried several times to spell them out. In one of his letters to the *Georgia Citizen,* he speaks of his "recently written *Theory of a true Poetical Language,*"[65] and it may be presumed that this essay, were it extant, would lead up to a full understanding of his hopes to create a diction depending more upon connotation that denotation, and of his onomatopoetic attempts.

The presence of a strong rhythm in much of Chivers' experimental poetry is best accounted for by remembering his boyhood among his father's slaves. He writes that "there is absolutely more *real* and *soul thrilling* music made audible, (but still unwritten,) by the impassioned utterance of the *negroes* in the South . . . than can be found . . . in these whole Northern regions. . . ."[66] Earlier he had noted that he had a large collection of such songs, and had praised them for their "simplicity" and natural perfection of rhythm."[67] Cultural historians and jazz enthusiasts of the twentieth century have agreed, and Chivers' own day of course saw the beginning of the famed Christy minstrels. Whether the "Corn Shucking Song" Chivers published in 1855 in his own work and the result of many hours listening to work songs, or whether it is a literal transcription is difficult to tell. An earlier Negro melody, "De Ole Gray Hoss,"[68] contains the lines, "Oh! whar did you kum fum/ Kum fum, kum fum—," the substance and rhythm of which can be found in many of that race's songs today, and the rhythm of the following seems legitimately derived from Negro melody:

Shuck de Cawn, Niggers! oh! shuck de Cawn, Darkies!
De Mawnin' Staws a-risin' to bring de brake o' day;
Shout aloud, Darkies! oh! shout aloud, Niggers!
De Oberseer's watin' to cawl us awl away.

· Wawk yore tawk, Jawbone! oh! wawk yore tawk wakin'!
  . For old Massa's dreamin' about de brake o' day;
  Bress yore soles, Darkies! de Oberseer's akin!
     To gib us awl de cowhide, before we go away!
  Git away de Cawn, Boys! git away de Cawn!
     Oh! git away de Cawn, Boys! git away de Cawn!
  Linkydum-a-hydum, a linkydum-a-ho!
     Holler, Boys! holler! de Cawn is gettin' low.[69]

Chivers evidently delighted in such exaggerated colloquialisms, for
"De Ole Gray Hoss," mentioned above, is a comic lyric, and "The
Death of the Devil," a low comedy farce built around one man's
efforts to hoodwink another, makes use of exactly such stage-darky
diction as we have above, unfortunately lacking the rhythms that
make the "Corn-Shucking Song" successful.[70]

Rhythm and onomatopoetic diction came together again in
Chivers' attempt to reproduce the effect of a railroad train leaving
the station. This is tour de force work, but nonetheless interesting
as it exhibits his deep interest in an experiment with hypnotic
effects. The images that are scattered throughout the poem resemble some of those he used to produce the sweeping effects of "The
Poet of Love" or "Apollo" in that they are entirely suggestive, and
totally unrelated to the realistic scene portrayed.

> All aboard! Yes—Tingle, tingle,
> Goes the bell as we all mingle—
> No one sitting solely single—
> As the steam begins to fizzle
> With a kind of sighing sizzle—
> Ending in a piercing whistle—
> As the fireman builds his fire,
> And the steam gets higher, higher—
> Thus fulfilling his desire—
> Which forever he keeps feeding
> With the pine-knots he is needing,
> As he on his way goes speeding—
> Till the Iron Horse goes rushing,
> With his fiery face all flushing—
> Every thing before him crushing—
> While the smoke goes upward curling,
> Spark-bespangled in unfurling
> And the iron wheels go whirling,
> Like two mighty millstones grinding,

When no miller is them minding—
All the eye with grit-dust blinding—
And the cars begin to rattle,
And the springs go tittle-tattle—
Driving off the grazing cattle—
As if Death were Hell pursuing
To his uttermost undoing,
Down the iron road to ruin—
With a clitta, clatta, clatter,
Like the Devil beating batter
Up in Hell, in iron platter....[71]

These poems emphasize the continual necessity Chivers felt to expand the limits of poetic theory and practice as he knew it. They are not uniformly successful, but they are strong indication of his distinction from the common. He had imagination, an ear which could catch tonal differences and melodic rhythms, and often the talent to turn what he heard and felt into effective poetry. His diction varies from the dream world of "The Little Boy Blue" to such realism as we have just seen, a scope indicative of his interest in deriving meaning from the manipulation of sound itself.

POETIC DEVICES

Chivers' creative process was a religious one; his moments of inspiration are akin to the mystic's consciousness of his at-oneness with God. Chivers made the relation between the artistic and the religious experience concrete and factual by proclaiming that his poetry was an evocation of divinity, of the divine presence. Unlike most mystics, he felt no sense of awe upon establishing this identification. Supremely confident of his own abilities, he comments on the fact of the nature of poetry rather than on the technique used to create the poetry.

Expressing himself in exultant terms in his prefaces and prose statements, Chivers seldom speaks of his conscious effort to achieve something new in form and technique. Indeed, the majority of these statements have proved to be his efforts to explain the true quality of his subject matter, rather than explications of his method.

In line with this silence about his technical experiments is the absence of any general statement on imagery, beyond his assertion that "the more palpably [Divine Beauty] is made manifest in the

· 239

IMAGE, through Art, the more lucid will be the *Revelation of the Divine Idea.*"[72] In introducing this comment, Chivers insisted that the image is derived "by glorying sensation, which is finite, into thought, which is infinite. . . ."[73] Such a statement could come only from a poet who reacted to experience, to stimuli of any sort, by his senses alone. A ratiocinative poet, for example, would place his emphasis upon the Art, which Chivers does include in his theorem, rather than upon the sensation. When Chivers said Poe failed in certain poetic areas because he lacked passion, what he meant was that the Art, the craftsmanship of the poet, had become too obvious, that the fire of inspiration had been extinguished before the calculation of means to achieve the desired effect.[74] Such an objection sums up the failure of certain of Poe's poems quite exactly; it also clarifies Chivers' own theory and practice. For while he objected that Poe stressed the necessary Art to the exclusion of the necessary Passion, Chivers himself delighted in the Passion to a point where some of his poems lose form and shape before its onslaught.

But it is not to be imagined that Chivers held entirely to the notion that Passion, or exalted emotion, was a poem's only necessary ingredient. His experiments in diction and form have already testified to his interest in technical matters, and his use of imagery furthers the belief that while he could speak of poetry only in terms of its ultimate purpose and divine nature, he was deeply if silently concerned with the problems of the working artist. Just as we have seen that his efforts to extend the boundaries of poetic form and language resulted from certain basic beliefs which he held, so will we see that his use of imagery derives from his insistence that an image is basically sensation "glorified" or raised into thought.

The explication of such a statement is relatively simple once Chivers' prose is understood: sensation, the reaction of the poet as he stands in the face of the given experience, when placed in the context of the poem's theme becomes more than simply emotional response; it becomes the true interpretation of the experience, for the poet sees with the eyes of the seer. His reaction, then, expressed in terms of imagery, gives the facts or details of the experience the inspired quality which makes them the "Revelation of the Divine Idea."

With such a belief behind it, Chivers' poetry takes on new meaning, particularly when his subject matter is concerned with divinity or the divine, that which is in some way at a remove from this earth. His more conventional pieces, those devoted to standard romantic themes of earthly love, parting, or sorrow, for example, seldom make use of imagery. But the poems which transcend the earthly toward the divine contain images which are distinctly unusual in the work of an American poet of the 1840's and 1850's.

While this theory lies behind virtually all of Chivers' more unusual imagery, his use of the simile seems to derive directly from an outside influence rather than from his poetic theory. In many of the poems following the middle years of the 1830's, presumably after he had seen Shelley's collected works for the first time, Chivers depends wholly upon the parallel construction made possible by repetition of the simile. Shelley's influence seems clear, for his work abounds in such usage; this has already been noted in reference to Chivers' "To Allegra Florence in Heaven."[75]

Yet in another way Chivers' use of the simile derives from the emotional and sometimes erratic quality of his mind. Where a poet like Edward Taylor, rational in at least certain elements of his Puritan thinking, seldom leaves an image until he has exhausted all its involutions and possibilities,[76] Chivers, moved by emotion and not by intellectual or rationalistic stimuli, seldom investigates an image beyond its surface connections with the subject at hand. One aspect of a comparison catches his attention, and he builds a simile about it; another, perhaps illustrating a second comparison, may be added to the first—and so on. Rather than utilizing a single fully developed metaphor or image, Chivers' poetry is characterized by a loose, inclusive structure, typical in many ways of Shelley. Borne upward by emotion, his mind and imagination play over a series of comparisons, delighting in each for a moment before going on to the next. The effect of such composition is sometimes erratic, while at other times the spread of his series of pictures gives just the quality of totality which he desired. "The Dying Beauty," a poem written soon after he had first studied Shelley, is typical:

> She died in meekness, like the noiseless lamb
> When slain upon the altar by the knife,
> And lay reclining on her couch so calm,
> That all who saw her said she still had life.

> She died in softness, like the Dorian flute,
> When heard melodious on the hills at night,
> When every voice but that loved one is mute,
> And all the holy heavens above are bright.
> And like the turtle that has lost her love,
> She hastened quickly from the world to rest;
> And passed off gently to the realms above,
> To reign forever in her FATHER'S breast.[77]

The majority of Chivers' similes utilize the word *like*, and frequently it is given a primary position in the line.[78] Others use a moderately extended simile bounded formally by *as* and *so;* apparently the strict format of such a construction helped Chivers to achieve a tighter structure. "Caelicola," an elegy on Poe, begins,

> Like that sweet bird of night,
> Startling the ebon silence from repose,
> Until the stars appear to burn more bright
> From its excessive gush of song which flows
> Like some impetuous river to the sea—
> So thou did'st flood the world with melody.
>
> For as the evening star
> Pants with its "silver lightnings" for the high
> And holy Heavens—the azure calm afar—
> Climbing with labor now the bending sky
> To lead Night's Navy through the upper sea—
> So thou did'st pant for immortality.[97]

Such usage is not always effective, for the structure of the stanza dominates its content instead of containing it.

Chivers' mind, with a wide enough grasp to delight in virtually unrelated similes,[80] occasionally achieved a yoking of disparate elements reminiscent of John Donne. When lust attacks virtue, Chivers says in *Conrad and Eudora,* "Then fix a pivot in thy heart for doubt to turn on!"[81] Violent and forceful images of this sort do not occur often in his work, but their presence, as in the following example, is another instance of that facility of imagination which characterizes Chivers' poetry:

> Thou wert as mild as an incarnate Moon,
> Making his soul the satellite of mine—
> Round which thou didst revolve in joy,
> as soon
> As my fond soul could shed its light on thine.[82]

The Path of Sorrow (1832) and *Conrad and Eudora* (1834) do not develop in this imaginative usage very far. Generally, the poems in the first volume utilize direct statement of emotion or reaction rather than the indirection of the simile or metaphor. "Songs of the Heart" of *Conrad and Eudora* contains fewer of such personal revelations, but the format normally involves an artificial situation or theme, and such notable imagery as is found there seems orthodox romanticism. Occasionally Chivers developed an atmospheric effect through the use of an imaginative image: his sister's dying eyes mirrored sights to him which were "the whisperings of bliss, / Uttered by silence. . . ."[83] The significance of silence seems to be the beginning of his almost mystic insight into sensory reaction:

> my chamber has become an alcove
> For the watchers of the sky! and in my
> Bed, at midnight of my sleep, I people
> Worlds, and dream unnumbered things; till silence
> Wakes from lethargy, and shocks my burning
> Brain. . . .[84]

In these two random examples, Chivers has had comparative success with a device which he was to use more and more frequently. By personalizing or animating the abstract, he attaches a physical dimension to his otherwise prosaic statement.

This same device is elaborated in *Nacoochee* (1837), and we find "An angel fondling with the locks of even . . ." or with "the locks of love!"[85] His Heaven is made physical, if not visual, and thus susceptible to sensory reaction. He came to use this device most frequently when he attempted to envision vast or distant or indistinct forces. The earth, in her last convulsion at Judgment Day, is seen as an animated being:

> the far-stretching solitudes were torn
> By the tempestuous whirlwinds, as they came
> From out the nostril of the dying sea!
> And when the pantings of his collapsed sides
> Gave out the last Lunarian sigh to heaven,
> That sent prolific torpor through his limbs;
> And when the voiceless confines of his waves
> Lay back within the pulseless arms of his
> Peninsulas, with one far-spreading seethe
> Of songless palsy—down his bosom sank![86]

He attempts the same visual effect in "The Death of Time":

> A mournful anthem comes from out the moon!
> For she has found her grave-clothes in the clouds!
> And frightened at the widowhood of earth,
> She wanders blindfolded from her wonted path,
> And, wailing for her ocean-lord, she puts
> On sackcloth for the dying sun, and sets
> Behind Eternity to rise no more![87]

Such an image is both pictorial and suggestive; the reader cannot visualize its full extent, but because of the animation of forces and bodies not normally capable of feeling or emotion, Chivers has made an otherwise unimaginable circumstance vivid.

Imagery of this sort depends for its effect upon and helps explain extensions beyond the normal boundaries of experience. When Chivers says "Before [God] laid the world's foundation stone / High on the nothing of primeval night,"[88] he intends that the reader understand by visualizing the action. God fixing the cornerstone of the world led to more unusual work. By the same token that Chivers is able to accept and utilize the metaphor of an artisan construcing the world is he able to provide an almost surrealistic effect when he imagines his own death:

> The great golden hand on the Adamant Dial
> Of the Clock of Eternity pauses in Heaven!
> From Death's bony hand I now empty the Phial—
> And the Morning is just like the Even![89]

It is a sensory reaction that Chivers demands of the reader. By an extension of the physical reality of this world to a plane which is usually dealt with only in abstract terms, he presents an image which can be visualized by the imagination. I say "by the imagination," because Chivers seldom uses intimate detail of the physical world in his imagery. The scene set by "Death, from out Hell's bars, / Looked lean for want of life!"[90] is one which can be seen, but seen only by the inward, imaginative eye. The following description of a dead woman's hair moving slightly in the wind sets a scene clearly enough, but it is one which draws the imagination into the reader's reaction; where much romantic imagery provides a familiar or quickly visualized setting, the following scene exists in a separate world, a world which, I believe, existed within Chivers' own consciousness:

> the whispers of the odorous Breeze,
> Lifting her raven locks with spirit-hands,
> And weaving, with their glossy curls, the woof
> Wherein to hide the fragrance he had stolen—[91]

Or, more exactly, when he speaks of his own emotions Chivers turns to an imaginative world which is not far distant from that which provided such imagery as we have been examining. Here the metaphor is standard in its limits, until the final lines:

> The last dark wave that lashed affection's shore,
> Is pausing now upon my weary soul!
> Thy syren mistress of its tides shall be
> A lamp hung out beyond eternity![92]

Chivers' imagination and mind were extensive enough to grasp such an image, and through the use of them in his poetry he hoped to achieve the revelation of the nature of his reaction to certain situations. When the situation was one which included Heaven, then his inward reactions became the true image of that Heaven, or when it was of lesser import, as the one above, he could suggest the extreme nature of his reaction by images which immediately force the reader to abandon his grasp upon the physical world and to enter into Chivers' consciousness, which, partially at least, becomes just as visible and real as the world the reader has left.

The images we have examined so far have all dealt in visual and sometimes imaginative terms; they are the sensory reactions Chivers has spoken of which both explain the poet's response and demand intuitive comprehension by the reader. But Chivers depended less upon his visual sense for his most striking images, than upon a combination of his auditory and olfactory senses. At times such imagery approached sense confusion, but almost always such multiplicity of sensory response is intentional. It might better be called ambiguity than confusion of sensory response. When Emily Dickinson described a humming bird as "A resonance of emerald,"[93] she was uniting the reaction of her eye with that of her ear; such unification is of course intentional and it suggests the totality or the multiplicity of her understanding of the bird. Chivers also makes use (perhaps to a greater degree even than Emily Dickinson) of this totality of the senses.

When Chivers speaks of the "Incense-smoke of pain"[94] arising

· 245

from the crucified Christ, he combines odor with emotion, as it were, in almost symbolic terms, demanding that the reader experience as well as understand the scene. A more complicated image attempts to describe the murmur of a sea shell when held close to the ear: "Here, in its labyrinthine curve, it leaves / The footprints of its song in many dyes; / And here, incessantly, it ever weaves / The rainbow-tissue of its melodies."[95] Song, personified, is equated with color in such an image, and the effect is one of purposeful ambiguity or sense confusion.

It would seem that Chivers' ear supplied him with virtually all the ambiguities of sense imagery which he uses. This fact perhaps explains as well as depends upon his understanding of Heaven as a state of music. The inward world out of which almost all his more vivid imagery comes was one in which abstractions could have their own particular sound (and sometimes odor), and where vast forces are understood best in terms of their sound. Only once did Chivers attempt to describe his reaction definitively: entitled "The Voice of Thought," the following poem presents an explanation of what occurred during his moments of inspiration.

Faint as the far-down tone
   Beneath the sounding sea,
Muffled, by its own moan,
   To silent melody;
So faint we cannot tell
   But that the sound we hear
Is some sweet rose's smell
   That falls upon our ear;
(As if the Butterfly,
   Shaking the Lily-bell,
While drinking joyfully,
   Should toll its own death-knell!)
Sweeter than Hope's sweet lute
   Singing of joys to be
When Pain's harsh voice is mute,
   Is the Soul's sweet song to me.[96]

The poem's title helps us understand Chivers' method of sensory perception; thought, an abstraction, is given a voice, and that voice is best understood by Chivers when likened to the odor of a rose. The voice, he says ambiguously, is silent, yet that silence stirs a certain sensory reaction within him.

By such reaction as this, Chivers could achieve a variety of effects. The vastness of space and Heaven, which he so often spoke of in his poetry, gathers sound unto itself, much in the manner of the belief of Pythagoras in the music of spheres:

> the rolling spheres
> Diffuse their circular orbit-tones on high—
> Spreading till they embrace th' Eternal Years
> With their dilating, wave-like melody—
> Winnowing the calm, clear, interstellar air—[97]

Or he can turn the device about and give physical qualities to sound itself:

> Tempestuous whirlwinds of deep melody
> Dash from his orb-prow on his spheric road—
> Rolling in mountain-billows on Heaven's sea
> Against the white shore of the feet of God.[98]

The image becomes vast and all-inclusive as the singer's melody becomes a vessel moving through an ocean; the poem from which the image comes is an attempt to recreate an astronomer's sense of exultation as he discovers a new planet, and in its context the image serves to increase and broaden the reader's response to the poem.

But such sensory effects as Chivers desires were not always of such huge size. By taking the physical quality of one physical situation and giving it to another, he produced a visual image which is at once real and imaginative:

> Silver twilight softly snowing
> On the earth and on the sea,
> All the darkness overflowing—
> Rode the moon. . . .[99]

This entire image depends for its effect upon the use of the word *snowing* in connection with *twilight;* indeed, many of Chivers' most interesting images stem from his ability to snatch a word from a familiar context and put it in another, where it both describes the image and suggests the one from which it was taken.

But sound imagery, which is the particular fascination of so many of his poems, can be carried further, sometimes too far. A harpist is described:

> While from his fingers' ends the dews of sound
> Dript, changing into Jewels as they fall,
> Bright as stalactites of crystal. . . .[100]

The imagery which has been described here is not unusual in Chivers' poetry; it is not chosen with any purpose other than to present his most typical and yet most unorthodox images. There are, of course, numbers of poems which are wholly standard in imagery: here the wind is personified.

> Thou wringest, with thy invisible hand, the foam
> Out of the emerald drapery of the sea,
> Beneath whose foldings lies the Sea-Nymph's home—
> Lifted, to make it visible, by thee. . . .[101]

But even as standard a romantic image as this indicates Chivers' primary interest and effect; it is an imaginative, visual, yet suggestive world out of which he would write. His attempt to re-create the totality of his sense response to particular situations through ambiguity is only a symptom of the completeness with which his emotions responded to certain stimuli.

The manner in which Chivers often strings a series of similes together to illustrate his reaction to an experience indicates further his attempt to make the Divine Idea, to use his words, clear to the reader. By comparing his subject with a variety of partially similar subjects or experiences, he hopes to illustrate the basic quality of that subject. These similes, as well as certain of his almost metaphysical conceits, frequently deal in terms of the poet's senses, for, as has been noted, Chivers would change sensation into thought or understanding, and one of the surest ways of achieving such a change is to force the reader to respond with his own senses in a variety of ways until the subject of the poem becomes an actual experience for him just as it was for the poet.

 Notes

Numbers in brackets at the top of the following pages indicate the pages in the text to which these notes refer.

The following abbreviations are used for some of Chiver's published volumes: C&E, *Conrad and Eudora;* EofR, *Eonchs of Ruby;* LP, *The Lost Pleiad;* M, *Memoralia;* N, *Nacoochee;* PofS, *The Path of Sorrow;* SofU, *The Sons of Usna;* V, *Virginalia.*

Preface

1. There is disagreement over the date of Chivers' birth. His wife said he was 52 at his death in 1858; the dates on his tombstone corroborate this evidence. But Chivers successfully defended himself against a suit brought against him by his first wife by establishing the fact that he was a minor at the time of their separation in 1828 (Records of the Taliaferro Superior Court, Wilkes County, Georgia, January term, 1832). Thus he was not born in 1807. Two poems provide evidence for what I believe to be the correct date: "To My Precious Mother, on the Anniversary of my Twenty-Fifth Year," *C&E,* pp. 90-92, dated 1834; and "Hymn to Death," *C&E,* pp. 102-103, dated 1834, line 57 of which, "My four and twentieth year," indicates his age at the time of composition. See S. Foster Damon, *Thomas Holley Chivers* (New York, 1930), p. 30n, and James A. Harrison, ed., *The Complete Works of Edgar Allan Poe* (New York, 1902), VII, 268 and 281, for further discussion of this point.
2. Purchased from Chivers' great-nephew's wife, Mrs. Percy Hoyle Adams, these mss. are now housed in the Chivers Collection, hereinafter referred to as Chms.
3. See particularly Joel Benton, *In the Poe Circle* (New York, 1899), and Harrison, *Works of Poe,* VII.

Chapter I

4. The first anthology to include any of his poems, interestingly enough, was W. M. Rossetti's *American Poems* (London, n.d.).
5. Edmund Clarence Stedman, *Poets of America* (Cambridge, Mass.), 1855, p. 250.
6. See stanza 4, "Lily Adair," *V,* pp. 26-26.
7. For a discussion of the possibility that Rossetti may have derived the concept of "The Blessed Damosel" from Chivers, see Damon, *Chivers,* pp. 270-272. A copy of *EofR* with Rossetti's signature on the fly leaf is in the Dewitt Miller Library, Forest Glen, Maryland.
8. Horace E. Scudder to William Rossetti, *Rossetti Papers 1862 to 1870* (London, 1930), pp. 180-181.
9. E. C. Stedman to J. K. Adams, July 3 and September 15, 1888; Chms.
10. Andrew D. White, *Autobiography* (New York, 1905), p. 359.
11. "Literary Chat," *The Times* (Chattanooga, Tenn.), March 5, 1899.
12. For a discussion of these circumstances, see pages 113-114; [cross-references (such as this one), to this study itself, have been provided throughout].
13. There is a photostat of this copy in the Harris Collection of Brown University.
14. Records of Transylvania University, Lexington, Kentucky.
15. "Kosciusko's Resignation," *PofS,* pp. 124-125, dated April 10, 1829; "Anastasius," *PofS,* pp. 114-118, dated July 10, 1829; "Though the Rose of my Eden is Blasted,"

PofS, pp. 122-123, dated April 10, 1830; "On the Death of Adaline," *PofS,* pp. 18-30, dated August 20, 1830.

16. See pages 218-220 for a discussion of these experiments.

17. "An Elegy," *PofS,* pp. 128-129, written on the death of one of his tutors, Thomas Lacey, suggests that his reading was in some part directed by this man. It was a normal circumstance for a wealthy plantation owner to have his son tutored at home rather than sending him to school. One of Chivers' daughters recalls that Chivers' mother was reputed to have tutored him also.

18. Chms. Preface to ms. of *Songs of Sorrow.*

19. Many of the clippings from such a file are in the Chivers scrapbooks in Chms.

20. Chms. Preface to the ms. of *Songs of Sorrow.* Chivers crossed the lines out in the manuscript.

21. Ms. in Chms.

22. Included without change are: "Anastasius," "Kosciusko's Resignation" as " (Fragment of a War Lyric)." Revised are: "On the Death of Adaline" as "The Death of Adaline," "The Prophet's Dream" as "Eleusis," "The Lament of Youth" as "April Drops of Lode," "Though the Rose of my Eden is Blasted" as "To One Dearly Beloved, But Early Lost."

23. "The Separation," Chms. in the ms. of *Songs of Sorrow,* 11, 65-70, 74-78.

24. See, for example, "To * * * *," *PofS,* pp. 126-127.

25. See "To Idealon," *N,* opposite p. 1.

26. "Song," *N,* p. 103; of the *PofS* text it uses 11. 1-14 as its first 14 lines; the remaining lines are new.

27. Chms.

28. *Western Monthly Magazine,* I (July, 1833), 321-325.

29. *Ibid.,* p. 322.

30. *Ibid.*

31. *Ibid.,* p. 324.

32. "Lines written on Receiving the *New Monthly Magazine,*" *Western Weekly Review,* February 7, 1834.

33. Constance Rourke, in her *American Humor* (New York, 1935), develops the thesis of the bitterness which lay behind many of the western tales.

34. The 1834 volume of the *Western Weekly Magazine* contains the following pieces: "Lines Written on Receiving the *New Monthly Magazine,*" February 7; "Squire Bunkley of Sandy Cross," February 14 and 21; "Western Beauty," March 6; "Lines on Parting, Dedicated to the Ladies," March 6; "The Burial at Sea," April 25.

35. Such is the date of the original Preface; this Preface, although written for *Conrad and Eudora,* was first published as the Preface to *Leoni, or The Orphan of Venice (Georgia Citizen,* May 17, 1851), a play which is a recasting of *Conrad and Eudora.*

36. Printed in Philadelphia, 1834; no printer or publisher is indicated.

37. Marion Lee Steinmetz, *The Sharp-Beauchamp Case in American Literature,* unpublished Master's thesis, Brown University, 1951, p. 6. See "An Elegy on the Death of my friend, Mr. Thomas Lacey," *PofS,* pp. 128-131, for proof of Chivers' close acquaintanceship.

The details of the murder have been culled from the above-mentioned thesis, and from the unpublished Master's theses of Ardrew Shields McIlwaine, *The Beauchamp Tragedy in American Drama,* University of Chicago, 1927, and of Kate Tipton Irvine, *The Beauchamp Tragedy in American Fiction,* University of Kentucky, 1932.

38. Preface to *Leoni, Georgia Citizen,* May 17, 1851; Act I appeared in this issue,

Act II on May 24, Act III on May 31, Act IV on June 7, and Act V on June 14, 1851.

39. The Pamphlet is not dated; it was apparently republished by H. T. Goodsell, of Kentucky, in 1854.

40. "A New Tragedy," *New-York Mirror,* IV (July 29, 1826), 7.

41. *C&E,* II, ii, 11. 25-26.

42. Besides *Conrad and Eudora,* Poe's *Politian,* written in 1835, Charlotte M. S. Barnes' *Octavia Bragaldi* (1837), and John Savage's *Sybil* (1856), are based on the Sharp-Beauchamp case.
    See McIlwaine, *Beauchamp Tragedy.*

43. *C&E,* II, i, 11. 55-56.

44. The sight of the American Indian in his native habitat did inspire Chivers temporarily.

45. One William Parker, in testimony gathered for Chivers' wife's suit to obtain alimony, mentions his "Doctor's shop" in Sandy Cross. (Records of the Talia-ferro Superior Court, Wilkes County, Georgia, January term, 1833.)
    J. Q. Adams, "Thomas H. Chivers," *Atlanta Constitution,* March 14, 1897.

46. There is evidence of the influence of Edward Young.

47. The poems dated from Philadelphia are: "The South," pp. 92-93, "To a Ladye," pp. 139-140, "To Ellen," pp. 110-111, and "To Miss W * * * *," p. 130; all may be found in *C&E.*

48. "Hymn to the Deity," *M,* pp. 24-25, is dated "Oak Grove, Ga.," in 1834.

49. "The Broken Heart" and "A Forest Hymn," December 12, 1835.

50. There is a Chms. clipping of "Atala's Prayer," published in *V,* pp. 70-71, indi-cating a publication in the *Atlanta Enterprise* which has not been traced; it is dated 1836.

51. "The Dying Year," *Knickerbocker,* IX (January, 1837), 62; "Morning Hymn," *New Yorker,* IV (December 9, 1837), 594.

52. "To Correspondents," *Southern Literary Messenger,* I (March, 1835), 387.

53. See page 138.

54. "To Readers and Correspondents," *New York Mirror,* XII (May 16, 1835), 367.

55. *Ibid.,* XI (June 27, 1835), 414.

56. See pages 118-120.

57. See pages 117-118.

58. See Damon, *Chivers,* p. 92; the poem referred to is "The Dying Beauty," (*N,* pp. 45-47), which appeared as "Euthanasia" in *V,* pp. 69-70.

59. For an explanation of the symbolism, see page 268, note 42.

60. See both George White, *Historical Collections of Georgia* (New York, 1854), and Lucian Lamar Knight, *Georgia's Landmarks, Memorials, and Legends* (Atlanta, Georgia, 1914).

61. "Tuccoa," *Baltimore Literary Monument,* I (March, 1839), 217-218.

62. "Notes and Queries," *The Criterion,* I (February 23, 1856), 269.

63. William Bartram, *Travels through North and South Carolina* (Philadelphia, 1791), p. 372.

64. *Ibid.,* pp. 365-366.

65. These explorations and the mound's history are described by George G. Heye, F. W. Hodge, and George H. Pepper, "The Nacoochee Mound in Georgia," *Con-tributions from the Museum of the American Indian* (New York, 1918), IV, No. 3.

66. "Notes and Queries," *The Criterion,* I (February 23, 1856), 269. Chivers' He-brew is correct, but he is mistaken in believing that the Cherokee *Nacoochee* is derived from the Hebrew.

67. Preface to *Nacoochee.*

68. For a discussion of his theory of poetry, see pages 211-217.

69. Preface to *Nacoochee*.

70. *Ibid*.

71. This copy is privately owned.

72. *Chivers' Life of Poe*, Richard Beale Davis, ed. (New York, 1952), p. 73, HEH HM 24272, contains proof of Chivers' acquaintance with early *Southern Literary Messenger* texts of Poe's poems. Mr. Davis takes his text from mss. in the Henry E. Huntington Library; throughout I will cite Huntington mss. numbers and the appropriate pages from *Chivers' Life*.

73. Chivers to Poe, July 12, 1842; the ms. is in the Griswold Collection in the Boston Public Library.

74. Thomas Ollive Mabbott, "Kilmer and Chivers," *The New York Times,* June 4, 1933, section 4, p. 5, recalls having seen Kilmer's name when he himself borrowed the Columbia University copy in about 1918.

75. Chivers' first wife, Frances, began proceedings against him in 1841, and was granted a divorce in 1842. (Records of the Superior Court, Troup County, Ga., 1840-44.) He could legally marry a second time before having been divorced from his first wife because of a Georgia law which allowed such action if husband and wife had been separated for five years. (Oliver H. Prince, *Digest of the Laws of the State of Georgia* [Athens, Ga., 1837], p. 645.)

76. Recorded in a Chivers family Bible now owned by Mrs. Buford Smith of Savannah.

77. Chivers to E. Connor, Esq., March 7, 1838: Chms.

78. "Sonnet. On hearing of the Death of My Mother," *LP,* p. 24, dated "April 1, 1838" from Philadelphia; "Lament on the Death of My Mother," *LP,* p. 18, dated "April 9, 1838," from Oaky Grove, Georgia.

79. "To One Beloved," *Philadelphia Saturday Courier,* June 16, 1838, is dated "Off Cape Hatteras"; apparently Chivers had decided to return by boat.

80. "To Allegra," *Sentinel and Witness,* June 26, 1839.
    One poem, "The Dying Year," had been reprinted from the *Knickerbocker,* IX (January, 1837), 62, in the *Sentinel and Witness,* January 25, 1837.

81. *The National Magazine and Republican Review* is a good example; his first poem appeared there in February, 1839; by the end of June, ten had been published there.

82. "My Spirit's Bride," *National Magazine and Republican Review,* I (March, 1839), 260.

83. "The Grave of Dade," *Sentinel and Witness,* November 13, 1839.

84. "Wreck of the Home," *Sentinel and Witness,* December 4, 1839. "Burning of the Lexington," *The Brother Jonathan,* January 25, 1840, and "Loss of the Central America," *Georgia Citizen,* May 21, 1858, show the same interest. "Hymn to the Ocean at First Sight," *C&E,* p. 127, is the best of his poems on the ocean's effect upon his imagination.

85. "Virtue," *National Magazine and Republican Review,* II (May, 1839), 76.

86. "To Allegra, Two Weeks after Her Birth," *Sentinel and Witness,* June 26, 1839, is dated "June 23rd, 1839."

87. See pages 180-182 for a discussion of Chivers' visionary experience.

88. *Sentinel and Witness,* July 17, 1839.

89. *Sentinel and Witness,* August 14, 1839.

90. *Ibid*.

91. *Sentinel and Witness,* August 21 and September 11, 1839, respectively.

92. See chapter three.

93. "John Newland Maffitt," *Sentinel and Witness,* September 1, 1841.

94. "Buzzards," *Sentinel and Witness,* September 8, 1841.

95. "Awful Death," *Sentinel and Witness,* September 15, 1841.
96. Only one poem was published in 1844.
97. Chivers' family Bible records the date of her death, as well as those of three other children. Chivers told Poe that Allegra Florence had died after an illness of only two days. (Chivers to Poe, December 7, 1842; the ms. of the letter is in the Griswold Collection of mss. in the Boston Public Library.)
98. For a discussion of Chivers' visions, see pages 180-182.
99. *LP,* pp. 15-16.
100. The Bible record gives the following names and dates: Allegra Florence, died October 18, 1842; Eugene Percy, died January, 1848; Ada Lallage, died April 2, 1848; Thomas Holley, died April 7, 1848. I believe that 1848 should be 1843, for the original family Bible is said to have been burned during the Civil War. In court testimony in 1873, Mrs. Chivers, trying to establish the dates of her children's births, said that the Bible record had been altered at least once, and that she was not at all certain of its correctness. Left poverty-stricken after the Civil War, she had difficulty enough clothing and feeding her surviving children without concerning herself with their birth dates. (See *Reports of Cases in Law and Equity, Argued and Determined in the Supreme Court of Georgia,* Atlanta, 1912, XLVIII, 219-220.) If they did occur in 1848, there is certainly no evident reaction to the triple tragedy in Chivers' writings of that period.
101. They are: "The Invocation," August 11; "To Ianthe in Heaven," August 25; "The Lover's Lament for His Mistress Lost at Sea," September 1; and "Noises of the Night," October 6.
102. "The Lover's Lament for His Mistress Lost at Sea," September 1.
103. For example, "Spring," pp. 21-22, "The Voiceless Earth," p. 24, and "Song to Spring," p. 30.
104. See page 153.
105. See, for example, the *Federal Union* [Milledgeville, Georgia], September 23, 1845.
106. *Southern Patriot,* August 7, 1845, and August 19, 1845.
107. Chms. fragment, untitled.
108. "Editorial Bureau," *Southern and Western Monthly Magazine and Review,* II (October, 1845), 277-281.
109. Chivers to Poe, September 9, 1845, speaks of this happiness. The ms. is in the Griswold Collection of mss. in the Boston Public Library.
110. Chivers to Sims, April 10, 1852: George E. Woodberry, "The Poe-Chivers Papers," *The Century Magazine,* LXV (February, 1903), 553.
111. Poe to Chivers, August 29, 1845: John Ward Ostrom, ed., *The Letters of Edgar Allan Poe* (Cambridge, Mass., 1848), p. 296. He had noted receipt of the article as early as September, 1845.
112. Chivers to Poe, September 9, 1845: the ms. is in the Griswold Collection of mss. in the Boston Public Library.
113. His dead children still appear; "The Violet in the Valley of Rest," *Christian Index,* February 10, 1848, and "The Bruised Reed," *Ibid.,* October 7, 1847, are both concerned with Allegra Florence's death.
114. *The Magnolia,* N.S. II (January, 1843), 52-53.
115. *Graham's Magazine,* XX (June, 1842), 329.
116. *Search after Truth,* pp. 35-37.
117. "To couch" an eye (an old surgical term) was to remove a cataract. (See *New English Dictionary.*) This is one of the very few evidences in Chivers' work of his medical training.
118. *Search after Truth,* p. 19.
119. *Ibid.*

120. *Ibid.*, p. 58.
121. A. J. Davis, *Principles of Nature* (New York, 1847).
122. *Univercoelum,* September 16, 1848.
123. "Letter to the Editor," *Univercoelum,* II (October 28, 1848), 346.
124. "Scene from 'Via Coeli,'" *Univercoelum,* III (December 9, 1848), 22-23.
125. "Shelley," *Univercoelum,* III (March 31, 1849), 285-286.
126. "Orphic Truths," *Univercoelum,* III (May 5, 1849), 356.
127. *The Spirit Messenger* received a letter of praise from Chivers on August 31, 1850 (I, 30-31), because it so much resembled *The Univercoelum.*
128. "Letters from New York," *Georgia Citizen,* April 19, 1851.
129. "The Greek Slave," *Georgia Citizen,* May 17, 1850.
130. "Letters from New York," *Georgia Citizen,* March 8, 1851.
131. Chivers to Poe, April 4, 1847: the ms. is in the Griswold Collection of mss. in the Boston Public Library.
132. "Letters from New York," *Georgia Citizen,* April 19, 1851.
133. "Letters from New York," *Georgia Citizen,* September 20, 1850.
134. "To Jenny Lind," *Waverly Magazine,* II (October 12, 1850), 45.
135. "Letters from New York," *Georgia Citizen,* February 1, 1851.
136. "Letters from New York," *Georgia Citizen,* April 5, 1851.
137. "Letters from New York," *Georgia Citizen,* February 1, 1851.
138. The "frog pond" is Boston, an oblique and critical reference originally made by Poe to New England Transcendentalism.
139. *New York Tribune,* December 27, 1850.
140. "Letters from New York," *Georgia Citizen,* February 22, 1851.
141. "Letters from New York," *Georgia Citizen,* March 15, 1851.
142. *Ibid.*
143. In his *Dream of a Day* (New Haven, 1843).
144. The files of the *Philadelphia American and Gazette* have not been found.
145. "The Patriot Dead," *Georgia Citizen,* May 31, 1850.
146. *Ibid.*
147. "The Valley of Diamonds," *Georgia Citizen,* June 14, 1850.
     Fredrika Bremer was a well-known Swedish novelist who was joyously received by the New York literati upon her arrival in 1849.
148. "The Valley of Diamonds," *Georgia Citizen,* July 5, 1850.
149. "The Valley of Diamonds," *Georgia Citizen,* July 5, 1850.
150. "The New School of Poetry," *Literary Union,* April, 1850.
151. "The Valley of Diamonds," *Georgia Citizen,* July 12, 1850.
152. Chivers says "To Allegra Florence in Heaven" was published in the *Southern Literary Messenger;* there is no evidence that it appeared publicly before 1845 except at it was reviewed in the *Orion,* II (March-April, 1843), 370-372.
153. One of these, "The Departed" (*Broadway Journal,* II [July 12, 1845], 7), Chivers later said was Poe's; others have believed it Chivers'. At bottom right, just beneath the poem as it is printed in the *Broadway Journal,* appears a mark resembling the letter "L." Under a magnifying glass, it becomes little more than a misplaced printer's mark, for the upright part of the letter is too grossly elongated to be read as an "L," and the seeming period is too far above the line to be interpreted as such. I believe its presence contributes nothing toward identifying the poem.
154. "To My Angel Daughter," *Boston Museum,* I (March 17, 1849), 313, 11. 1-10. Chivers omitted the two final lines when he quoted this stanza.
155. "The Valley of Diamonds," *Georgia Citizen,* July 19, 1850.
156. Chivers to Poe, August 27, 1840: the ms. is in the Griswold Collection of mss. in the Boston Public Library.

157. "The Valley of Diamonds," *Georgia Citizen,* August 2, 1850.
158. "Letters from New York," *Georgia Citizen,* April 5, 1851. The original collection of Chivers' manuscripts still contained, in 1888, letters from Willis not extant today. (See J. Q. Adams, "Edgar Allan Poe," *Atlanta Constitution,* March 3, 1888.)
159. "Letters from New York," *Georgia Citizen,* February 22, 1851.
    Bryant's trip to South Carolina was recorded in the eleventh of his *Letters of a Traveller* (New York, 1850).
160. *Parnassus in Pillory* (New York, 1851), p. 79, 11. 1-2.
161. Preface to *Woodland Melodies,* ACms.
162. The only copy I know of is in the Huntington Library.
163. Chivers to Poe, April 4, 1847: the ms. is in the Griswold Collection of mss. in the Boston Public Library.
164. "Eonchs of Ruby," *Georgia Citizen,* June 28, 1851. "Correspondence" refers to Emanuel Swedenborg's theory that the word of God could be known by a true understanding of the natural world, for every natural object is seen as the "effect" of a spiritual "cause." Thus a series of correspondences between the natural and the spiritual world is created by which the latter may be known.
165. *EofR,* pp. 117-119 and p. 145.
166. "Book Table," *The Message-Bird,* December 16, 1850.
167. *Whitaker's Magazine,* I (December, 1850), 624-631.
168. *Ibid.*
169. *American Whig Review,* N.S. VII (January, 1851), 96.
170. See, for example, *Arthur's Home Gazette,* December 28, 1850.
171. Edith Lindsey, "Dr. Chivers' Poems," *Georgia Citizen,* January 4, 1851.
172. J. Hunt, Jr., "Eonchs of Ruby," *Georgia Citizen,* May 24, 1851.
    A disturbing question arises concerning this review. A series of letters exchanged between Hunt and Chivers just before the review appeared suggests that Chivers himself may have dictated at least part of Hunt's criticism.
173. "Letters from the North" extended in the *Georgia Citizen* from April 26, 1851, to March 24, 1854, and included forty-two articles.
    "Letters from the North," New Series, extended from June 2, 1854, through eight numbers until November 17, 1854.
174. "Letters from the North," New Series, *Georgia Citizen,* September 22, 1854. This is Chivers' only reference to Melville.
175. "The Belles of Tontine," *V,* pp. 22-23, 11. 28-36.
176. "Letters from the North," *Georgia Citizen,* June 28, 1851.
177. "Letters from the North," *Georgia Citizen,* August 16, 1851.
178. The same belief is expressed in *Search after Truth.*
179. *Ibid.*
180. "Letters from the North," *Georgia Citizen,* June 12, 1852.
181. "Letters from the North," *Georgia Citizen,* May 14, 1853.
182. "Letters from the North," *Georgia Citizen,* June 5, 1852.
183. "The Great Know Nothing," *Georgia Citizen,* April 7, 1854.
184. *Ibid.* Thus it becomes clear why Charles A. Dana (of the *Tribune*) thought Chivers "a literary freak." ("Thomas Holley Chivers," *The Times* [Chattanooga, Tenn.], March 5, 1899.)
185. G. K. Dickinson to Longfellow, May 27, 1852, and June 18, 1852: Longfellow Collection, Craigie House, Harvard.
186. Horace Elisha Scudder, *James Russell Lowell* (Boston, 1901), p. 375.
187. Simms to Chivers, April 5, 1852, and Chivers to Simms, April 10, 1852; Woodberry, "The Poe-Chivers Papers," pp. 552-554.
188. "Editorial Notes," *Putnam's Monthly,* I (May, 1835), 583.

189. *New York Quarterly,* II (April, 1853), 161-163.
190. "Miscellany," *Georgia Citizen,* March 26, 1853.
191. "New Works," *Waverley Magazine,* VI (April 9, 1853), 233.
192. One of the most extraordinary examples of these characteristics is bound with the Harris Collection's copy of Edwin Augustus Atlee's *Essays at Poetry* (Philadelphia, 1828). Entitled "The Religion of the Sun, A Posthumous Poem," supposedly by Thomas Paine, it contains many of the elements which make Chivers' poetry successful.
193. January 8, 15, and 22, 1853. Copies of the printed text at Harvard and in the British Museum have corrections in Chivers' hand. The *Georgia Citizen* deleted various lines descriptive of the physical union of the two lovers.
194. Chivers may have obtained the word from Young's *Night Thoughts,* Book Two, 11. 172-173, or possibly from Poe's "Morella."
195. See pages 178-180.
196. Simms to Chivers, April 5, 1852: Woodberry, "The Poe-Chivers Papers," pp. 552-553.
197. This copy is in the British Museum.
198. "A Paul Epic," *Southern Literary Messenger,* XIX (June, 1853), 379-382.
199. *Dodge's Literary Museum,* V (October 30, 1852), 334.
200. *The Spiritual Telegraph,* III (September 9, 1854), 75.
201. "The Valley of Diamonds," *Georgia Citizen,* July 12, 1850.
202. *Spirit Messenger, N.S.,* I (January 15, 1852), 47-48.
203. "Letters from the North," *Georgia Citizen,* June 26, 1852.
204. *Boston Museum,* IV (February 28, 1852), 300.
205. *Dodge's Literary Museum,* V (June 19, 1852), 26.
206. "Apollo," *V,* p. 24, 11. 1-2: quoted in "Letters from the North," *Georgia Citizen,* July 3, 1852.
207. *Lily of the Valley for 1853* (Boston, 1853), p. 159.
208. For example, his "Invocation to Spring," *V,* pp. 87-89, he believed had been plagiarized in "Summer Friends," *Lantern,* I (May 22, 1852), 202, ["Letters from the North," *Georgia Citizen,* July 10, 1852]; the same poem he thought had been used by John Townsend Trowbridge in his "The Mill Pond," *Putnam's Magazine,* I (April, 1853), 369-370, ["Letters from the North," *Georgia Citizen,* May 14, 1853].
209. "Letters from the North," *Georgia Citizen,* February 26, 1853.
210. *Waverley Magazine,* VII, 73. This pseudonymn, and another Chivers used, "Dr. Eugene Percy," still fool literary historians; see Bertram Holland Flanders, *Early Georgia Magazines* (Athens, Georgia, 1944).
211. "A Croak from the Raven," *Waverley Magazine,* VII (August 13, 1853), 105.
212. "Edgar A. Poe," *Waverley Magazine,* VII (August 13, 1853), 108.
213. "Honey from Hybla," *Waverley Magazine,* VII (August 20, 1853), 120.
214. "The True Odin," *Waverley Magazine,* VII (August 20, 1853), 121.
213. "Honey from Hybla," *Waverley Magazine,* VII (August 20, 1853), 120. The article is signed "M."
216. E. H[erbert]. L[ancey], "Plagiarism," *Waverley Magazine,* VII (September 3, 1853), 152.
217. "Poe's Plagiarism," *Waverley Magazine,* VII (October 1, 1853), 216.
218. *Ibid.*
219. *Waverley Magazine,* VII (October 29, 1853), 284. Chivers' article was apparently either "The Mastix," or "More Honey from Hybla," both in Chms., and both extreme in statement and tone.
220. *Waverley Magazine,* VII (July 2, 1853), 11.
221. Chivers to J. R. Snead, Esq., June, 1853: the letter is in the Chms.

222. IX, 91.
223. "Cape Island Correspondence," *Waverley Magazine,* IX (July 29, 1854), 73.
224. "Plagiarism," *Dodge's Literary Museum,* IX (August 5, 1854), 141.
225. "Editorial Chit-Chat," *Waverley Magazine,* IX (August 5, 1854), 88.
226. Grace LeBaron Upham, "A Memoir of Mrs. Jane Ermina Locke," in *Contributions of the Old Residents' Historical Association,* of Lowell, Mass., (Lowell, 1890), IV, No. 3.
227. Mrs. Jane E. Locke, *Waverley Magazine,* IX (August 5, 1854), 88.
228. *Dodge's Literary Museum,* IX (August 19, 1854), 169.
229. This controversy began shortly after the poem's publication. Thomas Conrad Porter (*National Intelligencer,* XLIII [November 25, 1855], 2) accused Longfellow of having derived "Hiawatha" from the "Kalevala." Moncure Daniel Conway replied in defence on November 29, (XLIII, 2); he had reviewed the poem favorably on November 23, (XLIII, 2).
230. "Professor Longfellow's 'Hiawatha,'" *Georgia Citizen,* January 19, 1856. This article was continued on February 16.
231. See pages 268-270.
232. "The Dignity of the Medical Profession," I (June, 1858), 76-82; "Life," I (August, 1858), 129-133; "Theurgia," I (October, 1858), 211-220.
233. One draft of the letter, addressed to L. F. W. Adams, exists in the Chms. How much of Chivers' energy went into the writing of plays in the last decade of his life is impossible to say. There is one play in manuscript in the Chivers Collection, entitled *Charles Stuart,* which the *Literary Museum,* V (August 3, 1852), 60, announced had been sold to "Dickinson, the English tragedian, for the sum of $1,000." Letters from Dickinson to Chivers indicate he was to have been paid out of the profits of its projected performance. There is no record of its ever having been produced.
234. *Georgia Citizen,* April 20, 1858.
235. Harriette H. Chivers to L. F. W. Andrews, December 20, 1858: the letter is in Chms.

CHAPTER II

1. The review is quoted by James D. Hart, in his *The Popular Book* (New York, 1950), p. 92. See Randall Stewart, *Nathaniel Hawthorne* (New Haven, 1948), pp. 95-99 for details of publishing and reception.
2. Quoted by Willard Thorp in his critical edition of *Moby Dick* (New York, 1947), p. x.
3. Hart, *Popular Book,* p. 68. Many of the details of the literary scene noted here have their source in *The Popular Book.*
4. For a summary of Davis' activities and beliefs see Damon, *Chivers,* pp. 155-159.
5. "Avalon," *EofR,* pp. 49-56, 1, 106.
6. "Letters from the North," *Georgia Citizen,* August 16, 1851.
7. Hart, *Popular Book,* p. 27.
8. "Letters from the North," *Georgia Citizen,* June 14, 1851.
9. "The Mighty Dead," *EofR,* pp. 27-48, 1, 224.
10. "A Longing to Know," *LP,* p. 31, ll. 7-8.
11. Only once, in "The Gospel of Love," *EofR,* pp. 103-106, did Chivers preach directly on ethical matters; in this poem he suggests the parent should love, not punish the child to develop correct manners. It concludes, interestingly enough, with a plea for the abolishment of "death-punishment."
12. "The Lost Pleiad," *LP,* pp. 5-12, ll. 628-641.
13. Edward Young, *Night Thoughts,* "Ninth Night," ll. 264-269.
14. "The Death of Time," *N,* pp. 32-35, ll. 18-33.

15. Proof of this is in Chivers' use of the name Narcissa in "The Vestal's Tomb," *C&E*, p. 107; "Narcissa" is the title of the Third Night of *Night Thoughts*.
16. "The Consolation," *Night Thoughts*, 11. 1258-1259.
   Young took his image, as he indicates, from Joshua, X, xii, & xiii. It is entirely possible that Chivers found the image there independently. Tennyson also used it in "Locksley Hall," 1. 180: ". . . like Joshua's moon in Ajalon!"
17. "Avalon," *EofR*, pp. 49-56, 11. 45-55.
18. "Western Beauty," *Western Weekly Review*, March 6, 1834, contains quotations and paraphrases from Books V and VIII of *The Course of Time:* "The Broken Heart," *Augusta Chronicle*, December 12, 1835, takes its theme from Book V, 11. 421-422.
19. *The Course of Time*, Book Sixth, 11. 46-48, 54-62.
20. "The Death of Time," *N*, pp. 32-36, 11. 47-54, 68-73.
21. Rollin G. Osterweis, *Romanticism and Nationalism in the Old South* (New Haven, 1949), pp. 98-99.
22. *PofS*, pp. 124-125.
23. Preface to *Atlanta*.
24. "To Thekla," *National Magazine and Republican Review*, I (March, 1839), 299; Moore's footnotes are numbers 214 and 223. Chivers also uses the phrase "gul-scented"; its definition is in footnote number 316.
25. "To Allegra, Two Weeks After Her Birth," *Sentinel and Witness*, June 26, 1839.
26. For a comprehensive analysis of the *Israfel* controversy, see pages 161-163.
27. "The Veiled Prophet," *Lalla Rookh*, 11. 722-725.
28. "The Heavenly Vision," *Graham's Magazine*, XX (June, 1842), 329; it was one of two poems Poe praised as being among "the finest I have *ever read*." (Poe to Chivers, July 6, 1842: Ostrom, *Letters*, pp. 207-208.) It was republished in *LP*, p. 19.
29. "Uranothen," *V*, pp. 97-99, 11. 45-48.
30. *Western Weekly Review*, March 6, 1834.
31. *Dodge's Literary Museum*, V (October 23, 1852), 318.
32. "Sonnet. The Release of Fionnuala," *EofR*, p. 146. Chivers repeats the substance of Moore's note, without adding its source.
33. Chivers' use of an obscure literary reference from this review is noted by Mr. Davis in his edition of *Chivers' Life of Poe*, p. 115.
34. "Sonnet on Reading Mrs. Browning's Drama of Exile," *V*, p. 118.
35. *A Drama of Exile*, 11. 207-209.
36. "The Chaplet of Cypress," *EofR*, pp. 117-119, 11. 1-6.
37. "Song of Le Verrier," *Ladies National Magazine*, XIV (December, 1848), 215.
38. "Uranothen," *V*, pp. 97-99.
39. A. C. Newcomer, "The Poe-Chivers Tradition Re-examined," *The Sewanee Review*, XII (January, 1904), 20-35.
40. "The Prophet's Dream," *PofS*, pp. 44-72, 11. 8-9.
41. *Ibid.*, stanzas XL and XLI.
42. In *PofS*, "The Minstrel's Valedictory," p. 36, "The Prophet's Dream," p. 44, "The Lament of Youth," p. 84. Almost all of these poems with liberty and freedom as their theme have a certain biblical cast. One important difference is that Chivers' poems do not speak of the future; the prophecies of which he speaks are always at hand.
43. "The Prophet's Dream," *PofS*, stanza XC.
44. "The Lament of Youth," *PofS*, Canto II, stanza 11, pp. 104-105.
45. "On the Death of Adaline," *PofS*, p. 29, 11. 2-6.
46. "The Retrospect," *PofS*, pp. 113-114.

47. See pages 175-182.
48. "The Lost Pleiad," *LP*, pp. 5-12, 11. 223-232.
49. See particularly *Psalms* 49, 80, 107, 136.
50. "Song to Isadore," *The Univercoelum*, III (December 16, 1848), 39, 11. 22-28.
51. "Lily Adair," *EofR*, pp. 164-166, 11. 56-66.
52. "The Chaplet of Cypress," *EofR*, pp. 117-119, 11. 1-6.
53. Preface to *Virginalia*.
54. *The Western Review*, III (November, 1820), 235.
55. "The Lament of Youth," *PofS*, Canto I, p. 93, 1, 22.
56. In "The Farewell," contained in the Chms. of the *Songs of Sorrow* collection. The note was probably added when Chivers attempted to revise *The Path of Sorrow* in 1837.
57. This summary has been gathered from obviously autobiographical details in "The Dream," "The Minstrel's Valedictory," "The Lament of Youth," "Let My Name Still Survive," "To a Friend," "Though the Rose of my Eden is Blasted," and "To * * * *." All are in *The Path of Sorrow*. Furthermore, the records of the Taliaferro Superior Court, Wilkes County, Georgia, for 1832, contain an alimony bill brought against Chivers by his wife. She charged extreme cruelty; his answer protests that she has been falsely persuaded to leave him by relatives unfriendly to him.
58. See "An Elegy," *PofS*, pp. 128-129.
59. See stanza XLIV.
60. In *Ladies' National Magazine* XII (November, 1847), 159.
61. 11. 21-24.
62. Chivers, no Augustan, felt no temptation to follow Byron's satiric bent. "Satire," he said, "belongs to the province of prose—not to poetry." ("Letters from New York," *Georgia Citizen*, April 5, 1851.)
63. Damon, *Chivers*, pp. 64-65.
64. "The Minstrel's Valedictory," *PofS*, pp. 36-43, 11. 113-118.
65. The suffering of the just man wronged appears also in "The Prophet's Dream," *PofS*, pp. 44-71, a poem but slightly influenced by the Byronic figure.
66. Canto IV, 11. 1228-1229.
67. "Lament of Youth," *PofS*, 84-105, 11. 332-334, and in 11. 413-416.
68. 11. 1207-1215.
69. "The Dream," pp. 9-17, "On the Death of Adaline," pp. 18-19, "The Lament of Youth," pp. 84-108, and "The Retrospect," pp. 109-113.
70. A. G. Newcomer, "The Poe-Chivers Tradition Re-examined," mistakenly says it is "a curious jumble of religious hymns, Byronic blank verse, and Shelleyan lyrics," (p. 22).
71. "To * * * *," *PofS*, pp. 126-127, a poem reminiscent of Byron's refusal to stoop to curse his wife; and "Though the Rose of my Eden is Blasted," *PofS*, pp. 122-123, which is modeled, even to the repeated structural use of the conditional "Though," on Byron's "Stanzas to Augusta" ["Though the day of my destiny's over"]. The Columbia University copy of this poem has "Directly from Byron" pencilled in above it.
    Chivers caught the Byron fever in three other poems, all of which follow Byron's successful romance-adventure formula: "Anastasius," *PofS*, pp. 114-118; "Chactas," *V*, pp. 9-12, an Indian adaptation of the method; and "Schamyl," *Georgia Citizen*, November 19, 1853. None of these poems is effective.
72. See William Ellery Leonard, *Byron and Byronism in America* (Boston, 1905), for details. Chivers' poems should be added to his listings.
73. No influence of "Don Juan" appears in his work; for all Chivers' experimentation in verse forms, he uses the *ottava rima* only once, in "To My Sister on

Hearing That She Had Borne Twins," *N*, pp. 101-102. The poem's content suggests a composition date of *c.* 1831. "The Dying Beauty," first published in *N*, pp. 49-51, opens with "She died in beauty!"; Byron's "She Walks in Beauty" *(Hebrew Melodies)* may have been the inspiration, although a contemporary popular song, "She died in Beauty! Like a rose blown from its parent stem," seems a more probable influence.

74. Hyder Edward Rollins, *Keats' Reputation in America to 1848* (Cambridge, Mass., 1946), p. 2. and p. 29.
75. Damon, *Chivers*, pp. 90-91.
76. See page 114.
77. See below, note 92.
78. See Chapter IV and page 231.
79. "The Dying Beauty," *N*, pp. 49-51, stanzas 3 and 4.
80. *Atlanta*, Lustrum the Second, 11. 145-161.
81. To Emerson's belief in the beauty inherent in every object, for example.
82. In "The Bright New Moon of Love," *V*, pp. 43-44, Chivers offers proof of his acquaintance with the "Grecian Urn":
     For the Truth she loved was Beauty,
         Because Beauty was her Truth;   [11. 25-26]
83. "Endymion," Book 4, 11. 691-700.
84. "The Eve of St. Agnes," stanza XXX.
85. *Atlanta*, Lustrum the Third, 11. 110-118.
86. Bayard Taylor, *The Echo Club and Other Literary Diversions* (Boston, 1876), "Night the Third," pp. 53-54.
87. "Apollo," *V*, p. 24, 11. 19-27.
88. "Hyperion," Book I, 11. 127-131.
89. *Chivers' Life*, p. 94, HEH HM 2530.
90. Noted by Horace Scudder in a letter to Willam Rossetti, *Rossetti Papers 1862 to 1870* (London, 1930), pp. 180-181.
91. For example, Shelley's *adamantine, hyaline,* and *jasper* appear in Chivers.
92. Chivers must have seen "Adonais" before 1832, for in "The Prophet's Dream," *PofS*, pp. 44-71, 1, 101, he refers to Byron as "The Pilgrim of Eternity"; the phrase is Shelley's coinage. However, there is no evidence of further influence until after the publication of *Nacoochee.*
93. X (February, 1844), 104-106. The letter is in the Griswold Collection of mss. in the Boston Public Library.
     In 1844 he also published "The Wife's Lament for Her Husband Lost at Sea," in the *Ladies' National Magazine*, VI (August, 1844), 54, which he later revised and published *(EofR,* pp. 114-116) as "Mary's Lament for Shelley Lost at Sea."
94. *New York Daily Tribune*, February 14, 1844.
95. "Shelley," *LP*, p. 17. The poem was enlarged to thirteen stanzas in the *United States Journal*, October 15, 1845.
96. *EofR*, pp. 27-48.
97. Stanza LV, 1. 1.
98. "Kosciusko's Resignation," in *PofS*, p. 124, is a lament over the death of the Polish hero. It has a motto from Byron.
99. "Letters from the North," *Georgia Citizen*, October 18, 1851.
100. *The Univercoelum*, III (December 9, 1848), 22.
101. "Exile of Heaven," 11. 49-56, in "Nacoochee," *N*, pp. 1-31.
102. "To a Skylark," 11. 6-10.

It is·interesting to note that Chiver's description of the swan in "The Soaring

Swan," *N*, p. 36, is apparently derived from Alastor's wry comments on the swan, 11. 275-290.

103. "The Soaring Swan," *N*, p. 36, 11. 69-77.
104. "Song of Le Verrier," *EofR*, p. 145, 11. 13-16.
105. *National Magazine and Republican Review*, I (April, 1839), 386-392.
106. *LP*, pp. 25-26.
107. "Una," *V*, pp. 13-15, 11. 16-20, 41-45, 66-70.
108. For a detailed analysis of this technique see pages 241-242.
109. There are two poems which contain lines from Shelley: "Tuccoa," *Baltimore Literary Monument*, I (March, 1839), 217-218; 1. 33, "an amphisbenic snake" from *Prometheus Unbound*, III, iv, 119: "The Evening Land," *LP*, pp. 25-26, dated "Middletown, Connecticut, Sept. 25th, 1841," 1. 9, " 'follow Love's folding star' " from *Hellas*, 1. 1029.

The nine pieces which either deal with Shelley as subject or show his influence are: "The Soaring Swan," *N*, p. 36: "To My Sister's Child while Dying," *The New-Yorker*, VI (February 23, 1839), 355: "Idealon," *National Magazine and Republican Review*, I (April, 1839), 386-392: "A Child's Question," *The Sentinel and Witness*, August 25, 1841: "The Wife's Lament for Her Husband Lost at Sea," *Ladies National Magazine*, VI (August, 1844), 54, dated "Middletown, Conn., Feb. 17th, 1842": "To Marion in Heaven," *LP*, p. 27, dated "Middletown, Conn., April 8th, 1842": "To Allegra Florence in Heaven," noted and criticized but not published in *Orion*, II (March & April, 1843), 370-372, dated "Oaky Grove, Ga., Dec. 12th, 1842": "Shelley," *LP*, p. 17, dated "Oaky Grove, Ga., August 10th, 1843": "Shelley," *United States Journal*, October 15, 1845.

110. In III, iii, of *Prometheus Unbound*, Prometheus gives the Spirit of the Hour (of his freedom) a "mystic shell," saying,

> Go, borne over the cities of mankind
> On whirlwind-footed coursers: once again
> Outspeed the sun around the orbed world;
> And as thy chariot cleaves the kindling air,
> Thou breathe into the many-folded shell,
> Loosening its mighty music; it shall be
> As thunder mingled with clear echoes . . . . [11. 76-82]

Chivers' famous use of *Eonchs* may well have been inspired by this scene, for he says it "is used, as a title, by metonymy, for Songs." (*Georgia Citizen*, June 28, 1851.) In "Isabel," *EofR*, pp. 65-74, his loved one draws sweet music from an "eonch" shell.

111. Julia Power, "Shelley in America in the Nineteenth Century," *University of Nebraska Studies*, 1940, p. 93.
112. *Ibid.*, p. 93.
113. Bayard Taylor, *The Echo Club*, p. 54.
114. If there is one principal difference in the poetry of Chivers and Shelley, it is in the presence of strong, often dominant rhythm in the former's work.
115. Noted by Meade Minnigerode, *The Fabulous Forties* (New York, 1924), p. 117.
116. For a detailed discussion of Tennyson's reception in America, see John Olin Eidson's *Tennyson in America* (Athens, Ga., 1943). I have relied heavily on Mr. Eidson's description of the years preceding the 1842 volume.
117. Poe, *Works*, XI, 176. Poe often quoted Bacon's statement; see "Ligeia," *Marginalia*, etc.
118. *Chivers' Life*, p. 47, HEH HM 2528.
119. The Boston Public Library's collection of Griswold correspondence includes

a ms. letter from Chivers to Griswold, asking for the return of his letters to Poe for inclusion in a *Life of Poe*. The letter is dated October 30, 1850.

The conclusion that Chivers continued to work on the *Life of Poe* until 1857 is Mr. Richard Beale Davis'.

The accuracy of Chivers' memory in recalling what was said in his conversations with Poe is testified to by the similarity between Poe's statements as Chivers quotes them and as they appeared elsewhere.

120. Chivers to Poe, September 9, 1845: the ms. is in the Griswold Collection of mss. in the Boston Public Library.

Chivers goes on to object to Tennyson's diction, saying that because of it, Tennyson does not appeal "to any of the universal feelings of the heart of Man." Apparently Tennyson's diction was no inspiration for Chivers' own extremes in language.

121. Chivers to Poe, Oct. 30, 1845: the ms. is in the Griswold Collection of mss. in the Boston Public Library.

122. *Chivers' Life*, p. 94, HEH HM 2530. It should be noted that "Gothic," to Chivers, meant "True."

123. See page 271, note 42.

124. See Eidson, *Tennyson.*, p. 107 and note 79, p. 237.

125. See "Childhood," p. 119, "Lines to Inconstancy," p. 120, and "Voice of the Spirit," p. 122. That Chivers knew he was using a meter uncommon at least to his own practice (the volume consists largely of poems in iambic pentameter, variously rhymed) is suggested by his placing the three so close together. None of these three poems is successful; and Chivers did not use the meter again until his 1853 volume.

126. *V*, pp. 28-29. Like the three poems noted above, it uses the single quatrain scheme, *abab,* the *b*'s being catalectic, but unlike them it uses an eight-stress trochaic line.

127. Eidson, *Tennyson*, p. 105.

128. *EofR*, p. 97, 11. 1-7.

129. *Chivers' Life*, p. 95, HEH HM 2534.

130. "The Vigil in Aiden," *EofR*, pp. 5-26, 11. 1-3.

131. "Evening," *EofR*, pp. 109-110, 11. 5-8.

132. Eidson, *Tennyson*, p. 104.

133. Women's or girls' names had long been favorite titles for Chivers; in *PofS*, he uses Adaline (his sister); in *C&E*, Ada Medora (three times), Adaline, and Ellen; in *N*, Nacoochee, Inez, Liza, and Irene; in *LP*, Allegra-Florence (his daughter) (twice), Isa (seven times), Marion, and Jesse. There are nine titles using girls' names in *EofR* and in *V*.

134. Damon, *Chivers*, p. 217; Professor Damon notes specifically *Aiden, Politian, Auber, Weir*.

Chapter III

1. Alexander Lindey, *Plagiarism and Originality* (New York, 1952), p. 22.

2. *Chivers Life*, pp. 73-78, HEH HM 24272 and HEH HM 2535.

3. *Southern Literary Messenger*, I (March, 1835), 387.

4. Damon, *Chivers*, p. 86 and note. David K. Jackson's *The Contributors and Contributions to the Southern Literary Messenger (1834-1864)* (Charlottesville, Va., 1936), does not list it as Poe's.

5. Ostrom, *Letters*, p. 207. The letter is dated July 6, 1842.

6. Chivers to Poe, August 27, 1840: the ms. is in the Griswold Collection of mss. in the Boston Public Library.

7. Mr. Hervey Allen (*Israfel* [New York, 1934], p. 373) says, "Chivers has already published poems which had attracted Poe's notice. . . ." This might refer to those sent to the first volume of the *Southern Literary Messenger* (never published there), to *Nacoochee*, or to Chivers' magazine publication before 1840.

8. *Graham's Magazine*, December, 1841.

9. Poe to Chivers, July 6, 1842: Ostrom, *Letters*, pp. 207-208. The letter is generally dated June; for proof of the July date, see Ostrom, p. 498.

10. Chivers to Poe, July 12, 1842; the ms. is in the Griswold Collection of mss. in the Boston Public Library.

11. Poe to Chivers, September 27, 1842: Ostrom, *Letters*, pp. 214-216.

12. Chivers to Poe, June 15, 1844: the ms. is in the Griswold Collection in the Boston Public Library, incorrectly dated May; for proof of the June date see Ostrom, *Letters*, p. 506.

13. For this information I am indebted to Mr. Davis' researches in his edition of *Chivers' Life*. Before its publication it was not known why Clark reopened his quarrel with Poe in the *Knickerbocker* (XXVII, 71) in January, 1846. Mr. Davis' complete text of this meeting in the summer of 1845 indicates the source both of Poe's anger (Clark's criticism of his anonymous *Broadway Journal* article in the *Knickerbocker*, XXVI [July, 1845], 76) and of Clark's resumption of the quarrel.

14. *Chivers' Life*, p. 59, HEH HM 2529.

Clark continued his attacks on Poe after the latter's death. Chivers sent "The Rappings / A Wise Cap for a Fool's Head" to the *Georgia Citizen* (March 20, 1852). It begins

> In New York— (I grieve to say so—)
> In his narrow room in Nassau,
> Sat the 'Editor of the Knickerbocker Magazine,'
> Lewis Gaylord Clark, the go-it,
> Writing nonsense— (all men know it—)
> When he thought of Poe, the Poet,
> And his yellow face turned green—
> Finally settling down to greenness which absorbed all other green.
>   [ll. 1-9]

15. Poe to Chivers, August 29, 1845: Ostrom, *Letters*, pp. 295-297.

16. Chivers to Poe, Sept. 9, 1845: the ms. is in the Griswold Collection of mss. in the Boston Public Library.

17. Poe to Chivers, November 15, 1845: Ostrom, *Letters*, pp. 302-303.

18. Poe to Chivers, July 22, 1846: Ostrom, *Letters*, pp. 325.327.

19. For proof of its existence, see Ostrom, *Letters*, pp. 527-528.

20. Chivers to Poe, February 21, 1847: the ms. is in the Griswold Collection of mss. in the Boston Public Library.

21. Chivers to Poe, April 4, 1847: the ms. is in the Griswold Collection of mss. in the Boston Public Library.

22. Poe to Chivers, July 13 [14?], 1848: Ostrom, *Letters*, p. 375. For proof of Poe's error in dating, see p. 527.

23. Poe to Mrs. Clemm, August 28, 1849: Ostrom, *Letters*, pp. 458-459.

24. Woodberry, "The Poe-Chivers Papers," p. 558.

25. There are indications that Chivers began such experiments as early as 1836. "Ellen Aeyre," HEH HM 2532, which Chivers said appeared "In a Philadelphia paper, in 1836" (*Waverley Magazine*, VII [September 17, 1853], 189), has elements of diction, rhyme, and structure typical of Chivers' later work.

26. "The Valley of Diamonds," *Georgia Citizen,* July 12, 1850.
27. "Letters from the North," *Georgia Citizen,* October 11, 1851.
28. "Origin of Poe's 'Raven,' " *Waverley Magazine,* VII (July 30, 1853), 73.
29. In 1845, Chivers wrote to the editor of the *Federal Union* (Milledgeville, Ga.) that he had already seen six imitations of "To Allegra Florence in Heaven"; he does not cite the poems: Chivers to [Herschel V. Johnson], November 1, 1845, HEH HM 24228.
30. See Ostrom, *Letters,* p. 303n. Percy Hoyle Adams, great-nephew of the poet, told the late Dr. Lewis Chase that Poe had sent Chivers a ms. copy of "The Raven"; Adams searched for it unsuccessfully and it has not been found since.
31. "Editor's Department," *Orion,* II (March-April, 1843), 370-372.
32. Chivers to Poe, June 15, 1844, refers to his last letter as having been written in "strawberry time," probably May-June of 1843. The ms. of this letter is in the Griswold Collection of mss. in the Boston Public Library.
33. Ostrom, *Letters,* p. 260n, suggests "To Allegra Florence in Heaven." But Poe had before referred to Chivers' line, "She came from Heaven to tell me she was blest," (Poe to Chivers, July 6, 1942: Ostrom, pp. 207-208) which is from Chivers' poem "The Heavenly Vision," published later in *LP,* p. 19. Mrs. Clemm's letter to Chivers on December 8, 1852, (Woodberry, "Poe-Chivers Papers," p. 551) repeats the line and Poe's statement that he often recited the poem from which it comes.
34. Poe, *Works,* VII, p. 212.
35. See, for example, "Childhood," "Lines to Inconstancy," and "Voice of the Spirit," all in *C&E,* or "Nacoochee's Prayer," in *N.*
36. This note was included in the poem's publication in the *Sentinel and Witness,* of Middletown, Conn., July 24, 1839, and when it was republished in the *United States Gazette,* August 1, 1839; it was omitted in *LP,* p. 18.

    Later, in defending Poe against charges that he had copied his "To One in Paradise" from Tennyson ("Letters from the North," *Georgia Citizen,* February 26, 1853), Chivers quoted 1. 16, "No more—no more—no more—," saying it contained "the profoundest insight into the essential laws of a true *Poetical Language.*" He was still sure Madame De Steel was right.
37. *The Knickerbocker Magazine,* IX (January, 1837), 62.
38. "Origin of Poe's 'Raven,' " *Waverley Magazine,* VII (July 30, 1852), 73. This is signed "Fiat Justitia," a pseudonym which the editor soon recognized.
39. "The Valley of Diamonds," *Georgia Citizen,* July 12, 1850.
40. *Broadway Journal,* August 2, 1845.
41. Poe to Chivers, August 29, 1845: Ostrom, *Letters,* pp. 295-296.
42. *Chivers' Life,* p. 74, HEH HM 2510. The poem appeared in the *Broadway Journal* (II, 7), on July 12, 1845.
43. Killis Campbell, "A Bit of Chiversian Mystification," *Studies in English, University of Texas Bulletin* (Austin, 1930), No. 3026, p. 152.
44. *Chivers' Life,* note 148, p. 76. In their review of *Chivers' Life,* Lois Ferry Parks and Emma Chase note that the copy must have been made after 1849, not in 1845 as Mr. Davis suggests, for it is in the hand of Jedediah Hunt, whose acquaintance with Chivers began at that time. *(Journal of Southern History,* XVIII [November, 1952], 549-551.)
45. "Origin of Poe's 'Raven,' " *Waverley Magazine,* VII (July 30, 1853), 73.
46. Woodberry, "Poe-Chivers Papers," p. 552.
47. *Ibid.,* p. 553.
48. *Whitaker's Magazine,* I (December, 1850), 624-631.
49. *The Message-Bird,* No. 34, Second year (December 16, 1850), 561-562. This re-

view was excerpted in *The Portland Transcript*, XIV (January 1, 1851), 310, and in the *Western Literary Magazine*, XV (February, 1851), 288.

50. Woodberry, "Poe-Chivers Papers," p. 554.
51. Chivers used this theme, one in which he may well have taken a personal interest, in four poems: "The Dying Wife," *The Sentinel and Witness*, October 30, 1839; "Sonnet.—The Dying Husband to His Wife," *LP*, p. 24; "The Vigil in Aiden," *EofR*, pp. 5-26; and "Isadore," *EofR*, pp. 97-10[2].
52. "Isadore," *EofR*, pp. 97-10[2], ll. 22-28.
53. There were apparently various sources for Richardson's article. Comparison of his datings of Chivers' poems with dates furnished in *The Lost Pleiad* show he obtained most of them from that source. "Isadore" was not published there. However, J. Q. Adams had stated, a month before Richardson's article appeared, that "Isadore" had been published in the *Sentinel and Witness* in 1841. ("Thomas H. Chivers," *Atlanta Constitution*, March 14, 1897.) That paper's files do not indicate any such publication, but Adams' statement was probably Richardson's source.
54. Damon, *Chivers*, p. 210n. Chivers' letter is in the Griswold Collection of mss. in the Boston Public Library.
    One other point indicates a date earlier than 1850 for "Isadore": Chivers published "Song to Isadore" in *The Univercoelum*, (III, 39), on December 16, 1848. It has the same meter (even to the catalectic lines) and the same rhyme scheme as "Isadore." The concluding line of both stanzas, "Back to Heaven, dear Isadore!", is equivalent to "Back to Hell thou ghostly Horror!" from "Isadore," which suggests "The Raven's" 8th stanza.
55. Damon, *Chivers*, p. 216.
56. "The Mother's Lament on the Death of Her Child," *LP*, pp. 26-27, ll. 1-4.
57. "Morcia Funebre," *V*, pp. 45-46, ll. 1-15. An earlier but still post-"Bells" use of the repeated word for sound effect is "Love," *EofR*, pp. 155-156. Benton, *Poe Circle*, p. 20, speculates that it may have helped Poe, *if* it preceded "The Bells"; there is no evidence to that effect.
58. Damon, *Chivers*, pp. 214-216.
59. *Chivers' Life*, pp. 76-77, HEH HM 2535. Mr. Davis adds the information that Chivers' *Ul-Erin* is the product of his own imagination, or that of "some Irish or Scottish eccentric who knew nothing of Celtic". (p. 116).
60. Poe, *Works*, VII, pp. 274-275.
61. In "The Beautiful Silence," *V*, pp. 19-21, l. 12, and "Bessie Bell," *V*, pp. 84-86, ll. 17-18.
62. In "Song to Isa Singing," *LP*, p, 25, "The Mighty Dead," *EofR*, pp. 27-48, "To Cecilia," *EofR*, pp. 81-82, and "Israfelia," *V*, pp. 62-63. Poe corrected a grammatical error in "Song to Isa Singing" (see Ostrom, *Letters*, p. 208n); he, at least, found nothing untoward in Chivers' use of *Israfel*.
63. In "To Allegra," *Sentinel and Witness*, June 26, 1839.
64. *Chivers' Life*, pp. 77-78, HEH HM 2535.
65. "Letters from the North," *Georgia Citizen*, October 18, 1851.
66. "The Song of Seralim," *Magnolia*, N.S.II (January, 1843), 52-53. "God Dwells in Light" appeared as a separate poem in *LP*, p. 27.
67. "The Song of Seralim," *The Christian Index*, February 11, 1847; *V*, pp. 123-125.
68. See pages 97-98.
69. Poe, *Works*, VII, p. 275.
70. The same sort of separate inspiration by a third source, but not interaction or stimulus, occurred when both Poe and Chivers were each inspired by A. J. Davis' *The Principles of Nature* to attempt an explanation of the relation of God

to man or the universe; the resulting essays, *Eureka* (1848) and *Search after Truth* (1848), are completely unlike one another, although Chivers paid Poe the compliment of naming his questioner in his Socratic dialogue "Politian."

71. In January, 1834. His admiring comment in *Chivers' Life*, p. 78, HEH HM 2535, is an indication of how closely and how early he followed Poe; in his summary of the poem's appearance he even quotes comparative texts. He defended Poe's poem vigorously in "Letters from the North," *Georgia Citizen*, February 26, 1853, when Poe was falsely accused of having copied the poem from Tennyson.

72. *Auber* is used in "Love," "The Lusiad," and "Lord Uther's Lament for Ella," all in *EofR; Weir* occurs in "The Lusiad." It may be noted here that Chivers' "Rosalie Lee," *V*, pp. 31-33, has nothing in common with Poe's "Annabel Lee."

73. Louis Untermeyer, ed., *American Poetry From the Beginning to Whitman* (New York, 1931), p. 388. A. G. Newcomer, "The Poe-Chivers Tradition Re-examined," suggests the same comparison.

74. Poe to Griswold, March 29, 1841, quoted in George E. Woodberry, *The Life of Edgar Allan Poe* (Boston, 1909), pp. 351-352.

Chivers' second line is "Long time ago"; Poe's twelfth is "Time long ago." Of this phrase Chivers wrote, "You are, probably, aware of the fact that the *Long time ago* of G. P. Morris's '*On the lake* where drooped the willow," is of '*nigger*' origin," ("Letters from the North," *Georgia Citizen*, March 24, 1854). Morris' song, entitled "Southern Refrain," is probably the basis of Chivers' poem, which has the same meter (although it adds a refrain) and theme.

75. These allegations are expressed in James A. Harrison's "Poe and Chivers" in his edition of Poe's *Works*, 1902, (VII, 266-288). It should be noted, however, that this was virtually a pioneer effort in the field of Poe-Chivers criticism. The only regrettable fact is that it probably still serves as a source work for scholars interested in Chivers.

A symbol of the confusion existing in Poe-Chivers scholarship is Professor Harrison's inclusion of the phrase *red-litten* in his comment on Chivers' unusual diction (p. 283); the phrase is from Poe's "The Haunted Palace," 1. 42.

76. "The Vigil in Aiden," *EofR*, pp. 5-26, stanza VII.

77. Chivers to Simms, April 10, 1852: Woodberry, "Poe-Chivers Papers," p. 553.

78. As, for example, in the use of *Aiden* in "Isabel" (*V*, pp. 66-67) or in "Song of Una to Auster" (*V*, pp. 73-74).

CHAPTER IV

1. "The Retrospect," *PofS*, p. 109, 11. 12-13.
2. "To a China Tree," *N*, pp. 51-53.
3. "Childhood," *C&E*, p. 119, 11. 21-22.
4. "To My Sister," *N*, pp. 101-102, 11. 9-22.
5. See, for example, "Sonnet.—My Mother's Love," *LP*, p. 22, and "The Place Where I Was Born," *V*, pp. 80-81.
6. Chivers' anger at his first wife was never really dissipated; in his will he bequeaths her and their daughter a dollar each.
7. See "Voice of the Spirit," *C&E*, p. 122. Considering his feeling of kinship with Byron, it is possible that the name may be only a literary one.
8. "To a Friend," p. 121, and "To****," p. 126, both of *PofS*, present these opposites.
9. "Lines to Inconstancy," *C&E*, p. 120, 1. 45.
10. "The Voice of the Exile," *N*, pp. 61-63, 11. 69-72.

11. "The Lament of Youth," *PofS*, Canto I, stanza XIII, 11. 7-12.
12. Only one poem, "Zephyrus," *C&E*, p. 95, contains mention of his father, and that a distant, if friendly, reference. *PofS* contains only one poem to her, "To My Mother," p. 130: *C&E* contains five; "To My Precious Mother," pp. 90-91, "To My Mother," pp. 93-94, "To My Mother on Hearing of Her Illness," p. 113, "The Boy's Return," pp. 114-115, and "Sonnet [sic] to My Mother," p. 133. Her death occurred in 1838, and *LP* contains five elegies to her: "Lament on the Death of My Mother," p. 18; "Sonnet—On the Death of My Mother," p. 20; "Lament on the Death of My Mother," pp. 20-21; "Sonnet.—My Mother's Love," p. 22; "Sonnet.—On Hearing of the Death of My Mother," p. 24. Two other elegies appeared in magazines: "To My Mother in Heaven," *New-Yorker*, V (June 10, 1838), 195, and "Sonnet to My Mother," *Graham's Magazine*, XXI (July, 1842), 32.
13. "To My Mother," *C&E*, pp. 93-94, 1. 47.
14. "To My Precious Mother," *C&E*, pp. 90-91, 11. 48-50.
15. "Sonnetta," *C&E*, p. 133, 11. 14-21.
16. "Stanzas for Music," *N*, pp. 105-106, 1. 17.
17. "Song to a False One," *LP*, p. 29, 11. 19-20.
18. "Zephyrus," *C&E*, p. 95, 11. 21-30.
19. "Song" ["Fain would I sit in this untented cave,"], *C&E*, p. 143.
20. The late Dr. Lewis Chase determined the place of Chivers' marriage; See Damon, *Chivers*, p. 108n. Chivers' family Bible records the date.
21. Thomas Holley, Jr. (the second son of that name), Fannie Isobel, and Emma Isadore, the three surviving children, all married, Isobel to R. M. Brown, of Decatur, Georgia, and Emma to Jerome C. Potter, of Guilford, Conn.
22. "Valete Omnia," *V*, pp. 26-27, 1. 38.
23. See pages 180-182.
24. "To Allegra Florence, on the Morning of Her Birth," *LP*, p. 24, 11. 5-12.
25. "To Allegra Florence in Heaven," *LP*, pp. 15-16, 11. 73-81.
26. In "Monthly Chat with Readers and Correspondents," *Orion*, II (March and April, 1843), 370-372.
27. "Avalon," *EofR*, pp. 49-56, stanza XVI.
28. "The Lost Pleiad," *LP*, pp. 5-12, 11. 354-363.
29. "On the Death of Adaline," *PofS*, pp. 18-19, 11. 121-125.
30. Occasionally the results are ludicrous; in "Avalon," *EofR*, pp. 49-56, Chivers' Heaven is a very natural one; his dead children have grown up. In "The Chaplet of Cypress," *EofR*, pp. 117-119, the Heaven is a personal one; his sister Adaline's spirit, ascending into Heaven after death, is guided by his daughter, Allegra Florence.
31. *Search after Truth*, p. 23. See also Rosignol Suedois," [sic] *V*, pp. 33-34.
32. "The Mighty Dead," *EofR*, pp. 27-48, 11. 19-24.
33. "The Song of Seralim," *V*, pp. 123-125, 11. 13-36.
34. "The Chaplet of Cypress," *EofR*, pp. 117-119, 11. 1-6.
35. "Song of Le Verrier," *EofR*, p. 145.
36. *Search after Truth*, New York, 1848, p. 37.
    Professor Damon has made a definitive precis of Chivers' theories; See Damon, *Chivers*, pp. 160-164.
37. See particularly "The Soul's Destiny," *LP*, pp. 16-17.
38. *Ibid.*, p. 32.
39. Preface to *Atlanta*.
40. *Ibid*.
41. For a further elaboration of the poem's symbolic meaning, see Damon, *Chivers*, pp. 244-249.

42. It is interesting to note the difference in theme between "Nacoochee" (1837) and *Atlanta* (1853); the former is, clearly enough, a tragedy, for Ostenee, Julian's counterpart, does not succeed in uniting himself with Nacoochee, the Ianthe of the poem. Instead, she expresses strong dislike and fear at his approach, emotion so strong that the symbol of the Angel of Death appears and takes Nacoochee up to Heaven just as Ostenee arrives at the Island. Ostenee then realizes that he must wait until after death (purification) to find her.

The temptation to conclude that Chivers experienced some sort of psychic reassurance between the writing of these two poems is strong, although there is no written evidence of it. Perhaps he had experienced some sort of purging in the tragedy surrounding the deaths of his four children in the 1840's, and now felt possessed of the unity Julian finds.

In any case, this marked difference in the two poems, understood in terms of their similarity, solidifies the argument for intentional symbolism in both poems.

43. For a discussion of Chivers' knowledge of his own limitations, see page 99.
44. *Atlanta*, "Lustrum the Third," 11. 119-127.
45. *The Univercoelum*, III (December 9, 1848), 22.
46. See "To My Mother on Hearing of Her Illness," *C&E*, p. 113.
47. "Vision of the Heavenly Ones," *V*, pp. 115-117, 11. 21-42.
48. See, for example, "The Heavenly Vision," *LP*, p. 19, "The Spirit's Yearnings," *LP*, p. 32, or "A Vision of the Night", *V*, p. 65. Such poems are generally unsuccessful.
49. "Stanzas for Music," *N*, pp. 105-106. The quotation is from 1. 9.
50. "The Poet of Love," *V*, pp. 103-104, 11. 12-22.
51. See "The Mighty Dead," *EofR*, pp. 27-48, stanza LI particularly.
52. "The Rising of the Nations," *V*, pp. 46-48, 11. 33-40.
53. *PofS*, pp. 72-83.
54. *V*, pp. 110-111.
55. The metaphor of the "Liberty tree" is used again in "Song of the True Sons of Liberty," *Georgia Citizen*, August 25, 1855. Here it is used in the more conventional manner; the tree, firmly rooted in the United States, sows its seed over the world.
56. *Georgia Citizen*, May 14, 1858, 11. 1-4.
57. "Where Liberty was Born," *Georgia Citizen*, August 18, 1854, 11. 101-105.
58. "The Roll of Fame," *Spiritual Telegraph*, III (September 9, 1854), 75, 1. 1.
59. *Ibid.*, 11. 41-44, 69-72.
60. "Washington," *LP*, p. 18.
61. *V*, pp. 108-110.
62. *LP*, pp. 30-31.
63. "Sonnet," *V*, p. 112.
64. *Georgia Citizen*, August 25, 1855.
65. *EofR*, pp. 27-48, 11. 43-48.
66. 10th of 31 stanzas of "The Mighty Dead," not published until November 13, 1854, in the *Georgia Citizen*.
67. Stanzas 19, 22, and 23, *EofR*, pp. 27-48.
68. Preface to *Birth-Day Song of Liberty* (Washington, Ga., 1856).
69. Stanza 23.
70. "Ganymede," *V*, pp. 15-19, note.
71. "The Falling Garden," *C&E*, p. 134, 11. 21-22.
72. "Malavolti," *N*, pp. 117-143.

73. See L. C. Knight, *Georgia's Landmarks, Memorials and Legends* (Atlanta, Georgia, 1914), pp. 1031-1033.
74. "Nacoochee," *N*, pp. 1-31, 11. 64-72.
75. *C&E*, pp. 137-139.
76. *Ibid.*, 11. 64-65.
77. The same concern over paganism is present in "The Indian Sachem Slain," *C&E*, p. 137.
78. *Peterson's Magazine*, XV (April, 1849), 143.
79. *Ibid.*, 11. 24-25.
80. "The South," *C&E*, p. 92, 11. 17-18.
81. "Tuccoa,"*The Baltimore Literary Monument*, I (March, 1839), 217-218, 1. 9.
82. "Rosalie Lee," *V*, pp. 31-32, 11. 23-33; Keats provided the basis for this catalogue in "The Eve of St. Agnes," and Sir Walter Raleigh's "His Pilgrimage" offered the *suckets-buckets* rhyme in much the same context.
83. *Atlanta*, "Lustrum the Second," 11. 166-188.
84. Much the same sort of description is present in "Nacoochee," *N*, pp. 1-31, from which *Atlanta* was derived.
85. "The Soaring Swan", *N*, pp. 36-39, 11. 103-109.
86. "Isabel," *EofR*, pp. 65-80, 11. 217-224.
87. "The Wilderness," *C&E*, p. 106, 11. 34-36, 43-44.
88. "Tuccoa," *The Baltimore Literary Monument*, I (March, 1839), 217-218.
89. "God," *C&E*, p. 126.
90. *Conrad and Eudora*, I, i, 1. 23.
91. "Spring," *LP*, pp. 21-22, 11. 13-16. "The Voice of Spring," *C&E*, p. 129, is much the same; "The Dying Year," *The Knickerbocker*, IX (January, 1937), 62, correspondingly uses autumn as symbol of death.
92. "Ode to the Mississippi," *C&E*, pp. 104-105, 11. 37-41.
93. "Hymn to the Ocean at First Sight," *C&E*, p. 127.
94. "Invocation to Spring," *V*, pp. 87-89, 11. 49-60.
95. "Evening," *EofR*, pp. 109-110, 11. 5-8.
96. But "Evening," *EofR*, pp. 109-110, 1. 27, takes Wordsworth's simile "The holy time is quiet as a Nun" ("It is a Beauteous Evening, Calm and Free," 1. 2) and changes it to "The pensive Nun in Heaven."
97. "Georgia Waters," *N*, pp. 74-75.
98. *Chivers' Life*, p. 52, HEH HM 2529.
99. *Ibid.*, note 68, pp. 52-53.
100. "The Raven," published when Poe was already known as editor and critic, was sold for ten dollars: Mary E. Phillips, *Edgar Allan Poe The Man* (Chicago, 1926), p. 878.
101. E. Douglas Branch, *The Sentimental Years* (New York, 1934), p. 115.
102. Hyder Rollins, in his *Keats' Reputation in America* (Cambridge, 1946), quotes *The Atheneum* as saying that "Mrs. Hemans has, perhaps, exercised a more visible influence upon the poetry of America than any other writer."
103. "Stanzas," *C&E*, p. 109, 11. 1-2, 5-8.
104. All from *C&E*, these lines, in the above order, are from: "To Donna Medora," p. 110, "To a Ladye," p. 114, "To a Ladye," p. 117, and "Song," p. 132.
105. "Thoughts on Early Days," *C&E*, p. 97, 11. 20-27.
106. "Medora of Ultramontane," *C&E*, p. 116.
107. "Rosalie Lee," *V*, pp. 31-33, 11. 1-22, 56-66.
108. "Eulalie," *EofR*, pp. 160-163, 11. 17-20, 29-32, 61-72.
109. "Song to Isa Singing," *LP*, p. 25, 11. 24-25.

110. See "To Irene,", *N*, p. 93, "Anacreontique," *LP*, p. 28, or "The Marvel of Arabia," *V*, p. 58.
111. "Sonnet,—To Isa Sleeping," *LP*, p. 20.
112. Hart, *Popular Book*, p. 128.
113. "Religion," *Christian Index*, June 3, 1847, 11. 15-16.
114. In prose, however, Chivers could reason with surprising logic; see *Search after Truth*.
115. "Paramuthia" (*Christian Index*, October 7, 1847) and "Drink and Away" (*N*, p. 71) ask man to reject life's temptations; "Song of Dependence on God" (*The Spirit Messenger*, I [October 5, 1850], 71), expresses his need for God's help.
116. "Words to the Unwise," *V*, p. 92, 11. 1-4, 13-24.
117. "Song of Adoration to God," *N*, pp. 64-65, 11. 7-12, 25-30, 37-48.

CHAPTER V

1. See "The Dream," *PofS*, pp. 9-17.
2. See "The Prophet's Dream," *PofS*, pp. 44-71.
3. "To a China Tree," *N*, pp. 51-53, 1. 54.
4. Preface to *Atlanta*.
5. "The Poet of Love," *V*, pp. 103-104. Chivers added a note explaining that *Norns* are three maidens dwelling in Heaven whose names are *Past, Present,* and *Future.*
6. Preface to *Nacoochee*.
7. Preface to *Nacoochee*.
8. Preface to *Birth-Day Song of Liberty*.
9. "Letters from the North," *Georgia Citizen*, October 18, 1851.
10. Poe's interpretation of the "soul" is not clear. He does not use the word in a theological sense. I believe he means that faculty which responds to sensory or emotional stimuli.
11. Preface to *Memoralia*.
12. Preface to *Atlanta*. Chivers spoke of Emerson only twice ("The Valley of Diamonds," *Georgia Citizen*, August 2, 1850), once to praise him as a "Literary Ganymede," an "ambrosial Eclecticist."
13. Preface to *Virginalia*.
14. Preface to *Virginalia*, and "The Poet," *M*, pp. 25-26.
15. Preface to *Virginalia*.
16. See, for example, "Death of Adaline," *C&E*, pp. 100-101, or "Song on Parting," *C&E*, p. 125.
17. Preface to *Virginalia;* although the essay is not extant, Chivers said he had written on the *Theory of a True Poetical Language* ("Letters from the North", November 6, 1852).
18. "Letters from the North," *Georgia Citizen*, October 18, 1851.
19. See Damon, *Chivers*, p. 103. Coleridge apparently had little direct influence on Chivers, although the exotic diction of "Kubla Khan" must surely have inspired some of Chivers' experiments in pure sound.
20. *LP*, pp. 24-25.
21. *Memoralia*, published in 1853, is *Eonchs of Ruby* with the first 26 pages replaced by new work.
22. "The Prophet's Dream," *PofS*, pp. 44-71, 11. 46-54.
23. "Apollo," *V*, p. 24, 11. 10-18.
24. "The Retrospect," *PofS*, pp. 109-114, 11. 126-146.
25. "The Soaring Swan," *N*, pp. 36-39, 11. 69-77.

26. "On the Death of Adaline," *PofS*, pp. 18-29; "The Lament of Youth," *PofS*, pp. 84-108.
27. "To a China Tree," *N*, pp. 51-53.
28. "Song," *N*, p. 88, 11. 1-8. "Boat Song," *V*, p. 79, is another of this type; lines 3 and 4 of a seven line stanza are repeated in lines 6 and 7.
29. "Choral Song of the Temperance Legions," *V*, pp. 102-103.
30. *V*, pp. 83-84.
31. "Ellen Aeyre," HEH HM 2532, 11. 34-44. Chivers said this appeared "In a Philadelphia paper, in 1836." (*Waverley Magazine*, VII [September 17, 1853], 189.)
32. "Lily Adair," *EofR*, pp. 164-166, 11. 12-22.
33. "Avalon," *EofR*, pp. 49-56, 11. 78-88.
34. "The Dying Beauty," *N*, pp. 49-50, 11. 1-24.
35. *New-Yorker*, V (June 16, 1838), 195.
36. "Uranothen," *V*, pp. 97-99, 11. 45-48.
37. "Threnody," *EofR*, pp. 120-125, 11. 17-19.
38. *PofS*, pp. 114-118.
39. *Christian Index*, July 1, 1847.
40. *Georgia Citizen*, July 14, 1954.
41. Two later experiments, "Song of the True Sons of Liberty" and "Song of the American Freeman," both in the *Georgia Citizen*, August 25, 1855, double the quatrain form and show his declamatory use of anapestic feet.
42. *LP*, pp. 15-16.
      John Olin Eidson (*Tennyson*, p. 107 and note 79, p. 237) suggests Chivers' use of octameters came from his study of "Locksley Hall."
43. *Georgia Citizen*, August 18, 1854.
44. "The Roll of Fame," *Spiritual Telegraph*, III (September 9, 1854), 75, 11. 1-4, 29-36, 43-46, 75-78.
45. "The Prophet's Dream," *PofS*, pp. 44-71, 11. 439-443.
46. *Conrad and Eudora*, II, i. 72-73.
47. *Ibid.*, 11. 129-133.
48. Published only in the *Georgia Citizen*, May 17, 24, 31 and June 7, 14, 1851. The ms. of the play, now at Harvard, shows the published version was much abridged.
49. *Leoni*, I, i, 79-81. Quotations are taken from the *Georgia Citizen* text as corrected by the Harvard ms.
50. A third play, *The Sons of Usna* (Philadelphia, 1858), is entirely unlike either of these earlier plays in language; its diction is that of his later style.
51. "The Soaring Swan," *N*, pp. 36-40, 11. 62-67.
52. "The Lusiad," *EofR*, pp. 57-64, 11. 112-117.
53. "The Dying Swan," *EofR*, pp. 93-96, 11. 76-80.
54. "Lily Adair," *EofR*, pp. 164-166, 11. 12-14.
55. "Rosalie Lee," *V*, pp. 31-33, stanza 3.
56. "To Cecilia," *EofR*, pp. 81-82, 1. 16 and note.
57. "Malavolti," *N*, pp. 117-143, stanza XXX, 1. 5.
58. "Alma," *V*, pp. 77-78, 1. 11.
59. "The Angelus," *V*, p. 108, 11. 1-6.
60. "The Poet of Love," *V*, pp. 103-104, 11. 12-22.
61. "Apollo," *V*, p. 24, 11. 19-27.
62. "The Little Boy Blue," *Waverley Magazine*, VII (July 30, 1853), 71, 11. 1-12, 41-60.
63. "Chinese Serenade," *Dodge's Literary Museum*, V (October 30, 1852), 344, 11. 1-8.

64. *Ibid.*, 11. 99-103.
65. "Letters from the North," *Georgia Citizen,* November 6, 1852.
66. "Letters from the North," *Georgia Citizen,* August 31, 1852.
67. "Letters from the North," *Georgia Citizen,* March 8, 1851.
68. *The Knickerbocker,* XXXVIII (August, 1851), 181.
69. "Corn-Shucking Song," *Georgia Citizen,* June 25, 1855.
70. "The Death of the Devil," *Georgia Citizen,* November 13, 20, 27, and December 4, 1852.
71. "Railroad Song," *Georgia Citizen,* June 21, 1851, 11. 1-30.
72. Preface to *Memoralia.*
73. *Ibid.*
74. "But one of [Poe's] unaccountable deficiencies was, his utter inability to see that any work, to be perfect . . . must be the result of an equal blending of Art and Passion—that is, the highest Passion with the most exalted Art—the passion moulding the Art." *Chivers' Life,* pp. 86-87, HEH HM 2530.
75. See pages 130-131.
76. See, for example, "Huswifery."
77. "The Dying Beauty," *N,* pp. 49-50, 11. 25-26.
78. See "Rosalie Lee," *V,* pp. 31-33, for example.
79. "Caelicola," *Peterson's Magazine,* XVII (February, 1850), 102, 11. 1-12.
80. "Ringgold of Love to Adelais Percy," *Georgia Citizen,* March 28, 1857, is a violent example of this.
81. *Conrad and Eudora,* II, ii, 11. 26.
82. "To Isa," *LP,* p. 29, 11. 1-4.
83. "On the Death of Adaline," *PofS,* p. 19, 11. 33-34.
84. "The Retrospect," *PofS,* pp. 110, 11. 11-16.
85. "Nacoochee," *N,* pp. 1-31, 1. 202 and 1. 141.
86. "The Last Wreck," *N,* pp. 40-42, 11. 13-22.
87. "The Death of Time," *N,* pp. 332-35, 11. 67-73.
88. "God Dwells in Light," *LP,* p. 27, 11. 8-9.
89. "Valete Omnia," *V,* pp. 26-27, 11. 36-39.
90. "Tohoo Vabohoo," *V,* pp. 86-87, 11. 15-16.
91. "The Raising of Tabitha," *M,* pp. 23-24, 11. 25-28.
92. "The Voice of the Exile," *N,* pp. 61-63, 11. 69-72.
93. "A route of evanescence," 1. 3.
94. "The Crucifixion," *V,* p. 21, 1. 6.
95. "The Shell," *EofR,* p. 92, 11. 9-12.
96. "The Voice of Thought," *EofR,* p. 157.
97. "The Mighty Dead," *EofR,* pp. 27-48, 11. 19-23.
98. "Song of Le Verrier," *EofR,* p. 145, 11. 9-12.
99. "Isabel," *EofR,* pp. 65-74, 11. 213-216.
100. "Bochsa," *M,* pp. 15-18, 11. 88-90.
101. "The Wind," *V,* p. 113, 11. 1-4.

Bibliography

I. CHIVERS' WORKS

1. *Books*

    The Path of Sorrow, or, The Lament of Youth: A Poem. [Printed at the office of the *Western Weekly Review*], Franklin, Tenn., 1832.

    Conrad and Eudora; or, The Death of Alonzo. A Tragedy. In Five Acts. Founded on the Murder of Sharpe, by Beauchamp, in Kentucky., Philadelphia, 1834.

    Nacoochee; or, The Beautiful Star, with Other Poems., W. E. Dean, Printer, [New York], 1837.

    The Lost Pleiad; and Other Poems., Edward O. Jenkins, New York, 1845.

    Eonchs of Ruby. A Gift of Love., Spalding & Shepard, New York, 1851.

    Memoralia; or, Phials of Amber Full of the Tears of Love. A Gift for the Beautiful., Lippincott, Grambo & Co., Philadelphia, 1853.

    Virginalia; or, Songs of My Summer Nights. A Gift of Love for the Beautiful., Lippincott, Grambo & Co., Philadelphia, 1853.

    Reprinted in facsimile by E. L. Schwaab, Research Classics, No. 2, Brooklyn, 1942.

    The Sons of Usna: A Tragi-Apotheosis, in Five Acts., C. Sherman & Son, Printers, Philadelphia, 1858.

    Chivers' Life of Poe., edited by Richard Beale Davis, New York, 1952.

2. *Pamphlets*

    The Constitution of Man, Memphis, Tenn., 1833. [Titled from the *Western Monthly Magazine* (I, 321-325), July, 1833.]

    Search After Truth; or, A New Revelation of the Psycho-Physiological Nature of Man., Cobb & Yallalee, New York, 1848.

    Atlanta: or, The True Blessed Island of Poesy. A Paul Epic—

In Three Lustra., Printed at the *Georgia Citizen* Office, Macon, Georgia, 1853.

Birth-Day Song of Liberty. A Paean of Glory for the Heroes of Freedom., C. R. Hanleiter & Co., Printers, Atlanta, Georgia, 1856.

3. *Magazine Publication*

A complete bibliography of the contemporary publication of Chivers' work in periodicals is to be included in the projected edition of Chivers' Complete Works. Compiled by S. Foster Damon, it indicates that Chivers published in over seventy-five periodicals. The variety of geographical location of these periodicals suggests that Chivers' poetry reached virtually every section of the country; very often his work was reprinted in outlying magazines after its original publication.

II. Works with Special Reference to Chivers

1. *Contemporary*

Professor Damon's bibliography of Chivers' contemporary magazine publication includes both reviews of his published volumes and general criticisms of his poetry.

2. *Later*

Aiken, Conrad, ed., *American Poetry 1671-1928,* New York, 1929.

Allen, Hervey, *Israfel,* New York, 1926.

Anon., "The Astonishing Chivers," *Duke University Alumni Register,* XVI (May, 1930), 162.

Anon., "Brown's Chivers' Project," *Providence Journal,* October 4, 1933.

Anon., "Chivers to the Fore," *Munsey's Magazine,* XXIV (December, 1900), 465-466.

Anon, "Dr. Thomas Holley Chivers," *Bulletin of the Georgia Medical Society,* V (March, 1936), 63-64.

Anon., "Thomas Holley Chivers," *Atlanta Constitution,* March 14, 1897.

Anon, "T. H. Chivers Project Put on View at Brown," *Providence Sunday Journal,* October 28, 1934.

Anon., "Valuable Acquisitions Made by Duke Library," *Durham Sun,* March 5, 1930.

Anon., "Was Poe a Plagiarist?", *Literary Digest,* XV (May 22, 1897), 99.

Badger, Kinsbury, ed., *American Literature for Colleges,* Harrisburg, Pa., 1952.

Bartlett, John, *Familiar Quotations,* Boston, 1948.

Beatty, Richard Croom, Randall Stewart, Floyd C. Watkins, Thomas Daniel Young, *The Literature of the South,* Chicago, 1952.

Bell, Landon C., *Poe and Chivers,* Columbus, Ohio, 1931.

Benton, Joel, *In the Poe Circle,* New York, 1899.

——————, "Thomas Holley Chivers," *Munsey's Magazine,* XVIII (October, 1897), 154-155.

——————, "Was Poe a Plagiarist?", *The Forum,* XXIII (May, 1897), 362-372.

Boynton, Percy H., *Literature and American Life,* Boston, 1936.

Bradshaw, Sidney E., *On Southern Poetry Prior to 1860,* Richmond, 1900.

Campbell, Killis, "A Bit of Chiversian Mystification," *Texas University Bulletin, Studies in English,* No. 10 (1930), 152-154.

——————, "The Kennedy Papers," *Sewanee Review,* XXV (August, 1917), 349-360.

Chase, Lewis, "Searching for a Lost Poet," *Atlanta Journal,* Magazine Section, October 1, 1933.

Coburn, Frederick W., "Catchall," *Lowell Courier-Citizen,* March 21, 1933.

Damon, S. Foster, *Thomas Holley Chivers, Friend of Poe,* New York, 1930.

Eidson, John Olin, *Tennyson in America,* Athens, Georgia, 1943.

Ethridge, Willie Snow, "Did Poe Plagiarize Georgia Poet?", *The Macon Telegraph,* Sunday Magazine, September 23, 1928.

Flanders, Bertram Holland, *Early Georgia Magazines,* Athens, Georgia, 1944.

Gallaway, John F., "Georgia's Forgotten Poet," *Atlanta Journal,* January 12, 1930.

G[ilder], J. B., "Poe and his 'Precursor,'" *The Critic,* N.S. XXVII (May 8, 1897), 327-328.

Griswold, William M., ed., *Passages from the Correspondence and Other Papers of Rufus W. Griswold*, Cambridge, Mass., 1898.

Harrison, James A., "Poe and Chivers," *The Complete Works of Edgar Allan Poe* (New York, 1902), VII, 266-288.

Hart, Bertha Sheppard, *Introduction to Georgia Writers*, Macon, Georgia, 1929.

Henry, Earl, ed., *Selected Poems of Thomas Holley Chivers, The Bookmark*, Monroe, N.C., 1935.

Higginson, Thomas W., *Henry Wadsworth Longfellow*, Boston, 1902.

[Hodges, Louise Thrette], "Atlanta Woman Rescues Name of 'Lost Poet,'" *Atlanta Journal*, July 1, 1923.

[How, Lewis], "Chivers in the Harris Collection," *Brown Alumni Monthly*, X (June, 1909), 14.

Hubbell, Jay B., *The South in American Literature 1607-1900*, Durham, N.C., 1954.

Hubner, Charles W., *Representative Southern Poets*, New York, 1906.

Huneker, James, "A Precursor of Poe," *The Pathos of Distance*, New York, 1913.

Irvine, Kate Tipton, *The Beauchamp Tragedy in American Fiction* [unpublished Master's thesis], University of Kentucky, 1932.

Jacobs, Thornwall, ed., *The Oglethorpe Book of Georgia Verse*, Atlanta, Georgia, 1930.

Kenyon, C. M., *Keats' Fame in America Before 1860* [unpublished Master's thesis], Brown University, 1934.

Knight, Lucian Lamar, *Georgia's Landmarks, Memorials and Legends*, Atlanta, Georgia, 1914.

——————, *A Standard History of Georgia and Georgians*, Chicago, 1917.

Littlefield, Louise Hall, "Former Maine Man Seeks Information Here on Georgia's Long Forgotten Poet," *Portland Sunday Telegram*, January 20, 1935.

Mabbott, Thomas Ollive, "Collation of a Book by Thomas Holley Chivers," *Notes and Queries*, CLIX (October 11, 1930), 257-258.

——————, "Kilmer and Chivers," *The New York Times*, Section 4, June 4, 1933.

—————, "Numismatic References of Three American Writers," *Numismatist,* XLVI (November, 1933), 688-689.

—————, "On Chivers' *Conrad and Eudora,*" *Politian, An Unfinished Tragedy,* Richmond, Va., 1923.

McDonough, Mary Lou, ed., *Poet Physicians,* Springfield, Illinois, 1945.

Minnigerode, Meade, *The Fabulous Forties,* New York, 1924.

Newcomer, Alphonso G., "The Poe-Chivers Tradition Re-examined," *Sewanee Review,* XII (January, 1904), 20-35.

Orgain, Kate Alma, *Southern Authors in Poetry and Prose,* New York, 1908.

Ostrom, John Ward, ed., *The Letters of Edgar Allan Poe,* Cambridge, Mass., 1943.

Parks, Edd Winfield, *Segments of Southern Thought,* Athens, Georgia, 1938.

—————, *Southern Poets,* New York, 1936.

Parks, Lois Ferry, and Emma Chase, *"Chivers' Life of Poe," Journal of Southern History,* XVIII (November, 1952), 549-551.

Pattee, Fred Lewis, *The Feminine Fifties,* New York, 1940.

Pitfield, R. L., "Thomas Holley Chivers, 'The Wild Mazeppa of Letters,' " *General Magazine and Historical Chronicle,* XXXVII (1934), 73-92.

Phillips, Mary E., *Edgar Allan Poe The Man,* Chicago, 1926.

Power, Julia, "Shelley in America in the Nineteenth Century," *University of Nebraska Studies,* 1940.

Reed, Langford, ed., "The American Poet Laureate of Bathos," *A Book of Nonsense Verse,* New York, 1926.

Richardson, Warfield Creath, "Who Was Chivers?" *The Boston Evening Transcript,* April 24, 1897.

Rollins, Hyder Edward, *Keats' Reputation in America to 1848,* Cambridge, Mass., 1946.

Rossetti, William M., ed., *American Poets,* London, n.d.

Rutherford, Mildred Lewis, *The South in History and Literature,* Athens, Georgia, 1906.

Scott, W. S., "The Astonishing Chivers: Poet for Plagiarists," *Princeton University Library Chronicle,* V (June, 1944), 150-153.

Scudder, Horace Elisha, *James Russell Lowell,* Boston, 1901.

Smythe, Albert H., *Bayard Taylor,* Boston, 1896.

Stedman, Edmund Clarence, "Edgar Allan Poe," *Scribner's Monthly,* XX (June, 1880), 107-124.

————, *Poets of America,* Cambridge, Mass., 1885.

Steinmetz, Marion Lee, *The Sharp-Beauchamp Case in American Literature* [unpublished Master's thesis], Brown University, 1951.

Taylor, Baylor, "Night the Third," *The Echo Club, and Other Literary Diversions,* Boston, 1876.

Townsend, John Wilson, *Kentucky in American Letters,* Cedar Rapids, Iowa, 1913.

————, *Kentuckians in History and Literature,* New York, 1907.

————, "Thomas Holley Chivers," *The Library of Southern Literature,* (ed. E. A. Alderman & J. C. Harris), New Orleans, 1907.

Untermeyer, Louis, ed., *Early American Poets,* New York, 1952.

————, ed., *American Poetry from the Beginning to Whitman,* New York, 1931.

Van Doren, Mark, ed., *American Poets 1630-1930,* Boston, 1932.

Walton, Clarke W., "Thomas Holley Chivers," *The Bookmark,* II, No. 10 (July, 1934), Monroe, N. C.

White, Andrew D., *Autobiography,* New York, 1905.

Williams, Samuel Cole, *Beginnings of West Tennessee,* Johnson City, Tenn., 1930.

Wood, Clement, *Poets of America,* New York, 1925.

Woodberry, George E., "The Poe-Chivers Papers," *Century Magazine,* LXV (January, 1903), 435-448, and LXV (February, 1903), 545-558.

————, *The Life of Edgar Allan Poe,* Boston, 1909.

Yonker, Sister Mary Philomena, O.P., *The Contribution of Thomas Holley Chivers to Lyric Poetry* [unpublished dissertation], Fordham University, 1932.

III. General Bibliography

Adams, Grace, and Edward Hutter, *The Mad Forties,* New York, 1942.

Branch, E. Douglas, *The Sentimental Years 1835-1860,* New York, 1934.

Hart, James D., *The Popular Book,* New York, 1950.

Heye, George G., F. W. Hodge, George H. Pepper, "The Nacoochee Mound in Georgia," *Contributions from the Museum of the American Indian,* IV, No. 3, New York, 1918.

Leonard, William Ellery, *Byron and Byronism in America,* Boston, 1905.

Lindey, Alexander, *Plagiarism and Originality,* New York, 1952.

McIlwaine, Ardrey Shields, *The Beauchamp Tragedy in American Drama* [unpublished Master's thesis], University of Chicago, 1927.

Schlesinger, Arthur M., Jr., *The Age of Jackson,* Boston, 1945.

White, George, *Historical Collections of Georgia,* New York, 1854.

Index

INDEX

285